Culture of Ambiguity

TRANSGRESSIONS: CULTURAL STUDIES AND EDUCATION

Volume 75

This book series is dedicated to the radical love and actions of Paulo Freire, Jesus "Pato" Gomez, and Joe L. Kincheloe.

Cultural studies provides an analytical toolbox for both making sense of educational practice and extending the insights of educational professionals into their labors. In this context *Transgressions: Cultural Studies and Education* provides a collection of books in the domain that specify this assertion. Crafted for an audience of teachers, teacher educators, scholars and students of cultural studies and others interested in cultural studies and pedagogy, the series documents both the possibilities of and the controversies surrounding the intersection of cultural studies and education. The editors and the authors of this series do not assume that the interaction of cultural studies and education devalues other types of knowledge and analytical forms. Rather the intersection of these knowledge disciplines offers a rejuvenating, optimistic, and positive perspective on education and educational institutions. Some might describe its contribution as democratic, emancipatory, and transformative. The editors and authors maintain that cultural studies helps free educators from sterile, monolithic analyses that have for too long undermined efforts to think of educational practices by providing other words, new languages, and fresh metaphors. Operating in an interdisciplinary cosmos, Transgressions: Cultural Studies and Education is dedicated to exploring the ways cultural studies enhances the study and practice of education. With this in mind the series focuses in a non-exclusive way on popular culture as well as other dimensions of cultural studies including social theory, social justice and positionality, cultural dimensions of technological innovation, new media and media literacy, new forms of oppression emerging in an electronic hyperreality, and postcolonial global concerns. With these concerns in mind cultural studies scholars often argue that the realm of popular culture is the most powerful educational force in contemporary culture. Indeed, in the twenty-first century this pedagogical dynamic is sweeping through the entire world. Educators, they believe, must understand these emerging realities in order to gain an important voice in the pedagogical conversation.

Without an understanding of cultural pedagogy's (education that takes place outside of formal schooling) role in the shaping of individual identity—youth identity in particular—the role educators play in the lives of their students will continue to fade. Why do so many of our students feel that life is incomprehensible and devoid of meaning? What does it mean, teachers wonder, when young people are unable to describe their moods, their affective affiliation to the society around them. Meanings provided young people by mainstream institutions often do little to help them deal with their affective complexity, their difficulty negotiating the rift between meaning and affect. School knowledge and educational expectations seem as anachronistic as a ditto machine, not that learning ways of rational thought and making sense of the world are unimportant.

But school knowledge and educational expectations often have little to offer students about making sense of the way they feel, the way their affective lives are shaped. In no way do we argue that analysis of the production of youth in an electronic mediated world demands some "touchy-feely" educational superficiality. What is needed in this context is a rigorous analysis of the interrelationship between pedagogy, popular culture, meaning making, and youth subjectivity. In an era marked by youth depression, violence, and suicide such insights become extremely important, even life saving. Pessimism about the future is the common sense of many contemporary youth with its concomitant feeling that no one can make a difference.

If affective production can be shaped to reflect these perspectives, then it can be reshaped to lay the groundwork for optimism, passionate commitment, and transformative educational and political activity. In these ways cultural studies adds a dimension to the work of education unfilled by any other sub-discipline. This is what Transgressions: Cultural Studies and Education seeks to produce—literature on these issues that makes a difference. It seeks to publish studies that help those who work with young people, those individuals involved in the disciplines that study children and youth, and young people themselves improve their lives in these bizarre times.

Culture of Ambiguity

Implications for Self and Social Understanding in Adolescence

Sandra Leanne Bosacki

SENSE PUBLISHERS
ROTTERDAM/BOSTON/TAIPEI

A C.I.P. record for this book is available from the Library of Congress.

ISBN: 978-94-6091-622-9 (paperback)
ISBN: 978-94-6091-623-6 (hardback)
ISBN: 978-94-6091-624-3 (e-book)

Published by: Sense Publishers,
P.O. Box 21858,
3001 AW Rotterdam,
The Netherlands
www.sensepublishers.com

Printed on acid-free paper

DEDICATION

To my mother, father, and sister. Thank you for being my lighthouse in this world of emotional fog.

TABLE OF CONTENTS

PREFACE

I have a strong affection for puzzles and exploration. One of my earliest memories of exploring puzzles involves my childhood summer holidays with my parents and sister on the Atlantic shore, exploring on the beach in Cape May, New Jersey searching for seashells. I always felt a sense of awe as I wondered how you could see different shapes in each seashell – and that this would change next time you looked at it. It also fascinated me that others would also see something different in each seashell.

One of my earliest fascinations with ambiguity during school stemmed from my interest as a young child in the ambiguous figures such as Garrow's duck/woman. Upon childhood visits to the Ontario Science Centre in Toronto on elementary school trips and with my family, as a young child I used to stare at the ambiguous diagrams – mesmerized and mystified by how these figures played tricks with my eyes. I could not believe my own eyes as I would see one image one time, then a completely different image the next. I was also interested and surprised that other viewed the image so differently – or the same. How did we learn how to interpret these images?

As a young child growing up in a family with extended family who spoke Polish and Ukrainian – although I could not speak the language, I was enthralled as well as puzzled, as I often stood on the periphery of the social circle and observed my family members interacting during family gatherings. Although the Polish and Ukrainian words did not make sense to me, I could glean a sense of the meaning behind the eyes and laughs of family members and feel some kind of emotional sense of the story. These exposures to puzzles and complex multilingual social interactions have laid the emotional and cognitive groundwork for me to explore the area of adolescent's understanding of social and self ambiguity as many questions remain unanswered.

As an older child and young adolescent, I was also interested in how people's facial expressions would not necessarily match the tone of their voice emotionally, or what they were literally saying, or what I felt from them regarding their emotional tone. During my school years, I felt challenged as a learner to try to 'predict' the inner worlds others were experiencing using the clues available such as words, facial expression, non-verbal communication such as actions, gestures, stance, tone of voice, etc. I was usually in fear of being judged as an incompetent social detective – that it, I aimed as a child, and then later as an adult to aim to be a competent social detective and understand other's messages with/or without verbal language.

Over the years, as I continued my educational journey as student, through graduate work and into academia, this combination of such puzzling and enchanted learning experiences have led me to continue to explore ambiguity in adolescents' social and emotional lives in others and one's self in my teaching and research. Given the diverse cultural and moral landscape of the Canadian population, as well as the rapid advances made in technology today and social media, I find that I am perplexed by an increasing number of ambiguities in everyday situations and I wonder what this means for our psychological understanding of others and ourselves.

As I continue my pursuit to discover that 'perfect' shell on the Atlantic shore, I also continue my pursuit of issues of silence, emotions, and ambiguity in the emotional lives of Canadian youth as I continue to learn from the expertise and knowledge of adolescent minds. I invite the reader to join me on my journey of exploring the ambiguous and unexplored landscape of the personal and social world of the adolescent.

S.L. Bosacki

ACKNOWLEDGMENTS

I could not have written this book without the invaluable support of numerous individuals. I owe a debt of gratitude to Brock University for providing a rich opportunity to learn from some of the finest scholars in education. I appreciated the timely response and constant support from my Publisher Peter de Liefde, and editors, Michel Lokhorst and Shirley Steinberg at Sense Publishers for their time in responding to my questions, and to helping me with the production during the manuscript production process. I also thank the members of the production team at Sense Publishers including Bernice Kelly for their guidance and patience.

I thank all those involved with the schools in which I have conducted my research studies on adolescents' and children's thoughts and emotions over the years including the children, teachers, principals, school staff, and parents. Throughout the years, at Dalhousie University, Brock University, and the University of Chicago at Illinois I have had the pleasure to work with numerous graduate student research assistants on various research projects and I thank them all for their assistance and support.

I have had the opportunity to discuss my ideas for this book in various classes that I have taught at Brock University and I thank all of my past and present students for furthering my thoughts around the many ideas discussed in this book. I also take this opportunity to thank my colleague and friends who have provided many inspiring conversations regarding ambiguity and silence in adolescence and have supported and furthered my thinking in the area of exploring adolescents' social and emotional lives.

I thank Fiona Blaikie, Dean of the Faculty of Education, Brock University and Renee Kuchapski from the Department of Graduate and Undergraduate Studies in Education, Brock University, and all of my colleagues and friends at Brock University for their warm support during the book preparation process, and the Faculty of Education, Brock University for their financial support of my communication with Sense Publishers.

Background research and reflection underpinning the ideas and data presented in this book was supported, in part, by funding from various grants and scholarships received from Brock University, Dalhousie University, Ontario Institute of Educational Studies of the University of Toronto, the Spencer Foundation, and the Social Sciences and Humanities Research Council of Canada Postdoctoral Fellowship and Standard Research Grants #410-2003-0950 and #410-2006-0361.

Above all, I thank my parents and sister for their patience, tolerance, and humour while I devoted my time and energy to this project. Their emotional support has made this book possible.

SCHOOLING THE AMBIGUITIES OF ADOLESCENCE

A Psychocultural Exploration

"All knowledge is ambiguous." J.S. Habgood

"If I don't know I don't know I think I know
If I don't know I know I think I don't know."
(Laing, D.H., 1969, p. 55)

How do we help young people make sense and meaning out of ambiguity and uncertainty during the transition between childhood and adolescence? How do we encourage youth to develop effective skills to help navigate through the culture of ambiguity during early adolescence? Given the increased recent surge in research on social cognition, the focus remains on the cognitive regarding aspects of learning and development (Olson & Dweck, 2009). Thus, this book focuses on theoretical and practical issues regarding emotional and social aspects of adolescents' educational experiences that may contribute to their emotional and spiritual health. Drawing on past and current research on theory of mind and also on shy/socially withdrawn and emotionally sensitive children and adolescents (Bosacki, 2005; 2008), this book expands on the increasing complexity of the social and personal worlds of the Canadian adolescent. In particular, this book focuses on the ambiguities regarding identity and relationships. that occur during the transitional developmental period between childhood and adolescence.

As educators become increasingly cognizant of the new realities of adolescents, this book aims to encourage educators to redefine and restructure their definitions of ambiguity within adolescence. In particular, this book will build on, and then move beyond the traditional cognitive-developmental representations of how adolescents learn, and provide recommendations that may inspire educators to adapt holistic and inclusive educational strategies that aim to help youth to develop healthy relationships with one another and themselves in the increasingly ambiguous contexts of the classroom, community and beyond. Overall, this book aims to encourage the expansion of new ideas that challenge the dominant discourse in educational psychology that tends to focus on the cognitive. This book encourages readers to focus on the importance of emotionality and spirituality regarding teaching and learning within the realms of the personal, social, and supernatural. Specifically, I will explore why is emotional and spiritual health important for adolescents in the classroom, what are these important educational health issues, and how can educators and researchers integrate the emotional and spiritual into the classroom and develop practical educational strategies that will enable adolescents to navigate the ambiguous landscape of the classroom.

This book attempts to bridge the gap between theory and practice in the fields of human development and education. I view the psychocultural notion of that development and learning includes aspects of cognitive, social, cultural, emotional, moral, and the spiritual through the lens of both an educational researcher and a practitioner or a developmental interventionist. Through the book, I will draw on empirical evidence from past and present research on adolescents' social and emotional worlds including psychological understanding, self-conceptions, and peer relations, and also practical educational implications. This book will combine the scholarly areas of theory, research, and practice. As a developmental interventionist, it is my goal to provide a book that will encourage educators and researchers to engage the two disciplines in an ongoing critical discourse.

This book investigates adolescents' ability to interpret, understand or make meaning of human thoughts and feelings, and its relation to their sense of self, peer relations, and socio-communicative competence within the school setting. Often referred to as Theory of Mind understanding (ToM), the ability to "read" others' minds or mental states in the context of social action can also be referred to as psychological understanding (Bruner, 1996). This ability to translate the social language exchanged between others helps us to make sense of the minds of others in that it helps us to understand multiple perspectives and to communicate with others (Nelson, 2007; Tomasello, 1999).

Within the larger context of folk psychology, or our culturally shaped notion in terms of which people organize their views of themselves, or others, and of the world in which they live. This folk psychology, according to Bruner (1990) is an essential base not only of personal meaning, but of cultural cohesion as well. This book builds on Bruner's (1996) description of the connection between folk psychology and folk pedagogy as folk psychology guides our social interactions, whereas folk pedagogy in part shapes our goals to help children and adolescents to learn about the world. As educators and researchers, how can folk psychology and pedagogy help us to explore our questions regarding what are adolescents' minds like and how can we help them learn within the culture of ambiguity in the current school context?

Past research makes clear that communication, understanding of mind and relationships are closely linked in normative development, especially when individual differences are considered. A wealth of research with young children has now shown that engaging in discourse about inner states is linked to later success in understanding of mind and emotion. Beyond the age of five, however, little is known about the links between the understanding other minds and relationships (Dunn, 2008; Hughes, 2011; Moore, 2006). The ability to solve such ambiguous puzzles may mark children's first realization that beliefs can have their origin within persons rather than exclusively in an external world. Given that children who possess high levels of psychological understanding are more likely to "think about their own and others' thinking" during the school day, such an ability has important educational implications for beyond the gradeschool into highschool (Wellman & Laguttata, 2004).

Research has shown that the ability to "read others" or to make sense of the signs and symbols evident in human communication has an influence on children's self-conceptions and their social interactions in childhood and adolescence (Nelson, 2007). Thus, given that psychological explanations play a key role in teaching and learning, further research is required, particularly on adolescents within the school context. This book will investigate what aspects of these discourse experiences foster the growth of understanding of spirit, emotion, and mind in the adolescent.

Accordingly, from a co-relational approach to the development of understanding mind and education (Bingham & Sidorkin, 2004, Dunn, 2008), this book will build on past and current research by investigating the social and emotional antecedents and consequences of psychological understanding in early adolescence (Bosacki, 2003; 2008; Bosacki & Moore, 2004). Specifically, this book will explore the question: How do adolescents use their ability to understand other minds to navigate their relationships with themselves and their peers? To address this question, this book will critically examine research on adolescents' ability to understand mind, emotion, and spirit, and how they use this ability to help them navigate their relationships within the school setting.

This book aims to bridge the gap between theory and practice in the fields of human development and education regarding the notion of ambiguity within the context of adolescence. Expanding on the Oxford Dictionary's definition of ambiguity as "open to more than one interpretation, having a double meaning; unclear or inexact because a choice between alternatives has not been made," (Oxford Pocket Dictionary – 2006, p. 18), Derived from the Latin word "ambi guous meaning uncertain, from ambi gere which means to go about or around, this book views the notion of "the ambiguities of the adolescent's world" through the lens of both an educational researcher and a practitioner. I will explore the meanings and functions of ambiguity experienced by adolescents in the classroom.

As we enter the second decade of the twenty-first century, I have become interested in exploring the questions around ambiguity and uncertainty within the secondary school context. For example, when language is capable of being understood in more than one way by a reasonable person, ambiguity exists such that words are ambiguous when their significance is unclear to persons with competent knowledge and skill to understand them. What does this mean for adolescents? Given that there are two categories of ambiguity: latent and patent, where latent ambiguity exists when the language used is clear and intelligible so that it suggests one meaning but some extrinsic fact or evidence creates a need for interpretation or a choice among two or more possible meanings. In contrast, a patent ambiguity is one that appears on the face of a writing or document because uncertain or obscure language has been used. Applying these terms to the adolescent classroom, and drawing on the legal definitions of ambiguity such as in the law of contracts where ambiguity means more than that the language has more than one meaning upon which reasonable persons could differ (West's Encyclopedia of American Law, 2008). For example, if there is an ambiguity, and the original writer or creator of the ambiguity cannot effectively explain it, then the ambiguity will be decided in the light most favorable to the other party. Applying this thinking to the adolescent classroom, what does this mean for social contracts made between peers, family members, educators and learners?

What does ambiguity mean for the adolescent and her experiences within her private and public worlds? What are the emotional and social functions, or what do we do with the verbal and nonverbal ambiguities? How do the functions differ if we create our ambiguities, or if they are imposed on us by others including those individuals for whom we care about, compared to those with whom with we are unfamiliar? What are the implications of the ambiguities of our Canadian society for the adolescent? Finally, looking toward the future, I end the book by exploring the question of where do we go from here and where is our path leading us to?

I aim to provide some future directions for adolescent students, and those who work with youth regarding what to do with classroom ambiguities and uncertainties. To answer some of these questions, this book provides empirical evidence and also suggestions for practice, both educational and clinical. Thus, this book aims to marry the theoretical and practical two scholarly areas regarding ambiguity in adolescence. As the author, it is my goal to provide a book that will inspire educators and researchers to engage in an ongoing discourse involving classroom ambiguities and continue to question the silences and contradictions found within the adolescent school context.

What does it mean when there is ambiguity in the secondary school classroom? What are the experiences of adolescents when they are being claimed to act, and/or communicate in ambiguous terms, or when they are exposed to ambiguities in the classroom? What is happening in the hearts and minds of adolescents facing complex contexts for which there are multiple meanings? What role do social messages play in the classroom through the use of Internet, Smart phones, etc. play in the classroom and what implications do these technological communication tools and social media contexts have for adolescents' sense of self and social relationships?

To answer these questions, this book will borrow from both psychoeducational research and holistic educational philosophies that explore the roots of classroom complexities and uncertainties. This book will examine how individual differences and classroom culture, including gender, ethnicity, and language may affect our experiences of ambiguities in school settings and suggest ways in which educators can redesign and rethink educational programs that acknowledge the notion of doubt, uncertainty, and multiple meanings. To explore the landscape of classroom ambiguities from the perspective of a researcher and educator, I will outline, multiple meanings of ambiguity that adolescents may experience within the classroom. To bridge the gap between theory and practice in the fields of human development and education, theoretical and practical implications are discussed. It is hoped that this book's attempt to unravel the meanings of classroom ambiguities will encourage educators and researchers to instill and foster the unspoken love of learning among the youth they work with.

ORGANIZATION AND FRAMEWORK OF THE BOOK

This book developed from own writing, research, conference presentations, teaching, and personal experiences during childhood and adolescence. Currently, I teach various graduate courses in education including developmental issues in children and adolescence, educational research methods, and cognition and learning. Throughout the past fifteen years, the questions and comments from my previous research participants, students, and colleagues have influenced my thinking around the topic of adolescents' emotional lives and social worlds. Accordingly, these multiple voices have been integrated throughout this book, as they have inspired me to think further on the concept of ambiguity and the implications it has for the classroom.

By providing a combination of research findings and practical applications, this book aims to inspire in a theoretical and conceptual sense and also practical (for both research and teaching purposes). This book may assist educators of all ages by presenting them with ideas to integrate the concept of ambiguity into their classroom, and to address issues of self-growth, especially the spiritual and emotional aspects. Although this book focuses on adolescence, the main ideas discussed in this book regarding ambiguity in self and social development are applicable to any age, thus, the audience could range from an early childhood educator to a university professor.

In particular, I hope that this book will interest educators or 'developmental interventionists' who are curious about exploring the needs of the 'whole adolescent' in education. I wrote this book intending to appeal to a variety of educators and researchers, ranging from early adolescent educators/researchers to university professors specializing in socioemotional and spiritual/moral development. This book may also have an international appeal given that the topic of ambiguity, emotionality, and education has become of interest to many educators across the globe.

This book is divided into three main chapters or sections, with each chapter highlighting an important aspect of classroom ambiguity in adolescents. Chapter 1 critiques theoretical issues that surround concepts and definitions of the culture of ambiguity in adolescence. I also connect the literature on developmental social cognition and spirituality to issues of ambiguities. Chapter 2 explores some of the possible contexts of classroom ambiguities, their characteristics and how they influence the lives of adolescents. In other words, why do some adolescents feel more confused and upset by ambiguities than others, or feel the need to understand ambiguous situations, and are ambiguities helpful or hurtful to the adolescents' personal and social lives? This section describes some examples of when and where adolescents may experience specific ambiguities in the classroom. To explore this question, the chapter outlines the extant literature on particular examples of current experiences of classroom ambiguities regarding the self, and within the social context as well as the cultural context such as experiences of personal silence and social silence including ostracism. In particular, the chapter focuses on ambiguities created by situations of exclusion and ostracism including status variables such as ethnicity/race, gender, and social class. Specific examples of research used to explore youth's understanding of interpretive ambiguity regarding humour, teasing and psychological bullying, deception, silence and ostracism. Chapter 3 explores the practical implications of classroom ambiguities, and examines the strategies and directions that educators and researchers could take in work aimed to support the development of a healthy voice and heart in adolescents.

Overall, this book aims to address the paucity of research on adolescents' concepts of ambiguity within the classroom and how this may be linked to self-growth and social relationships. Socioemotional and spiritual development are emphasized and provide current and relevant psychoeducational research that may hopefully lead to new questions and lines of inquiry. Following A.A. Milne's (1926, introduction) advice, "Perhaps the best thing to do is to stop writing Introductions and get on with the book."

WHY? (WHO, WHAT, AND WHERE) CONCEPTUAL FOUNDATIONS

"A little illusion is the only bond between mortals that never breaks."
(Capek, 1927, p. 63)

"everything that deceives may be said to enchant." Plato, *The Republic*
- (cited in Turkle, 2011, p. vi)

INTRODUCTION

Given the complexity surrounding the concept of ambiguity, this chapter aims to provide a roadmap to some of the meanings and definitions of personal and social ambiguities within the context of adolescent and education. That is, to explore the question of what ambiguity mean to adolescents, this chapter explores the multiple meanings and definitions of ambiguity within the psychocultural context. More specifically, I will review and connect the literature on ambiguity to related areas of inquiry including social cognitive development and emotionality in adolescence. I end this chapter with recommendations for educators to address the personal and social ambiguities in adolescence within the secondary school context..

WHY SILENCE, AMBIGUITY, AND EMOTIONALITY WITHIN THE HIGHSCHOOL CLASSROOM?

Why discuss the concept of ambiguity within the adolescent culture? What is specific about Canadian adolescents that provide the opportunity to explore the ambiguities and uncertainties of the personal, social, and cultural worlds. Building on the work of Bruner and others (Bingham & Sidorkin, 2004, Bronfenbrenner, 2005; Bronfrenbrenner & Morris, 1998; Bruner, 1996; Dunn, 2008; Olson, 1994), I take a psychocultural approach to development and schooling that views the importance of relationships as well as personal identity within the larger discourse of a learning community. As Yon (1994) notes, conceptualizing schooling as a discursive space enables us to recognize how individuals come from contradictory locations and occupy contradictory positions. Thus, binary categories will not work within a discursive space, as the connections between identity and community remain fluid as both learning and growing processes.

How do adolescents respond socially and emotionally to contexts of ambiguity? What emotional responses do socially ambiguous events evoke in youth within the school context. As I will discuss further on in Chapter 2, ambiguity and uncertainty may lead to feeling of positive and negative emotions as adolescents strive to make sense of contradictions and incoherency. Feelings of ambivalence may also arise as adolescents search for ways in which to express their emotions. Fitting within the culture of ambiguity, Yon (2004) discusses the school context as a place of incoherence and elusiveness accompanied by feelings of ambivalence and supports what Bauman (1991) describes as living with the tensions of opposing views and positions – however implicitly made.

Who: Why Canadian Adolescents in 2012?

> As the entomologist chasing butterflies of bring colors, my attention was seeking in the garden of gray matter, those cells of delicate and elegant forms, the mysterious butterflies of the soul, whose fluttering wings would someday – who knows? – enlighten the secret of mental life.
> Santiago Ramony Cajal [(1923/1981) cited in Battro, 2010, p., 163]

As Laing (1960) states in his description of the divided self during development, adolescence is the age where universally, the heightening or intensifying of the awareness of one's own being, both as an object of one's own awareness and the awareness of others (an awareness of oneself by oneself). Many researchers and educators agree that adolescence (approximately 9–18 years) is one of the most pivotal times in an individual's overall development (e.g., Berk, 2011; McDevitt & Ormod, 2004; Selman, 1980; Santrock, 1993). Regarding interpersonal relations and identity formation, according to the classical developmentalist G. Stanley Hall (1904), adolescence is the age when youths' shift their energy from themselves to their social relationships and experience the "storm" and "stress" of life. According to both Hall (1904) and Erickson (1968), the central task for the adolescent includes the development of one's own identity within the larger social and cultural context. Thus, the adolescent's task is to develop self-understanding within the nexus of social relationships.

As Fivush (2008) states, adolescence is a critical developmental period when autobiographical memories begin to coalesce into an overarching life narrative that defines self, others, and values. According to Fivush (2008), autobiographical memory is memories related to the self, and more specifically, these memories provide interpretative and evaluative information that transforms a memory from a simple *recounting* of what occurred to a *reminiscing* about what kind of personal meaning that event holds for the individual. As children develop through middle childhood and into early adolescence, they become increasingly able to think about multiple facets of an event simultaneously, to maintain cognitive and emotional ambiguity, and to infer and deduct both physical and psychological connections between events (Habermas & Bluck, 2000; Habermas & Diel, 2010; Habermas & de Silveira, 2008).

With these social cognitive skills, adolescents become capable of creating overarching life narratives infused with increasingly sophisticated perspective and evaluation. Thus, according to Fivush (2008), in adolescence, we see the beginning of a coherent life narrative that links events across time and places the self in relation to others, embedded in an unfolding human drama of interconnected stories. How these stories are constructed in family and friendship reminiscing remains critical for adolescents' developing sense of self and social understanding.

What: Definitions of Ambiguities in the Personal, Social, and Cultural Worlds

In this section, I will first discuss definitions of ambiguity as there is an ongoing conceptual discussion regarding ambiguity as a concept across various disciplines. Given on the application of ambiguity to all academic disciplines, this book will focus on the areas of inquiry related to adolescent development including psychology, psycholinguistics, and education among many others. Following definitions and areas of research on ambiguity, I will then discuss a selection of research on the development of children's reactions to ambiguity and will finish this section with how this study of ambiguity can help us understand how adolescents experience ambiguity in self and social contexts.

Derived from the Latin word ambiguus, *uncertain,* from ambigere, *to go about* : amb-, ambi-, *around*; see **ambi-** + agere, *to drive*; see ag- in Indo-European roots.], the Oxford Dictionary, The Pocket Book Dictionary of Current English (2006) defines ambiguity as open to more than one interpretation; having a double meaning, unclear or inexact because a choice between alternatives has not been made. The Merriam-Webster Dictionary defines ambiguous as "doubtful or uncertain from obscurity of indistinctness; capable of being understood in two or more possible senses or ways."

Ambiguity is often referred to as uncertainty or doubtfulness of the meaning of language. The word is associated with various synonyms and phrases such as: abstruseness, bewilderment, confounded meaning, confused meaning, confusion, disconcertion, doubtful meaning, doubtfulness, dubiety, dubiousness, duplexity in meaning, equivocalness, equivocation, incertitude, indefinite meaning, indefiniteness, indeterminacy, obscure meaning, puzzlement, reconditeness, uncertainty of meaning, unintelligibility, vagueness. Focusing on the meaning of language, where there is no ambiguity, one must abide by the words. Thus, when language (verbal and nonverbal communication) is capable of being understood in more than one way by a reasonable person, ambiguity exists. It is not the use of peculiar words or of common words used in a peculiar sense. Words are ambiguous when their significance is unclear to persons with competent knowledge and skill to understand them.

As I mentioned in the introduction, there are two categories of ambiguity, according to some legal texts (West's Encyclopedia of American Law, 2008): latent and patent. Both types of ambiguity have implications for the school context as such definitions help to guide educators strategies to deal with ambiguities in the classroom. Latent ambiguity exists when the language used is clear and intelligible so that it suggests one meaning but some extrinsic fact or evidence creates a need for interpretation or a choice among two or more possible meanings. For example, unknown to the parties to a social contract such as agreeing to go for a coffee, two individuals of the same name were to arrive from the same city during different months of the same year. This extraneous fact necessitated the interpretation of an otherwise clear and definite term of the contract. In such cases, extrinsic evidence may be admitted to explain what was meant or to identify the social contract.

A patent ambiguity is one that appears on the face of a document or writing because uncertain or obscure language has been used. In the law of contracts, ambiguity means more than that the language has more than one meaning upon which reasonable persons could differ. It means that after a court has applied rules of interpretation, such as the plain meaning, course of dealing, the court still cannot say with certainty what meaning was intended by the parties to the contract. When this occurs, the court will admit as evidence extraneous proof of prior or contemporaneous agreements to determine the meaning of the ambiguous language. Parole evidence may be used to explain the meaning of a writing as long as its use does not vary the terms of the writing. If there is no such evidence, the court may hear evidence of the subjective intention or understanding of the parties to clarify the ambiguity.

Sometimes, courts decide the meaning of ambiguous language on the basis of whom was responsible, or the creator of the ambiguity. When only one individual knew or should have known of the ambiguity, the unsuspecting party's subjective knowledge of the meaning will control. If both parties knew or should have known of the uncertainty, the court will look to the subjective understanding of both. Thus, the ambiguity no longer exists if the parties agree upon its meaning. If the parties disagree and the ambiguous provisions are material, no contract is formed because of lack of mutual assent. This knowing but not knowing is referred to as willful blindness, and although this language occurs within the context of the legal system, the concepts referring to ambiguity and interpretation can be applied to educational contexts and has implications for adolescents' social interactions within the classroom.

Ambiguity or the quality of being unclear due to optional interpretation is commonly used as the word to describe a situation that is hard to understand; although perhaps because the situation can be understood from more than one point of view. As Langdon claims, "all reality is ambiguous. Ambiguity is synthesis. The problem and the solution are one" (p. 35). As Harris (2010) notes, there are different types of uncertainty – expected uncertainty (where one knows that one's observations are unreliable), and unexpected uncertainty (where something indicates in the environment that things are not as they seem or appear to be). Ambiguous situations are related to unexpected uncertainty such as whether or not the look between two children are directed to one individual, and what does this look mean – acceptance? Rejection? Some researchers who explore behaviours within the context of economics found that expected uncertainty such as a situation where probably can be assessed is related to risk, whereas unexpected uncertainty is the uncertainty borne of missing information and relates to ambiguity.

Regarding communication and ambiguity, Empson (1947) notes "An ambiguity, in ordinary speech, means something very pronounced, and as a rule witty or deceitful" (p. 1). Empson used the word in an extended sense and applied it to "any subject with any verbal nuance, which gives room for alternative reactions to the same piece of language." (Empson, 1947; p. 1). He based his definition on the analytical mode of approach, and claimed that any prose statement could be called ambiguous in the sense that it needs to be analysed and interpreted. Interestingly - when Empson provides an example he refers to the statement, "the cat on a mat." – and when he refers to the emotional reaction a person may have to ambiguity in her/his life, he claims that it "has contradictory associations, which might cause some conflict in the child who heard it, in that it might come out of a fairy story." (p. 2). Given the ambiguities with the adolescent's world, to what extent does the adolescent experience emotional reactions to social and personal ambiguities and how can we look to developmental and educational research for clues?

Drawing on the connections to ambiguity and communication, Burke's (1970) approach to language claimed that language is used to persuade people to action and defined persuasion as "the use of language as a symbolic means of inducing cooperation in beings that by nature responds to symbols" (Burke, 1970, p. 43). According to Burke, persuasion could be referred to as the artful use of the "resources of ambiguity" that are usually revealed in an artistic, and frequently emotional format. Such an approach could help children to learn the techniques of persuasion and thus to co-create through the use of narrative a "common ground" as Aristotle stated, between the learner and the peer (audience). That is, how can adolescents create a shared understanding with their peers in that they influence their peers to feel they are being spoken to in their "own language" and hear references to their own beliefs and values. Thus, the audience (persuadee) will develop a sense of identification or mental and emotional connection with the persuader, believing that the persuader is like them – or share common ground. Thus, according to Burke's theory, when persuaders try to act, believe, and talk like the audience (her/his peers), they create an emotional bond with listeners, who will learn to trust and identify with them, and thus as their relationship or emotional bond strengthens, may follow their advice on issues. In terms of relationship building, Burke (1970) noted that such identification or bonding occurs most readily when wrapped in drama, a story, or other kind of narration.

This ability to persuade others involves the ability to understand the inner world of self an others as explained earlier when discussing the role of Theory of Mind. Thus, applying Burke's (1970) theory to the adolescent classroom, educators and researchers could explore the question of to what extent do youth use ToM and ambiguity as a means of communication with their family members, peers, and themselves? How does their ToM ability influence their decision to use ambiguity as a social strategy or device to influence adolescents' emotional, social, and moral selves? To help address these questions, in Chapter 3 I will describe how Burke's approach to the process of persuasion involving communication and ambiguity could help co-create a Theory of Mind (ToM) or social cognitive toolkit for adolescents that could be used to further their understanding of social and personal ambiguity within the classroom.

Regarding the connections between emotions and belief, Harris (2010) discusses neurocognitive research on disbelief and disgust that explores how the brain responds to uncertainty, or the mental state in which the truth value of a proposition cannot be judged or not knowing what one believes to be true. For example, various studies such as Wicker et al.'s (2003) research suggests disbelief was associated with bilaternal activation of the anterior insula, a primary region for the sensation of taste and this area is widely thought to be involved with negatively valenced feelings like disgust, harm avoidance, and the expectation of loss in decision making. For example, Wicker et al., (2003)'s research suggests that uncertainty prevents the link between thought and subsequent behaviour and emotion from developing. To help illustrate, when one believes what one sees and thus, she settles upon a specific, actionable representation of the world. However, applying belief to the social context, how can others be 'certain' of any social situation as we do not have access to all of the information necessary to lead to an informed social judgement.

However, on a note of caution, as Harris (2010) warns, we must be avoid drawing too strong a connection between disbelief and discussion (or any other mental state) on the basis of these data. Equating disbelief with disgust represents a "reverse inference" of a sort know to be problematic in the neuroimaging field. As we cannot reliability infer the presence of a mental sate on the basis of brain data alone, if and only if the anterior insula were active only if participants experienced disgust. But given the complexity of the brain and its responses, the research findings remain ambiguous in that the anterior insula appears to be involved in a wide range of neural, positive states such as music appreciation, self-recognition, smiling, and time perception (Craig, 2009; Poldrack, 2006). Thus, research findings on ambiguity remain ambiguous and contradictory, and in need of further research and study, especially regarding the development of cognitive and affective processes involved with the interpretation of ambiguous situations within adolescents. For example, how do adolescents respond emotionally to social and personal ambiguity? How do they cope with such uncertainties regarding social connections and identity?

Given the emphasis of linguistic representation in meaning and the need for clear, concise text and speech to minimize ambiguity, a growing amount of researchers are exploring the role technology plays in the ambiguities related to our social communication and personal development. As I will discuss the role technology plays in ambiguity and emotion throughout the book, I agree with educators and researchers who state the need to be cautious in how we interact with the contradictory and ambiguous nature of the moral landscape of the Internet (Harris, 2010; Hancock, 2009; Turkle, 2011). As Harris states, the Internet has simultaneously enabled two contradictory influences on belief in that it reduces intellectual isolation by providing more opportunity for people to learn the diversity of opinion on any topic, but at the same time allows others to share their beliefs – however valid or trustworthy their claims may be. How do we as adults cope with the paradoxical challenges the rapidly evolving technological landscape provides us with regarding the contradictions between freedom of speech, the right to privacy and safety? How do we as researcher and educators reconcile these contradictions and ambiguities, and how does this affect our youth today? As Harris notes, given that knowledge is increasingly becoming open-source, how does this accessibility shape our emotions and values? What are the implications for youth' social learning and developing a strong moral sense of self and identity?

Regarding the importance of clarity and reciprocity in meaningful social communication, research shows that one of the principal features of social feedback is that it systematically removes uncertainty. To explore this within a social and moral context, Delgado, Frank, and Phelps (2005) explored how adults' responses to feedback are influenced by their prior expectations. Delgado et al., explored our ability to accept or reject linguistic representation of the world within a game context where the participant played a trust game with three adults assigned a hypothetical moral character – (good, bad, and neutral). Overall, participants responded the most strongly to violations of trust in the neutral character, followed by the bad character, and were most wiling to trust the 'good' adults irrespective of their feedback within the game. The findings of this study have significant implications for adolescents within the classroom and how they interact with their peers, educators, and also family members outside of the school. That is, ambiguity affects not only how we communicate with others via written text and speech, but also in how we represent ourselves to others by either verbal or nonverbal communication. Given the importance of clearly valenced feedback for the development of trust to occur, future research needs to explore how perhaps remaining emotionally or morally neutral may have implications for how adolescents develop trust within social relationships with educators and their peers within the school context. I will return to the implications of Delgado's research in Chapter 2 when I discuss the links to education in more detail.

Developmental Foundations: In the Beginning…

Developmentally, in both the development of self-understanding and understanding social relations, both early toddlerhood (14–18 mos) and early adolescence are significant times of social cognitive learning. Research with young infants regarding ambiguity and social referencing are relevant to understanding self-knowledge and social relations, and may help to illuminate our understanding of how adolescents make sense of ambiguous situations regarding their sense of self and others. Studies with infants and their caregivers that explore infants' developing sense of self and their responses to ambiguous situations can help us to understand the origins of social cognition and identity development (Tamis-LeMonda and Aldoph, 2005), and thus could help us to make sense of the issue of ambiguity during adolescence.

As Tamis-LeMonda and Aldoph (2005) note, despite the centrality of ambiguity in the social referencing literature, the construct has been ill defined. Three interrelated problems influence extant studies of social referencing (1) definitions of ambiguity are problematic; (2) the role of infant's experience and age are not adequately examined; and (3) the meaning of infants' responses on social referencing tasks is unclear. We can glean information from research on infants and apply this to help us with research regarding ambiguity in adolescence. For example, Tamis-LeMonda and Adolph (2005) claim that studies with infants that explore the issue of ambiguity rarely consider individual differences in infants' experience and development. Researchers typically take a "one size fits all" approach to ambiguity. For example, the use of ambiguous stimulus may be used for all infants such as a visual cliff, select toys, animals, people, or the higher of the drop-off on the visual cliff (Sorce, Emde, Campos, & Klinnert, 1985). As Baldwin and Moses (1996) point out, the definition of ambiguity in traditional studies ends up being circular. As researchers claim, we can only know that a stimulus is ambiguous if infants seek social support from their mother and defer to mothers' social messages.

How does this research with infants' social referencing help us to understand social and self-ambiguity in adolescents? For example, what becomes meaningful ambiguous stimuli during adolescence, and how do adolescents differ in their interpretations of such ambiguous situations? Consider for instance the experimental paradigm of the visual cliff, or the strange toy experiment where the infant approaches an ambiguous situation with the main caregiver looking on and showing either positive or negative facial affect – the infant's task is to make a decision regarding how to act next, and how to cope with the situation – such as to take a risk, and to cross the visual cliff with the help of their mother's cues, or to take the risk of crossing, and/or approaching the strange to – irrespective of the mother's social cues.

Given that these social and personal experiences serve as parallels to markers of ambiguity during infancy when both the personal and social remain integrated and the infant is learning to differentiate between self and other, how can these experiences inform us of the developmental state of adolescence? What can findings from social referencing studies with infants tell us about the process of self-other differentiation and self-individuation during early adolescence? Who does the adolescent look to for social referencing cues when approaching an ambiguous situation and needs to make a decision regarding action?

As mentioned earlier, given that we can only know that a stimulus is ambiguous if infants seek social support from their mothers and defer to mothers' social messages, how does this finding translate to adolescence? Can we only know that a social situation is ambiguous if adolescents seek support from their peers and defer to peers' social messages? What implications does Tamis-LeMonda and Adolph's (2005) research on babies and social referencing have for the conceptualization and quantification of ambiguity in adolescence? As the infant studies may provide an ideal context for studying the emergence of infants' social referencing, what kind of studies would provide an ideal situation to study social referencing and the ontogeny of social information gathering in adolescence? What do these infant studies of ambiguity say about the adolescent's sense of self, confidence, and self-knowledge?

Whether and when infants seek and use social information will depend on their knowledge of self, as indexed in their evaluation of the situation as safe, ambiguous, or dangerous. To know that a situation is ambiguous, infants must be able to gauge the limits of their own abilities. As Tamis-LeMonda and Adolph (2005) claim, *in the absence of self-knowledge, there can be no ambiguity*. At least for motor abilities, self-knowledge depends on the duration of infants' motor experience.

Connecting this research to the adolescent experience in ambiguous situations, how do adolescents learn knowledge about themselves? How do they learn to gauge the limits of their own abilities – first motor, then emotional, social, cognitive, etc.? If there is no ambiguity in the absence of self-knowledge – how does this lay the foundation for the development of self-certainty, sense of competence, work, trust and confidence? In contrast to the lack of, or absence of self-knowledge such as inexperience, what happens when an adolescent has a sophisticated understanding of self-knowledge – does this increase their experiences of social ambiguity – are adolescents who acquire a sense of developed self-knowledge more likely to evaluate social situations as ambiguous and/or dangerous as compared to safe?

Overall, given that infants' intentional seeking and use of social information in ambiguous situations lies at the heart of social referencing, developmentalists and educators need to draw on social referencing research in infancy to help them make sense of self and social understanding later on in adolescence. However, to date, the one-size-fits all approach to social referencing exists, with little research examining individual differences, and thus the developmental emergence and continued longitudinal research of social referencing remains untested. Thus, such research will help to bridge the divide between infant social referencing and adolescent self and social understanding. Further on in this book, I will describe the theoretical and practical implications of exploring this connection between research in infants' social referencing and self-concept, emotional competence, and higher order ToM research (i.e., understanding recursive mental states, "She thinks that he thinks she likes him") in adolescents including work on understanding sarcasm and teasing (Banerjee, 2002; Barnett, Barlett, Livengood, 2010; Miller, 2009; Murphy, & Brewton, 2010; Happe, 1994; Hayward, 2011; Hughes; 2011; Keltner, 2009; Yuill, 2009).

Self-Ambiguity Continued: Sense of Coherence in Adolescence

To help adolescents with the task of self understanding and furthering one's own self knowledge, according to Antonovsky (1979)'s model of stress and health defined by 'salutogensis' or origin of health. This notion of health is characterized as a continuum, where each individual at a particular point of time exist somewhere on this continuum of health. To define where one stands on this continuum, people have 'general resilience resources' which can help them to conceptualize the world as organized and understandable. Sense of coherence (SOC) represents the motivation, and the internal and external resources one can use to cope with stressors, and plays an important role in the way one perceives challenges through life. SOC is a global orientation, an enduring tendency to see the world as more or less comprehensible (the internal and the external word are perceived as rational, understandable, consistent and predicable), manageable. Thus, the individual must believe and thus *have faith, confidence and trust* in oneself that s/he has available resources to deal with situations, and that the world is also meaningful in which one has the motivation to cope and the commitment to emotionally invest in the coping process.

SOC can also be perceived as a spiritual world view in dealing with the sources of stress, especially with regarding to the meaningfulness component (Braun-Lewensohn & Sagy, 2010). How adolescents create meaning in which some situations may be perceived as stressful, or by defining the ability to conceptualize stress a challenge or as 'fighting spirit' (Moore & Greer, 1989), one can also define SOC as a spiritual sources of coping with stress. However, what one individual perceives as a stressful event may not be considered by others as stressful. For example, some adolescents may find socially ambiguous situations stressful in that social roles and expectations remain implicit, unpredictable, inconsistent, and hidden.

According to Antovoksy's (1979) model, their ability to cope with this situation with regards to their resilience resources kit may influence their sense of self and well being. Further to this, how one perceives and copes with stress are also variable, as one individual may perceive a stressful event as a 'challenge' and 'puzzle' to solve, whereas another individual may react in a way that they perceive the stressful event as a threat to one's self and sense of safety. Educators and researchers need to develop educational programs that help youth to deal with these ambiguous and perhaps stressful events. In Chapters 2 and 3, I will describe examples of specific education models developed to help foster resilience and healthy decision-making aimed to promote well being and emotional health in adolescence (e.g., McGrath & Nobel, 2009).

As Dabrowski (1967) notes, an individual may have variable sensitivities to ambiguous and uncertain events that are unpredictable. According to Dabrowski's model of positive disintegration, some individuals may be considered to be very excitable or psychoemotionally overexcited within the context of personal, social and cultural ambiguity, and thus may experience feelings of isolation and vulnerability. Areas of future research need to focus on theses findings from within the field of applied sociocultural- neuropsychology, and need to explore ways in which educator-researchers can help adolescents to learn ways in which to effectively cope with such emotions.

As with the majority of psychological constructs, a sense of coherence is a multifaceted and dynamic concept in that may be affected by various individual and environmental factors, and thus remains flexible and vulnerable to change, especially at transition times during development. As adolescence is a crucial developmental stage in which youth further develop cognitive and emotional competencies, enabling them to take perspective, plan ahead, and see future consequences of an action, and manage emotions more effectively, all of which facilitate their abilities to deal with sources of conflict and stressful events in a variety of contexts. Additionally, early adolescence is characterized by confusion, unpredictability, and experimentation. In their longitudinal study of adolescents and mental health, Braun-Lewensohn and Sage (2010) from a developmental point of view expected stronger SOC (sense of coherence) in late adolescence. Several criteria during adolescence contribute to development of a strong construct of SOC. One of the most crucial is the stability of the community, since it helps adolescents to perceive the world around them as predictable and manageable (Antonovsky & Sagy, 1986). Furthermore, since the development of SOC in adulthood is based on adolescent experiences, adolescence seems to be a critical period. Facing ongoing stressful situations of political violence might influence adolescents' ability to develop a strong SOC.

This sense of coherence may also develop as adolescents develop their life narrative through autobiographical memories as noted earlier (Fivush, 2008). Recent research on narrative, memory, and family relations suggest that a shared collaborative perspective is related to higher adolescent self-esteem, whereas an independent perspective is related to higher adolescent self-efficacy (Bohanek et al., 2006). A closer examination of the emotional content of these narratives reveals that families that express and explain more emotion, providing a more embellished understanding and resolution of emotional experiences, have adolescents who display higher social and academic competence (Marin et al., in press). These patterns indicate that different aspects of family reminiscing are related differentially to adolescent's emerging sense of self and others.

Moral Ambiguities: Ambiguity within Canadian Culture and Values

As Grinder and Eglunde (1966) state in their review of research on adolescent development across various countries, intercultural research on adolescence offers great promise. Given that this research occurred almost 50 years ago, to what extent does transcultural research with Canadian youth in 2011 offer researchers further insight regarding their development and emotional health. Outlined below are some examples of some ways in which we can think about research with Canadian adolescents and continue to ask the questions regarding adolescents' perceptions and conceptualizations of Canadian values. For example, within the ambiguous moral and cultural Canadian landscape, what are adolescents' beliefs and feelings regarding Canadian values, and whom do they think has the power to decides which values provide the moral compass for Canadian youth today?

As Bruner (1990) mentions, if knowledge is relative to perspective, and if one considers all knowledge to be ambiguous, regarding the issue of values, how do we make sense of one's choice of perspective? To complicate matters furthers, give that everyone has a bias or cognitive frame which guides our meaning making, as Kahneman, Slovic and Tversky (1981) ask, how are we to judge the authenticity of others values and morals within the context of uncertainty or ambiguity? Are values and morals a matter of personal preference or choice? When does the personal moral domain intersect with the social conventional domain as many domain theories have discussed (see for example Nucci, 2001; Turiel). According to Bruner, values inhere in commitment to "ways of life" and ways of life in their complex interaction constitute a culture. Values are communal and consequential in terms of our relations to a cultural community and fulfill functions for us in that community. The values underlying a way of life, become incorporated in ones' self-identity and at the same time, they locate in one's culture. To the degree that a culture in Sapir's sense is no "spurious" the value commitments of its members provide either the basis for the satisfactory conduct of a way of life, or at least, a basis for negotiation. As a complete theoretical exploration of the philosophical underpinnings of moral and cultural development are beyond the scope of this book (see Harris, 2010 for further discussion regarding the complexity of moral landscapes), in this book, I will focus on some of the key questions raised by developmentalists and educational researchers and apply such questions to the context of adolescent development and educational context.

However, as Bruner (1990) cautions, the pluralism of modern life and the rapid changes it imposes may create conflicts in commitment, values, and therefore conflicts about the "rightness" of various claims to knowledge about values. Given that our world today contains ambiguities and uncertainties, I agree with Bruner in that we need to hope for a viable pluralism together with a willingness to negotiate differences in world-view. We need to be comfortable about these differences among others and ourselves, in an authentic, comparing, and compassionate way. As Bruner (1990) suggests, a psychocultural approach to educational and development emphasizes the need for us to develop and cultivate open-mindedness and demands that we be conscious of how we come to our knowledge and as conscious as we can be about the values that lead us to our perspectives. This ability to become aware of and care about other's perspectives, as well as the need to develop empathetic sensitivity or an awareness or sensitivity to one's emotional experiences as well as the experiences of others will be discussed in more detail in Chapter 3 when the educational implications of cultural, spiritual, social, and personal ambiguity are outlined and illustrate that the ability to develop open-mindedness and empathic sensitivity will remain a crucial component of any psychological program for youth.

A value system is the result of social environment and might provide aspiration for social goals through which actions can be judged, justified and motivated. Adolescence is a unique period in which values are being formed, re-evaluated and renegotiated. The formation of a value system also allows for identity development. Within the Israeli context, Sagy et al., (1999) identified three dimensions of values among adolescents: individual (e.g., personal friends, personal interests, money for self), in group collectivist (e.g., country, nationality, faith, solidarity with the poor in ones' country) and universal (e.g., international cooperation, democracy, solidarity with the poor in the world, environmental protection).

Regarding the specific Canadian context, as noted by Yon (2000) and his research, underlying the incompleteness and complexity of social interactions, as well as the tensions, contradictions and incoherencies, we need to be aware of Canada's focus on multiculturalism, as well as promoting behaviours that promote kindness, caring, and tolerance has consequences for adolescents' emotional and social development. Yon has noted that Canada's perspectives on multiculturalism can also be viewed as elusive and fluid, which also has implications for adolescents' identities and social relations with others concerning issues of diversity including gender and ethnicity. The addition of the increased use of technology and social media has also added to the culture of ambiguity within the Canadian context, as various communication levels remain unclear, especially the nonverbal communications. As Turkle (2011) notes, given that adolescents are increasingly using technological media such as social media and communication tools such as Smartphones, Twitter, Skype, texting, etc., the culture of ambiguity continues to expand. Thus, I agree with Dabrowski (1967) in that some children and adolescents may be more sensitive to ambiguity and thus, sensitivity to cultural ambiguity may also influence one's sense of coherence and emotional well being.

Consistent with the cautious attitude toward the relation between technology and education, various media thinkers such as Postman (1995) and more recently Sherry Turkle (2011) encourages educators and parents to question the social and psychological impact technology may have on youth's learning and development. As Turkle states in the book's subtitle, "We expect more from technology and less from each other," she claims that the Internet and digital age have changed since her 1995 book on created identity within the web. According to Turkle, she is now concerned with how electronic interaction may create constraints for our emotional expressions in that our range of emotional communication is controlled in a sense by our electronic interactions. Turkle mentions the work of Nass (2010) and his research with affective computing in which he claims his findings suggest that we interact with machines in the same way we interact with humans. That is, according to Nass

(2010), our brains cannot distinguish between interacting with people and interacting with electronic devices. I will elaborate on these issues of technology and moral and emotional ambiguity regarding social communication later in Chapters 2 and 3 when I explore questions such as, how do we know when we experience an authentic thought and feeling, and can electronic interaction create the same emotion and thought as a physical, face to face interaction? The implications of such possibilities for how we can help adolescents to communicate with themselves and others within this technological landscape will be explored further on in Chapter 3 when I outline the educational implications of emotional ambiguity and technology.

As the Canadian cultural context becomes increasingly diverse and complex, as Telzer (2011) notes, revisions to the theories on the acculturation gap-distress models are necessary to address the complex cultural landscape. This issue becomes an increasingly significant one regarding issues of ambiguity concerning a youth's cultural identity, particularly as the adolescent as compared to their parents, may experience different connections to their native or home country as opposed to their host country and vice versa. The acculturation gap-distress model purports that immigrant children acculturate to their new culture at a quicker pace than their parents, leading to family conflict and youth maladjustment. Telzer critiques the acculturation gap-distress model, showing that acculturation gaps function in unique ways depending on many social and contextual variables. According to Telzer, in contrast to the original model, which only discusses one type of acculturation gap, there are at least 4 types of acculturation gaps: (1) the youth is more acculturated than the parent in the host culture, (2) the youth is less acculturated than the parent in the host culture, (3) the youth is more acculturated than the parent in the native culture, and (4) the youth is less acculturated than the parent in the native culture. Thus, each of these types of gaps function in unique ways and have significant implications for youth in Canada with their social relationships and personal identity, as well as educational implications for the culturally diverse adolescent classroom.

Given the ambiguity surrounding the complex possibilities of these acculturation differences, how do adolescents learn how to make sense of such cultural ambiguities, and how are they to create trusting relationships and a coherent sense of self within such an ambiguous cultural context? For example, how does an adolescent Canadian-Ukrainian female who was born in Canada and has little knowledge of Ukrainian culture deal with parents who have limited knowledge of English, but are set against any use of Ukrainian language from their daughter, and discourage any reference to, or knowledge of the Ukrainian culture in favour of Canadian culture? Or picture the case of the same family, but reverse the scenario where the parents although fluent in the English language and Canadian culture, may encourage the use and learning of Ukrainian culture, whereas their daughter may prefer to learn English and only focus on Canadian culture? How is the adolescent female to develop a culturally coherent identity – does she consider herself to be Canadian? Ukrainian? Both? As one can imagine the numerous possibilities of this acculturation model and it will increase with complexity given the number of cultures within a family. As this particular example focuses on two of the models, there are many more complicated examples of multicultural families involving multiple cultural backgrounds, as well as considering how factors such as gender, age, level of education, financial status of the family among others may play a role in such models. Given the complexity of this issue, as Costigan (2011) and Phinney (2011) note, researchers and educators need to continue to explore these complex and ambiguous cultural models as they have critical implications for how a youth develops a coherent sense of self and social and emotional competence.

Surprisingly, despite the significance of this crucial transitory time, the majority of past research has focused on adolescents' cognitive abilities (Harter, 1999), and thus needs to further explore adolescents' emotional lives including their values and beliefs within a psycholocultural framework (Harter, 1999). Why have researchers continued to neglect the spiritual and socioaffective aspects of adolescent development? Is there anything distinctive about their affective development and the place of spirituality in their lives? To answer such questions, this book will consider how young adolescents make sense of themselves, and the world around them. As educators and researchers suggest (Damon, 2008; Twenge, 2006), as we enter a new millenium, researchers and educators who work with youth need to be open to new questions and new conceptions of adolescence as historically, scientific and lay conceptions of adolescents have diverged.

In addition to the reasons previously mentioned, early adolescence is often considered to be of developmental interest due to the emergence during this period of reflective/abstract thought (e.g., Piaget, 1962; Chandler, 1987), an increase in gender-role expectations and behaviours and the increase of self-contradiction and conflict (Blos, 1979; Harter, 1999). Furthermore, the lack of research on developmental, gendered social and self-understanding suggests that such an investigation would be fruitful. Early adolescence can also be viewed as a transitional phase, a discontinuous shift in the self-system. The characterization of the transition to adolescence as discontinuous is consistent with psychoanalytic, sociobiological, and sociocognitive-developmental models. Particularly during this time, conflict episodes may represent a rich microcosm through which novel self, peer, and parent relationships emerge and stabilize. Empirical and theoretical work supports the notion that early adolescence beings a period of shifting power dynamics, which may lead to competing goals and results in a higher density of conflict opportunities. As Baumrind (1991) suggests, adolescent maturity is thought to grow from "the balance between agency and communion, between separation and connectedness, and between conflict and harmony" (p. 120).

As adolescents struggle for balance, they may experience contradiction, conflict, which in turn may lead to experiences of ambiguities within themselves and others. That is, interpersonal conflict may lead to ambiguous social situations whereas intrapersonal the conflict may manifest as a lack of, or unclear and ambiguous private speech or inner dialogue. Thus, adolescents may begin to feel at conflict with themselves, and their own competing worlds of the public and private. Given that the adolescent needs to accomplish two main tasks, that of social connection and individuation, many researchers have noted the complexity and paradoxical qualities of this time which have implications for silence and voice.

Where: Adolescent Culture and Role of Technology in Self and Social Ambiguity

As Yon states (2000) Canada' culture of tolerance and diversity creates the context for a culture of ambiguity and ambivalence that adolescents must deal within the context of their learning journey to develop self and social understanding. Does tolerance and acceptance promote ambiguity and moral disengagement? For example, how do adolescents cope effectively with conflicting messages and increasing pressure to excel and cater to one's individual needs, although simultaneously, there is an increasing pressure to be tolerant, kind and compassionate towards diversity, and strive to meet the needs of others toward social justices and human rights.

According to Bandura (2001), times of uncertainty and contradictions within an ambiguous and complex larger cultural landscape may lead some adolescents to diseng morally. Bandura explains this process of moral disengagement in terms of social cognitive theory, in which one's moral behavior is a function of moral reasoning and the self-regulatory mechanism of self-monitoring, judgment, and self-reactions (Bandura, Barbaranelli, Caprara, & Pastoretti, 1996). This theory describes the cognitive processes by which moral disengagement (deactivation of internal controls) is used to justify behavior to self that is in violation of one's internal moral standards. Bandura also states that while moral disengagement occurs in a social and cultural context, such social circumstances can possibly weaken internal self-regulatory mechanisms and may hinder the development of moral and emotional sense of well being.

Regarding the role of emotions, to what extent does ambiguity lead to 'emotional disengagement' – and to what extent can an adolescent student appear to be cognitively and morally on the surface engaged – is there anyway to evaluate how the adolescent feels? What emotions are she/her experiencing toward oneself, others? As Laron (2011) note, how can researchers explore the connections betwen the feeling of boredom and disengagement? Can one be cognitively and morally engaged in an activity but remain emotionally disengaged – feeling no emotions, or perhaps experience negative emotions? As Larson (2011) notes, how can researchers explore the connections between boredom and disengagement? How do researchers and educators investigate this personal beliefs system and emotional framework?

The digital world in which youth socialize may also have the potential to serve as a social context that may promote moral disengagement (Hancock, 2009; Turkle, 2011). For example, the inability to observe the immediate reaction of the victim may allow the perpetrator to believe, "It was just a joke," or "He/she didn't really mind." The cyberbully might minimize the behavior by thinking, "I didn't hit her or anything. That would be bad, but this is not." The online disinhibition effect (Suler, 2004) noted above could be conceptualized as a variation of moral disengagement, as it allows the individual to behave in ways that are contrary to his or her usual moral code.

Regarding the process of disengagement, and I would further add to this by extending it to disenchantment - what role does belief and emotional experience in this 'en/disenchanted?" As Humphrey (2011) also notes - how can we protect our youth and ourselves from becoming disenchanted, or as Humphrey states "psychological zombies" who do not experiences or understand emotions. To what extent would we become emotional zombies? Further in the book during Chapter 3, I will return to the notion of disenchantment and the role technology may play in the classroom and creating emotional and social ambiguities within the adolescent context.

Related to feelings of enchantment, awe, and wonder as Humphrey (2011) and Keltner (2009) discuss, how does emotion play a role in our sense of awe? And I would build on this and ask, how are awe and emotional experiences related to en/disengagement? Regarding education - can we replace "engaged' with 'enchanted?" - how do children learn to become "enchanted with learning?" For example, within a religious and spiritual context, if one thinks believers are enchanted by religious icons - how do they learn to become to believe and what how does this belief develop into, or relate to enchantment? Applying this line of thinking to an educational context, how do learners become enchanted with the teacher/teaching/learning process?

As Damon (2008) discusses in his work regarding how adolescents find meaning in their path to purpose, how do young students become disengaged with their lives and how is this connected with their ability to find a sense of meaning and purpose in their lives? How did they become engaged or enchanted with learning in the first place, and what happened to allow them to become disengaged? Given the complex and ambiguous nature of engagement and learning, researchers need to explore how adolescents develop a sense of engagement and then for some, the process of disengagement and boredom in learning. What are the implications for the adolescent's social and personal lives?

According to Damon and his colleagues (2008), a sense of purpose refers to "a stable, and generalized intention to accomplish something that is at the same time meaningful to the self and consequential for the world beyond the self" (p. 33). This paradoxical and complex nature of purpose remains a puzzle for those who work with youth as it entails both a personal and social aspect and is simultaneously independent of one another, as well as dependent upon one another. For example – a sense of purpose according to Damon claims to be the foundation for one's goals in life and the reason for "why" we have goals and motivations to behave the in ways that we choose to move forward. Thus, this sense of purpose is connected to moving forward and to learning and growing, not only individually, but also for a genuine concern for others to grow and move forward as well.

Damon (2008) reflects on his research with American youth and their responses from interviews based on a questionnaire regarding the Youth Purpose study. In sum, Damon's research showed that the youth's responses could be divided in terms of the sense of purpose they expressed in their lives. And their responses allowed the researchers to divide the youth into four main groups [disengaged (25%), dabblers (31%), dreamers (25%), and purposeful (20%)]. Regarding the role of ambiguity in these youth's plans, interestingly, perhaps the purposeful group that experienced the least amount of ambiguity in their responses, stated that they have found meaningful goals in their life to inspire them to create a coherent future agenda, they know what they want to accomplish and why, and have made steps to achieve their goals. Ambiguity may have played a larger role in the plans of the dreamers and dabblers, as both groups appear to have purposeful aspirations but have taken few if any steps to act as in the case of the dreamers. Although the dabblers acted on various purposeful pursuits, they still may have experienced ambiguity they did not express a clear sense of why they are acting and whether or not they will stay with their interests.

Damon (2008) states his concern over the problem of youths who appear to be disengaged and do not appear to believe that they have a purposeful life, and appeared to express emotional ambiguity through their manner of ambivalence and nonchalance during the interviews. According to Damon (2008), this dis-engagement illustrated by these particular youth is a problem for society in that there appears to be an emotional disconnect between these youth and their caring for others and themselves. What would create the foundation for this sense of purposelessness or direction in life? How do such youth deal with the increasingly moral and cultural diversity North American society?

Damon (2008) states that the dabblers and the dreamers are the groups that perhaps remain in the greatest state of developmental flux they may be moving toward developing a purposeful life. However, to what extent can those who work with youth help to guide and support them so that they see the connection between intention and action? Damon (2008) builds on this concern and claims that the group of disengaged youth, and I would further build on this by claiming that they are disenchanted with learning, remains the most significant challenge for parents, researchers, educators and developmental and clinical psychologists. Working with youth to help them to feel a sense of meaning, direction, and purpose in their lives which will lead to well being remains a top priority for educators and schools that I will return to and elaborate on in Chapter 3 when I discuss how researchers and educators can collaborate to co-create a holistic, developmentally appropriate educational programs that promote both a personal sense of meaning as well as a sense of purpose for helping others and larger society.

In addition to the disengaged youth, I am also in agreement with Damon (2008), that perhaps the youth categorized as dabblers and dreamers may are also be at risk for failing to develop a coherent sense of self and meaningful life purpose. In contrast to disengaged youth who claim to have no sense of connection, those who are dreamers and dabblers both share ambiguities regarding their paths from intention to action as the dreamers may think about purpose but fail to act on their intentions, whereas the dabblers in a sense somewhat share a similarity to multitaskers regarding the use of technology. Dabblers who participate in various activities with little purpose and an overall plan could be viewed as remaining disconnected to others and their sense of purpose and meaning. As Turkle (2011) discusses in her reflections on her interviews with youth and adults regarding their experiences with technology, youth who participate in various tasks while interacting with others often experience a sense of emotional disconnect with others and a lack of meaning and direction regarding their personal lives.

In the case of youth who may be both dabblers or multitaskers, and dreamers, to what extent does technology help them to create purpose and meaning in our lives? If developing a sense of connection with self and others is necessary for leading a purposeful lives, to what extent does technology shape our emotional lives and interactions with others. What are the moral and emotional implications of remaining as Turkle (2011) states, "alone and together" (p. 14), or "there but not there." (p. 14). When interacting with others, and also ourselves, does the constant use of technology, or engaging in various activities with no overall purpose or goal prevent us from being alone with ourselves? To what extent are youth at risk for developing an ambiguous and incoherent sense of self and social connections within the current technological landscape? For example, why would an adolescent choose or prefer to take action that violates their personal moral and value codes – and is this process of moral decision making the same for virtual and real-life worlds? How do they develop and learn values and moral codes within a culture of multiple values and ambiguities and learn to decided which value is the preferred value and one that guides their personal and social worlds (both on-line and in real-time)? I will return to these questions in Chapters 2 and 3 when I discuss the research on adolescents' experiences with technology in relation to ambiguity, and the implications technology has for the youth's emotional, and moral, social lives.

Adolescents within Secondary School Culture in Canada

The secondary school context is a prime source for a host of multiple ambiguities and mixed messages regarding one's sense of self, social relations, and cultural issues. According to Suarez-Orozoco, Sattin-Banjaj and Suarez-Orozco (2010), in their description of the foundation for the Ross School, model, similar to Yon's (2004) notion of school a discursive place, schools are organized around a master narrative and animated by social practices and cultural models that align to the values, ethics, and worldviews encompassed in that narrative (Selman, 2003). Kroeber and Kluckhohn's (1952) synthetic work on the idea of culture is useful in suggesting how to think about the ways in which a school's culture can construct meanings, pattern interpersonal relationships, and shape institutional life. School cultures are organized around foundational narratives that are developed out of common experiences in the here and now but that also account for origins and a sense of mission in facing the future. School narratives are built on collective histories, stories, and the microrituals of belonging that communicate to every member of the school community. According to Rosaldo (1989), school cultures, like all cultures, are never monolithic, univocal, or static.

All cultures, especially the school culture, contain diversity, and contradiction – where cultural narrative suggest a plasticity where continuity and change contain and necessitate each other. As such, a cultural system that is able to adapt to new cultural realities and fuse the external forces with needs and values through internal symbolic logic will manage to navigate change in more productive ways and ideally lead to a culture of engagement and well-being. Given our emotional responses to change and contradiction within a larger context of ambiguity may lead to feelings of ambivalence that may influence how youth develop personally as well as socially. As noted by Yon (2004), living with such contradictory positions and opposing multiple subjectivities may lead to ambivalence or feelings that are mixed and uncertain. In Chapter 2, I will describe related research that explores the personal and social ambiguities experienced by adolescents in the classroom, during play and leisure time regarding virtual games, social networking, and involvement in extracurricular actives such as various sports, after school clubs, etc. The role of humour in ambiguity will also be discussed as it also plays a role in adolescents' experience. Finally, in Chapter 3, I will discuss educational programs that promote this pathway to the culture of engagement.

SUMMARY

In summary, how can we build on Grinder and Englund's (1966) claim that remains relevant almost fifty years later, "Major and rapid social and technological changes, as aspects of cultural contact, are disrupting traditional generalizations about socializing experiences, personality traits, and cultural patterns." (p. 459)? As I discuss in the next two chapters, as educators and researchers, we need to continue to investigate these complexities in the hopes that this research with adolescents may provide some practical educational strategies to help adolescents to develop a sense of personal well being and social and emotional competence within a complicated and ambiguous cultural context.

CHAPTER 2

WHAT? PAST AND CURRENT RESEARCH ON PSYCHOLOGICAL UNDERSTANDING AND AMBIGUITY IN ADOLESCENCE

"You know my method. It is founded upon the observation of trifles." (*Sherlock Holmes*, Doyle, 1892, p. 340)

"Everything there is, is worth observing." (Capek, 1927, p. 78)

Adolescence ←——→Ambiguity   ←→self, social, cultural, spiritual worlds

INTRODUCTION

In this chapter, I will provide a critical overview and discussion of past and current research on psychological understanding in early and middle adolescence. This chapter contains an outline of theories and research that support the notion that adolescents may begin to experience self and social ambiguity differently from younger children and adults, and these differences may be influenced by gender, cultural background, and age. I will describe related research that explores the personal and social ambiguities experienced by adolescents in the classroom during play and leisure time regarding virtual games, social networking, and involvement in extracurricular actives such as various sports, after school clubs, etc. I will outline research on self-development that shows that given an increase in adolescents' metacognitive abilities, the search for self often intensifies in early adolescence, including more advanced critical self-examination and social judgement. Connections will be explored between self-understanding and self-knowledge, building on higher order Theory of Mind in adolescents, as well as the adolescents' ability to understand ambiguous contexts containing humour, teasing, bullying, and deception.

The peer culture of the adolescent world also promotes an aura of ambiguity, especially regarding the social conversations that occur – both in-person, and more recently, and within the past decade, virtually through the use of social media via the Internet. Websites such as facebook.com and twitter.com have extended the landscape of ambiguity. This culture of ambiguity within the cyberworld is increasingly being examined by scholars as a possible context for further ambiguity to develop in both self understanding and identity development as well as our social relations with one another (Bauman, 2010; Postman, 2005; Twenge, 2006; Turkle, 2011). I will address some of the educational implications these virtual contexts may hold for adolescent self and social development further in Chapter 3.

Everyday conversations among teenagers provides multiple possible ambiguities, as Laing (1969) mentions in his discussion of discourse and relationships. Such ordinary discourse occurs in various contexts and these same arrangements of words,

27

smiles, groans, or gestures can function in many possible ways according to the context - but who 'defines' the context? As Yuill (2009) and others note (Olson, 1996, 2007; Bonitatibus & Beal, 1996), the group of studies that explore children's interpretive ambiguity in text may help us to begin to understand how and why adolescents become to understand the ambiguous landscape of social communication, particularly the ambiguous nature of social silences (Bosacki, 2005). As outlined later on in this chapter, studies on adolescents' interpretations of metaphor, irony and sarcasm show, the same form of words can be used as a plain statement of fact, as an attributions, as an injunction, as an attribution, as a joke, a threat, etc.

DEVELOPMENTAL RESEARCH ON CHILDREN'S UNDERSTANDING OF AMBIGUITY AND INTERPRETATION: SOCIAL DETECTIVES IN TRAINING?

"My dear doctor, this is a time for observation, not for talk." (*Sherlock Holmes*, p. 151, Doyle, 1892)

According to Yuill (2009), children in the early years of schooling show important changes in their understanding of the relation between text and meaning, as shown for example in the increasing ability to discriminate between verbatim and paraphrase (Lee, Torrance & Olson, 2001), the explicit recognition of interpretive ambiguity (Bonitatibus & Beal, 1996) and the judgement of spoken message adequacy (e.g., Robinson & Robinson, 1983). Olson (1996) argues that the acquisition of literacy brings the understanding that the wording of a text is fixed, but its meaning is subject to interpretation. The interpretive nature of text is particularly salient in the rather specific case of ambiguity deriving from lexical or structural properties of language, where there are two quite different interpretations of a text that are both plausible, as for example in the case of homonyms and of jokes based on linguistic ambiguity. Verbal jokes belong to a genre of language in which multiple interpretations are the explicit focus: to 'get' a joke is to appreciate how a particular context misleads us into the wrong interpretation of an ambiguous text. For example, take the joke: 'How do you make a sausage roll? – Push it down a hill.' The common meaning of 'sausage roll' is a type of savoury food, but the answer to the joke question does not make sense in this context, since an appropriate answer would mention cooking, pastry, and sausage meat. The answer can only be understood by reinterpreting the syntax of the question so that it refers to the more unusual, or uncued meaning of a sausage being rolled.

Children may understand the basic possibility of lexical and structural ambiguity at a relatively early age, but there seem to be marked individual differences over a wide age range in appreciating these aspects of ambiguity. For example, even in the basic understanding that one word can have different meanings, there is an early conceptual recognition of homonymy at the age of 4 (Doherty, 2000), but many children show poor performance, even up to the age of 10, in selecting referents for pseudohomonyms (Doherty, 2004). Similarly, children from the age of around 7 show competence in understanding at least some types of verbal humour (Hirsh-Pasek, Gleitman & Gleitman, 1978; Schultz, 1974; Schultz &

Horibe, 1974), but there are wide individual differences in 7- to 9-year-olds in the ability to recall and explain such jokes (Yuill, 2009).

These individual differences in understanding structural ambiguity in language may derive from two general types of process, both of which deserve further investigation. First, children may have difficulties in automatic aspects of processing that affect their interpretation of ambiguous text: for example, Gernsbacher and others (e.g., Gernsbacher, 1990) suggest that activation of irrelevant meanings of ambiguous words competes with the correct interpretation, and less-skilled readers may fail to suppress such irrelevant meanings, or to enhance activation of relevant meanings.

Second, Long, Seely and Oppy (1999) suggest that there may be more controllable and strategic processes affecting the selection of appropriate meaning in good and poor readers, which would be particularly evident in tasks that have metacognitive demands (e.g., judgements of meaning rather than lexical decision). Building on previous research on understanding of ambiguity at the strategic level in children with good or poor reading comprehension (e.g., Yuill, 2009), how can researchers apply these findings or help them explore adolescents make sense of ambiguity in their social context within the classroom. In addition, as I explore in the next section, how does this understanding of linguistic ambiguity relate to the understanding of humour in self and others and what does this means for the adolescent?

The Ambiguity of Interpretation: Humour and Neuromagic

Given (1947) claim that jokes have a moral component and depend on an ambiguity with both cases having contradictory meanings (e.g., scale of noble-naughty/intellectual/instinctual, p. 246) research on children's understanding of humour, cynicism, irony, and sarcasm may help us to uncover how adolescents make sense of social and personal ambiguity within the classroom (Pexman et al., 2005; Filoppova & Astington, 2008; Mills & Keil, 2005; Recchia, Howe, Ross, & Alexander, 2010; Winner, 1988). In relation to understanding sarcasm and irony, humour is an exclusive and complicated human phenomenon, which depends on many factors (McGhee, 1977; McGhee & Goldstein, 1983; Paulos, 1980, see Semrud-Clikeman & Glass, 2010 for a review). Thus, although most researchers generally agree that cognitive development is the basic element of appreciating and producing humour, although the role of humour and morality are less explored (Bergen, 2008; Chaney & Carolyn 1993; Johnson & Mervis, 1997; Lyons & Fitzgerald, 2004; McGhee, 1984; Pien & Rothbart, 1980; Schultz, 1972).

Drawing on research findings of children' understanding interpretive ambiguity within text and conversations (Beal & Bonitivus, 1996; Torrance & Olson, 1991), research on metaphor, irony, sarcasm, lying, and humour reveal that children in middle childhood and approaching adolescence are more likely to understand the meaning of ambiguous statements based on the intonation of the speaker. For example, studies on sarcasm found that if children heard an ambiguous statement with a negative intonation, this would be perceived as being a sarcastic statement (Capelli, Nakagaw, & Madden, 1990). More specifically, research on the development of understanding humour suggests that by the age of 6 to 7 years, children are beginning to understand the concept of double meanings which allows them to start appreciating jokes and riddles. Given that research suggests that development of cognition and humour are inextricably connected (McGhee, 1984), most of the work on humour focused on children's perception of humourous incongruities (Bariaud, 1989; McGhee; Pien & Rothbart, 1980; Schultz, 1974, 1976; Sroufe & Wunsch, 1972), with the majority of studies focusing on humour appreciation, comprehension, and cognitive development, and were conducted in experimental settings, using graphic stimuli as materials and smiling and laughter as indicators of humour. For example, Schultz (1972) used cartoons in an investigation of the role of incongruity and resolution in children's appreciation of humour, whereas Hoicka and Gattis (2008) found that 19-month-old children could differentiate between intentional jokes and unintentional mistakes. Similarly, research on humour and cognitive development investigated young children's humour using observation in natural circumstances, For example, Loizou (2005) examined the humour of young children under the age of two by observing them in a group childcare setting via an open and flexible method.

Given the complexity of the school context, developing understanding of jokes in early and middle childhood, and even in adolescence, has been examined by many authors (Bernstein, 1986; Bariaud, 1988; Cameron, Kennedy & Cameron, 2001; Abrahamsen, 2004; Radomska, 2007). As understanding humour, irony, and any other ambiguous statements suggests we need to step out of literal meaning, it is a very valuable way to research how children in adolescence understand mental states (Lalonde & Chandler, 2002; Filippova & Astington, 2008). Furthermore, humor comprehension may reflect a child's ability to differentiate between "what you said and what you really meant and how you feel." Thus, the perception that other people act intentionally plays a critical role in ToM and helps children to understand the meanings behind people's actions which will help them to decipher ambiguous social events..

Although the ability to create and understand jokes may help us to learn how children understanding of mental states in others in ambiguous situations, the processes of creating and understanding jokes are usually researched separately. Examples of past research involve exploring humor as a coping tool (Fuhr, 2002), and a weathervane for emerging cognitive abilities such as recognizing intentionality and understanding symbolism (for a review of developmental research see: Martin, 2007). To explore the relation between these two processes and how they relate to ToM, Kielar-Turska and Bialecka-Pikul (2009) explored 5- to 9-year-old Polish children's ability to generate and understand visual jokes as an expression of ToM. Kielar-Turska and Bialecka-Pikul asked children to draw a funny picture and then justify what made it funny, as well as provide a funny story. Two months later they were presented with selected drawings and they were asked to judge whether or not the drawing was funny. Overall, findings suggest that children's ability to understand the artist's intention increased with age, suggesting that the relation between a more complex, interpretive ToM and the ability to understand jokes increases with age. Moreover, findings suggested that children were more likely to find a drawing funny if their friend found it to be funny and thus supports Zygulski's (1976) claim that the community of laughter as reflected in family and peer environments may influence a child's perceptions of humour (Żygulski, 1976).

Given that cultural psychologists view culture and mind as inseparable, and argue that there are no common rules pertaining to how the mind works (Bruner, 1996; Tomasello, 1999; Johnson & Mervis, 1997; Lillard, 1997; Wellman et al., 2006; Xeromeritou, 2004). it would be interesting to conduct Kielar-Turska and Bialecka-Pikul's (2009) study in a variety of countries and compare findings, Thus, what is found to be humourous in one culture may not be viewed as such in another culture. Martin (2007) maintains that humour and laughter are universal in all cultures, but that cultural approaches may vary. However, there has been little cross-cultural comparison of humour as it relates to cognitive development. For example, Americans were found to have a higher sense of humour in the area of creativity than their Spanish counterparts (Thorson, Valero, & Carbelo Baquero, 2006). Chinese university students, as compared to Canadian norms, were reported to have significantly lower scores on humour styles and coping humour (Chen & Martin, 2007). In Western cultures, especially American culture, humour plays a main role in creativity and personality, unlike in the Chinese culture humour where it plays the least important role (Yue, 2008). Given these results, future research needs to continue to explore the role culture, age, and gender play in children's and adolescents' understanding of ambiguous contexts such as humour.

One important question for future research will be to establish the precise nature of younger children's and some youth's difficulty in detecting and reporting interpretive uncertainty and ambiguity in text passages that may or may not contain elements of humour. One possibility is that second graders' difficulty in this area reflects monitoring difficulties resulting from a confusion of literal and intended meaning (Beal & Flavell, 1984). For example, Yuill (2009) notes that exposure to ambiguities in joking riddles might in itself be a useful experience to increase 'sensitivity to meaning', but the role of discussion in fostering improvement may also be important. There is a large literature on the role of peer discussion in learning, much of it based on Vygotskyan ideas. Vygotsky (1930/1978) argued that cognitive development occurs through social interaction, and that this development is mediated by language. Higher mental processes (such as comprehension) first appear through dialogue with others, and the language of these dialogues becomes internalized as private speech.

As I will discuss further in Chapter 3 several intervention programmes in the area of reading comprehension incorporate peer tutoring and the use of humour as a tool to cope with stressful and challenging experiences (e.g., Fuchs, Fuchs, Mathes & Simmons, 1997; King, 1990; Palincsar & Brown, 1984). Such programs challenge children to further their own understanding and to make elaborated explanations to their peers. There is also evidence that readers can be trained in explaining text to themselves, as an aid to reading comprehension (e.g., SERT; McNamara, 2004). Given that research findings suggest that the ability to understand humour within ambiguous situations may lead to positive learning experiences and help children to develop a sense of resilience. I will outline strategies to incorporate humour into holistic, inclusive educational programs for adolescents.

Researchers need to continue to explore children's understanding of complex and ambiguous situations within the context of peer relations, especially during early and middle adolescence when the subtleties of language are sometimes used by others to sometimes mask negative and hurtful judgemental statements about others within humour through the use of teasing and irony. Given the linguistic ambiguities of such statements – children who have the competence to understand these double meanings may be more sensitive to such emotionally ambiguous in that they are interpreted as hurtful statements which may possibly may have a negative and damaging influence on their sense of self.

Given that most adolescents are co-constructing a sense of self or possible selves (Markus & Kitayma, 1994; Markus & Wurf, 1987), and that "every relationship implies definition of self by other and other by self" (Laing, 1969, p. 86), they may be cautious or hesitant to communicate their authentic self with feeling and thoughts. A person's 'own' identity or identities cannot be completely abstracted from her/his identity for other. Her identity-for-herself, the identity others ascribe to her; the identities she attributes to them; the identities she thinks her friends and family attribute, in other words, what she thinks her friends think she thinks they think (about her).

During adolescence as the self continues to develop, the definition of self becomes problematic as it becomes increasingly complex to imagine one's true self – given the multiple definitions of the self. In addition to Markus and Wurf's (1985) notion of dynamic and changing selves, Harter's (1999) explores multiple selves such as social, academic, athletic, behavioral conduct, physical appearance and also a general sense of well being and in addition to the task of juggling these multiples selves, adolescents also have the tasks of negotiating between their 'real' or 'ideal' self - and how do they relate to one another. As Kahneman (2003) also writes, we have our experiencing selves and our remembering self, as our experiencing selves are what we experience during life events such as a social interaction including which may be associated with particular thoughts and emotions. We also have our remembering self which takes into account the cognitive markers of the event and how this influences our sense of personal well being regarding our thoughts and emotions. As Kahneman asserts, these selves may not correlate with each other, and the individual will need to negotiate these selves within the personal landscape. This task of negotiating the various selves further adds to the complex emotional landscape of the adolescent, particularly during the school context, with implications for our emotional well being including our feelings of happiness (Harris, 2010).

SELF-AMBIGUITY

"Who are you?" said the Caterpillar. Alice replied, rather shyly, I-I hardly know, sir, just at present-at least I know who I was when I got up this morning, but I think I must have changed several times since then." (Caroll, 1916, p. 67)

Given that this ability to understand what others think of one's own mental states and emotions may also be considered to reflect a higher order ToM understanding (Astington, 1993; Homer et al., 2011; Hughes, 2011), such an ability may also have implications for an adolescent's own identity, which defined by Laing (1969, p. 86) is where "one feels one is the same, in this place, this time as at that time and at that place, past or future, it is that by which one is identified." How do adolescents make the connection between the ability to understand social messages and how does this ability affect one's identity and sense of personal well being.

As discussed in Chapter 1, Tamis-LeMonda and Adolph (2005) research with social referencing and the visual cliff with infants leads the researchers to claim that *in the absence of self-knowledge, there can be no ambiguity*. Within the context of adolescent experience in socially ambiguous situations, how do adolescents learn knowledge about their sense of self? How do they learn to judge the limits of their own competencies such as their moral and emotional skills? Does a more developed sense of self and ability to conceptualize as a person lead to a great sense of insecurity and self-doubt surrounding an incoherent or ambiguous self? If there is no ambiguity in the absence of self-knowledge – how does this create the foundation for the development of self-compassion and the ability to work and be compassionate towards others?

With the context of adolescence, as this developmental time is viewed by many theorists as a time of transition and stress which would entail ambiguity as the meanings of stress are multifaceted and multivalenced according to one's interpretation. As I first discussed the importance of Antovosky's (1979) model of sense of coherence (SOH) for adolescents, according to this model, youth with a well developed or strong sense of coherence are more likely to make meaning from situations that are ambiguous and stressful in that they are able to feel challenged by such events as they view these situations as valuable opportunities for growth and learning. In contrast to opportunities for growth and hope, youth with a weak sense of coherence are more likely to read the same ambiguous stressful situation as anxiety provoking and thus feel threatened by such situations. Their decisions to cope with such situations may involve self- harmful behaviours and negative social interactions. Researchers need to explore how adolescents decide to view such ambiguous situations, and how do they learn to develop these frame of minds or global orientations and which factors influence their ability to develop this frame of mind and heart? As Braun-Lewensohn and Sagy (2010) ask, how can we as educators and researchers learn to help youth to view ambiguity as a opportunity to see the world as comprehensible, rational, understandable, consistent and expected?

To help us answer such questions in terms of viewing ambiguous situations as language games, we could draw on Wiggenstein's (1953) two methods of representation and communication regarding 'showing' and 'saying' with the saying referring to propositionizing and is assertive and requires a tight coupling of logical and syntactive structure with what it asserts. In contrast, showing is not assertive, and presents information differently, in a nonsymbolic way with no underlying grammar or syntactic structure. As Wiggenstein (1953) discusses showing and saying, Kosslyn's (1973; 2006) work on imagery discusses imagers and verbalizers – with the former depicting or showing information to communicate with direct and unmediated representations, and verbalizers who describe or say their information with analytic representations that is mediated by verbal or other symbols. Similarly, Bruner (1986; 1996) discusses the two modes of thought as in narrative and logico-scientific or paradigmatic modes of thought as characterized by iconic visualization or the visualization of something outside oneself, and enactive visualization an integral feature of a performance (real or imagined) respectively. Further, according to Bruner (1986), the narrative mode of thinking requires the learner to make sense of meaning by understanding the landscape of action (arguments of action including the agent, intention and goal of the character), and the landscape of consciousness (understanding what those involved in the action are thinking and feeling), and within a particular social context. I will return to Wiggenstein's (1953) notion of language games further in this chapter when I describe how adolescents make sense of socially ambiguous situations between peers.

VISUAL NEUROSCIENCE RESEARCH AND AMBIGUITY

Research in visual neuroscience is also another area of research that is emerging and may help us to make sense of how adolescents interpret and understand ambiguous interactions. A newly developed area of research that stems from perception and neuroscience is that of Neuromagic. This area of inquiry involves research regarding visual illusions and how we interpret ambiguous and incomplete information and leading neuroscientists Macknik and Martinez-Conde (2010; 2011) explore what the neuroscience of magic and enchantment and how they reveal how we make sense of everyday deceptions in the new area of research referred to as neuromagic. Machnik and Martinez-Conde (2010) aim to understand how magicians work with our brains, and suggest that we can better understand how the same cognitive tricks are at work in advertising strategy, business negotiations, and all varieties of interpersonal relations. Their research aims to understand how magic works in the mind of the spectator and aims to uncover the neural bases of consciousness.

Machnik and Martinez-Conde's (2010) multi-year, world-wide research involved an exploration of magic and how its principles apply to our behavior. The authors claim how magic can reveal how our brains work in everyday situations. Their research supports the idea that the brain mechanisms that elicit perceived illusions, automatic reactions, and perhaps consciousness itself define in the most part who you are. They claim that visual illusions, a psychological principal refers to an illusion that occurs when physical reality does not match perception. In the visual perception process, our visual system makes inferences and guesses, your visual circuit amplify, suppress, converge, and diverge visual information. You perceive what you see as something different from reality. According to Machnik and Martinex-Conde, perception means resolving ambiguity. You reach the most plausible interpretation of retinal input by integrating local cues.

For instance, if their research is applied to the social ambiguous situations experienced during adolescence, if an adolescent behaves a particular way or makes a decision that she had never previously imagined and thus surprises herself, her peer was probably a master or expert at creating the "illusion of choice," a core technique of magic. Thus, the implications of neuromagic go beyond illuminating our behavior as their research points to new approaches for everything from the diagnosis of autism to educational strategies. The new area of neuromagic makes neuroscience fun and accessible by unveiling the key connections between magic, mind, and emotion and is another example of current researcher that can help us to understand how adolescents make sense of social and personal ambiguity.

Related to the area of neuromagic, cognitive neuroscientists such as Rudiger von der Heydt who study the emotion of love, explore the mismatch between physical reality and perception. They claim that love, as with all emotions, have no external physical reality and may be driven by neural events, but remains a subjective experience. For example, when shown a diagram with a heart through it, although there is no heart, an imaginary edge defined by the arrows, this effect is called an illusory contour. We perceive the shape of the heart only because our brains impose a shape on a very sparse field of data. Rudiger von der Heydt and colleagues have shown that illusory contours are processes in neurons with areas of the brain called V2, which is devoted to vision (Zhang & Rudiger von der Heydt, 2010). Thus, the researchers claim that this illusory contour helps us in much of our day-to-day experiences as the majority of your interactions consists of analogous feats of filling in the blanks as we take what we know about the world and use it to imagine what we do not know.

As researcher and educators continue to place the emotional well being and psychological safety of adolescents at the forefront of developmental research, such researchers need to be aware of the complex findings gleaned from the field of applied neuroscience. The strengthening of the connection between applied neuroscience and educational practice can help educators and researchers to develop educational programs that aim to help adolescents to make sense and derive a sense of purpose and meaning.

Within the context of this book's focus on social and personal ambiguity in adolescence, the application of findings from such cognitive neuroscience research may help educators to explore how adolescents makes sense of social relations, and how we can learn from this research to help adolescents make sense of, and to cope effectively with socially ambiguous situations. For example, research with the use of ambiguous graphic examples of we make sense of how experience may show us how experience affects our interpretations of ambiguous pictures. Such research includes the work on ambigrams or the words 'ambiguous' and 'anagram' or an artwork or typographical design that can be read from two different viewpoints (Machnik & Martinex-Conde, 2011).

Artists such as John Langdon and Scott Kim specialize in the visual presentation of words, playing with illusion and symmetry to create words that can be read in different ways or from multiple points of view (Langdon, 1992, Kim, 1981). These multi-directional words are called *ambigrams*. Many ambigrams are viewed as wordplay and puzzles with words that feature the same word seen from different directions such as 'love, and amor' (love spelled backwards). As I will discuss in Chapter 3, such research activities could be adapted to fit into an educational program for adolescents that promotes critical and divergent thinking abilities.

Regarding the exploration of pictorial ambiguity, as Wimmer and Doherty note (2011), researchers have been fascinated with how people perceive ambiguous figures for over two centuries. Ambiguous figures such as Jastrow's (1900) duck/rabbit, the vase/faces (Rubin, 1958) to name a few illustrate the fascinating aspect of ambiguous figures which is that the figure switches or reverses from one interpretation to the other – that is, the physical properties remain the same, yet multiple interpretations can be perceived. As Long and Toppino (2004) claim in their review of ambiguous figures research, researchers from various disciplines remain interested in ambiguous figures as they provide insights into the perceptual and cognitive processes underlying visual perception,

Given their puzzling reversible and representational natures, ambiguous figures continue to play a major role across various disciplines serving as a research tool within the fields of cognitive neuroscience, social psychology, philosophy of mind, among many others to explore how motivation affects perception as well as the ability to be cognitively flexible including research on bilingualism, autism, among others. However, as Wimmer and Doherty (2011) note, given their extensive use as research tools across various disciplines, particularly within cognitive psychology, few studies exist on how children's perceptions and interpretations of ambiguous figures develop over time. Although research on children's cognitive reversal abilities remains sparse, past studies support the finding that children under the age of 5 are unable to reverse, even when informed about the ambiguity (Doherty & Wimmer, 2005; Gopnik & Rosati, 2001; Rock, Gopnik, & Hall, 1994).

As the understanding of ambiguous figures can also help researchers and educators learn how children understand pictorial and linguistic representations, to what extent are they connected to metarepresentational abilities including Theory of Mind (ToM) or the ability to understand mental states in others and one's self. In their recent research, Wimmer and Doherty (2011) explored the development of children's (ages 3 to 5-year-olds) understanding of ambiguous figure perception in relation to social cognitive abilities including ToM understanding. Overall, Wimmer and Doherty found that children first learn the concept of pictorial ambiguity at ages 3 to 4, then the perception of ambiguity develops between ages 4 to 5 that enable children to learn the ability to reverse ambiguous figures. Lastly, Wimmer and Doherty's findings also revealed that children' conceptual understanding of ambiguity and the ability to perceive ambiguity is associated with

ToM understanding. Thus, Wimmer and Doherty's (2011) research suggest that ambiguous figure reversal develops among children in terms of distinction of ambiguity and reversibility as highlighted in adult research.

Interestingly, given the role that understanding perceptual ambiguity may be connected to understanding social and personal ambiguity within the adolescent classroom, at the time of writing this book, researchers have yet to explore how adolescents' understanding of ambiguous figures relates to ToM ability and self-perceptions. Thus, building on Wimmer and Doherty's (2011) findings regarding understanding perceptual ambiguity, as researchers and educators, how we can apply such findings to the adolescent classroom? How can such findings on graphic ambiguity help us to explore the questions of which specific cognitive abilities are required to understand social ambiguities within the secondary school context, and in what quantity? How will such abilities be useful to adolescents to help them to make sense of ambiguity regarding their identity and social relationships?

For example, is a particular combination of these abilities necessary to help the adolescent to make sense of ambiguity with the social context, and how will these abilities help adolescents to make sense of personal ambiguity and create a sense of well being? How educators and researchers help adolescents to learn become expert translators or decoders of ambiguous social messages? Is there a particular educational program that will promote this ability in adolescents, and is it possible to create a profile of an 'exemplar social decoder?' For example, could one be a verbalizer, preferring to share information verbally but also excel in enactive visualization? Or can one prefer to choose a particular mode of thought or thinking depending upon the particular task or situation. In Chapter 3, I will further explore such questions outlining ideas for future research studies on individual differences in these abilities within the context of ToM, as such differences may lead to different social experiences for the adolescent. Such cognitive abilities may help or hinder an adolescents' ability to make sense of the ambiguous social messages within the classroom.

IDENTITY AND SOCIAL RELATIONSHIPS: MEANINGS MASKED IN AMBIGUITY

"What do you mean by that?" said the Caterpillar, sternly, "Explain yourself!"

"I can't explain *myself*, I'm afraid sir," said Alice, "because I'm not myself, you see – being so many different sizes in a day is very confusing." She drew herself up and said very gravely, " I think you ought to tell me who you are first." (Carroll, 1916; p. 67)

According to Laing (1969), as identity sometimes may become an 'object' that an individual may feel that she has lost or is searching for, or in the midst of creating, adolescence is a unique time in human development, where most adolescents have the cognitive ability to understand interpretive ambiguity within text and explore their sense of self in the conceptual or cognitive sense (Yuill, 2009). However, applying Vygotsky's (1930/1978) thinking that cognitive ability is developed through social interactions, one of the main task of the adolescent to develop their sense of self and thus, this co-creation of the idea of oneself may develop through interactions with others. Given the various individual differences in intrapersonal and interpersonal competencies such as age, gender, cultural background, researchers need to continue explore how adolescents learn to understand and cope with the complex social ambiguities and silences to understand and engage in this self and social developmental process in an emotional and moral sense.

Emotional implications may occur when another person finds herself condemned to an identity as the complement of another she wishes to repudiate, but cannot. It may be difficult to establish a consistent and coherent identity for oneself, that is, to see oneself by others consistently in the same way – if definitions of oneself by others are inconsistent or mutually exclusive. The other may define self simultaneously in incompatible ways. Two or more others may identify self simultaneously in compatible ways. To fit in with them all or to repudiate them all may be impossible, which may lead to mystification, confusion, and conflict both intra- and interpersonally.

During the transitional developmental time of adolescent when adolescents are developing a sense of self, an adolescent may rebel or refuse to continue to define herself in terms of what Laing (1969) refers to as the 'nexus of bonds' (p. 86), or the personal web one has of their relationships or attachments with others. For example, an adolescent may no longer view herself as her 'mom's daughter' and may thus wish others to see her as that as well and to understand her perspective. However, when the adolescent feels that others are not understanding her view of herself, such inconsistencies may lead to miscommunication or no communication to avoid negative emotions that may emerge from feeling misunderstood and alone, and perhaps invisible.

Thus, given that some adolescents' developing sense of self may be fragile, and perhaps overly sensitive, some adolescents, perhaps those that have a more fragile or incoherent and contradictory sense of self may choose to mask their identity through ambiguous communication with others to mask meaning – both verbally and nonverbally. For example, verbally, adolescents may choose to remain silent in human conversation, or engage in talking with little affect, or have a preference for Orwellian double-speak that is, making an ambiguous statement with double or perhaps multiple meanings.

Regarding humour, perhaps some adolescents who prefer ambiguity may be more likely to engage in teasing, or speaking sarcastically or ironically. Such a verbal communicative style that focuses on speaking in riddles, may also be accompanied by ambiguous non-verbal communication and action, such as maintaining a stone face or statue-like, illustrating action devoid of emotion. Such a communication style, or that one that favours ambiguity, had implications for social relations, especially if as according to Laing (1969) other people may become "a sort of 'identity kit', in which adolescents define their sense of self identity where they can piece together a picture of oneself. Thus, we recognize ourselves in the face of others. Such 'emotional fog' may result from ambiguous interactions and those who experience such may find it difficult to get any sense of psychological grounding or safety.

This emotional fog can also be created by differences is our ability to recognize faces in others or what is known to be called as faceblindedness or prosopagnosia. The ability to recognize another person's human characteristics varies in individuals, and those with extreme ability are referred to as "super recognizers" (Sacks, 2010, p. 104), whereas those who experience a difficulty in recognizing others' faces (either acquired prosopagnosia by means of a brain injury, illness etc., or developmental prosopagnosia by means of a genetic tendency (Chen et al., 2010; Lee et al., 2010). It is caused by a problem with processing visual information in the brain, which can be present at birth or develop later due to brain injury.

People with prosopagnosia can become very good at using clues such as context, clothes, or voice to work out who people are. So people with proso-pagnosia may seem to recognise you one day, and then ignore you completely another day when they meet you unexpectedly, or you change your hairstyle. This ability may thus affect how children make sense of socially ambiguous situations, especially is they are not able to recognize the human face in others which provides many social clues to emotion and communication. Thus, an adolescent with prosopagnosia may have difficulty in interpreting socially ambiguous situations, as they may not be able to understand the connections between other people. In contrast, prosopagosics may be more sensitive to social visual clues other than the human face such as body posture, tone of voice. Fur-ther research needs to continue to explore the underlying mechanisms within prosopagnosia and apply the findings to all adolescents in the hopes of helping youth to understand the meanings within the complex and subtle interactions that occur during social exchanges. In the next section, I will outline research that explores this ability within the adolescent classroom.

Social Ambiguity in Adolescence: Personal and Social Knots

> "Piglet felt very miserable and didn't know what to say. He was still opening his mouth to begin something and then deciding that it wasn't any good saying that... (p. 162, Milne, 1926).

According to Laing (1969), all conversations include explicit meanings which may not be consistent with implicit levels, while on implicit levels, one person may convey two or more paradoxical messages or more. For example, a girl could say to her friend, "That is a nice dress." and depending upon both the context and the emotional valence of the intonation, her friend who listens, may have multiple interpretations of this simple sentence. According to Capelli et al.,'s (1990) res-earch, she could interpret this as a lie, sincere statement or a sarcastic one. Thus, given the complexities of everyday casual conversation, the teen is confronted with numerous opportunities to problem solve in terms of understanding mul-tiple meanings. Based on Capelli's findings, if the sentence was spoken with a negative tone, the girl receiving the comment would be most likely to interpret this interaction as a sarcastic statement.

Laing (1969) defines peer culture as a clique or groups of three or four persons in a closed nexus who will according to Laing (1969) create a status quo, which suits them, and create special rules for the members of the nexus to follow. This creates a collusive alliance to neutralize anyone who threatens its stability. In such a social nexus, any statement or gesture functions as something quite different from what it 'appears' to be and no action can be trusted to mean what it seems.

For example, an outsider to the group may not be able to understand what is 'really' going on for a long time. To an 'outsider' nothing may be going on. Exchanges are boring, repetitive, concerned only with trivia. The energy of the nexus is used to prevent anything from going on. Such naked ambiguity may lead the adolescent to wonder what is being meant by every sentence and may be sensitive to possible hidden meanings behind the sentences. Thus, many teenagers are constantly puzzling over the meaning of any statement, although this curiousity may be heightened due to the lack of clarity and increased complexity of the multiple layered social interactions.

It is important to note, though, that adolescents' dyadic friendships are often nested within larger social networks, for instance in cliques. Cliques can be defined as self-selective, friendship-based groups of peers who are highly interconnected (Shrum and Cheek 1987; Urberg et al., 1995; Kindermann 2007). As such research has noted, being isolated from cliques, which reflects not being a member of friendship groups of mainstream peers, may uniquely predict depressive symptoms. Because cliques are friendship-based groups, cliques can be distinguished from sociometric status. That is, sociometric status reflects how much a child is liked or disliked by his/her peers rather than the number of actual friends a child has (Parker and Asher 1993). A child with a negative peer reputation may still affiliate in cliques (Bagwell et al., 2000). In contrast, youth who are isolated from cliques may still be liked by their peers (Wentzel and Caldwell 1997).

Moreover, cliques may provide adolescents with resources, such as a sense of collective participation and group support, which dyadic friendships often cannot offer (Rubin 1980). Cliques have specific structural characteristics, such as cohesiveness, stratification, and transitivity that move beyond characteristics of dyadic friendships (Adler and Adler 1998; Wasserman & Faust, 1994). This conceptual distinction between dyadic friendships and cliques has also recei-ved empirical support. For instance, Wentzel and Caldwell (1997) showed that children's reciprocated friendships and their clique membership were differently related to their academic achievement in middle school. Consequently, children who are isolated from cliques are deprived of different assets (i.e., group support, a sense of belongingness) than children who are not part of dyadic friendships or who are rejected by peers.

As Brown and Lohr (1987) claim, being isolated from cliques may deny children positive group experiences and may therefore put children at risk for intensifying their depressive symptoms (Hoza et al., 2000). This may particularly be the case in late childhood and early adolescence. While close and intimate friendships may become more significant for children's development during adolescence (Sullivan 1953), achieving group identity and group acceptance is believed to be a central developmental task in late childhood and early adolescence (Parker & Gottman 1989; Buhrmester 1990; Buhrmester & Furman 1987). Consistent with this notion, initial evidence indicates that cliques isolates show more depressive symptoms than members of clique. That is, Henrich et al., (2000) identified clique members and clique isolates based on patterns of reciprocated close friendship nominations and found that sixth and seventh grade clique isolates show more teacher rated internalizing problems—including more depressed mood—than clique members. Nonetheless, the role of clique isolation in the development of children's depressive symptoms as well as other internalizing difficulties such as social anxiety remains uncertain.

In addition, it is unknown whether clique isolation is associated with depressive symptoms above and beyond other forms of peer relations. Although clique isolation, peer rejection and friendlessness are regarded as distinct peer relation problems, children who are isolated from cliques often have fewer reciprocated friendships and are less accepted by their peers than clique members (Wentzel & Caldwell, 1997). Most recently, Witvliet, Brendgen, van Lier, Koot, and Vitaro (2010) investigated whether being isolated from cliques from age 11 to 13 years predicted an increase in depressive symptoms at age 14 years, while controlling for other problems in the peer relations domain. In sum, their study found that loneliness influenced the association between adolescents' experiences of clique isolation and depression. Given that additional internalizing factors may also influence adolescents' experiences of clique isolation and depression, future studies could benefit from taking other internalizing problems besides depressive symptoms, such as social anxiety, into account. For example, perhaps adolescents with a more developed ability to interpret and understand social exchanges between others may be more sensitive to the emotional messages (positive and negative) portrayed in such exchanges. Thus, further research on adolescents' ToM ability and their reactions to ambiguous social messages within the peer culture and may help educators to understand how adolescents cope with the social ambiguities of adolescence.

Ambiguity and Psychological Pragmatics

Regarding the role silence and conversation play in the subtleties of social interaction, researchers remain challenged by the questions of how well children understand the mental states and emotions of others, how this ability influences their experiences of silence, and how these experiences connect in a way that influences their sense of self-worth and social behaviour. Understanding how adolescents co-construct their knowledge of others and what they do with this knowledge within social situations is similar to feminists' interests in how the sociocultural construction of knowledge is affected by sociopolitical structures. Given that feminist analysis often offers "a sharper articulation of the different strands—intellectual, imaginative, and affective—involved in human ways of thinking" (Lloyd, 1998, p. 172), I draw on the feminist lens to help unpack Nelson, Henseler, and Plesa's (2000) notion of psychological pragmatics.

Psychological pragmatics refers to a dynamic knowledge system comprised of self-views, emotions, and cognitions that undergoes constant creation and re-creation through social interaction (Nelson et al., 2000). This approach to psychological understanding is grounded in experiential knowledge gained in socioculturalinguistic contexts and is consistent with the principles of feminist epistemologies. This dialogical system allows us to understand the mental states of ourselves and others within a framework of action provided by cultural values, ideals, structures, and practices. Building on psychocultural theories of self-systems and social behaviour (e.g., Bussey & Bandura, 1999), researchers have started to explore the complex links between psychological pragmatics and self-worth within the ambiguous school culture. Thus, researchers have started to explore the claim that the sense of self may play an intervening role in the co-creation of youth's ability to be psychologically pragmatic (mental state understanding enacted through social interactions). Given the lack of research on the gendered links between social thought, peer culture (e.g., values, linguistic, and behavioural norms), and school behaviour (e.g., Bosacki, Varnish, & Askeer, 2008; Underwood, Galen, & Paquette, 2001), as Liben (2011) among others note, future research is needed.

As many scholars have suggested (Bruner, 1996), quite often, the focus of language educational programs is on the verbal components and promotes verbal and social skills that encompass verbal ability. In contrast, few language programs focus on fostering the nonverbal skills, including the art of listening and observation (e.g., Haynes, 2002). In addition, few educational programs for adolescents focus on the pragmatic or sociolinguistic skills involved in social and emotional learning. As I will discuss in Chapter 3, some holistic educators have mentioned this gap in both the developmental and educational literature, particularly regarding the lack of focus on the promotion of "intrapersonal skills," which entail periods of silent contemplation and reflection. Children and adolescents need the opportunity to "listen to themselves," including their thoughts, feelings, and physical sensations (Bosacki, 2008; Cohen, 1999).

As Piaget noted, "There is no cognitive mechanism without affective elements" (Piaget, 1981, p. 3); emotions play a critical role in learning and particularly in language development (Denham, 1998; Saarni, 1999). The connections among emotional development and language are complex and have strong implications for the educational context, particularly the elementary and secondary school classroom. As many emotion researchers note, sometimes the expression of emotion is contingent upon the particular label or emotion word. Thus, building on the previously mentioned Goldberger's (1996) notion of structural and strategic silence, both types of silences may have different emotional implications. Regarding the case of structural silence, an adolescent may feel "silenced," either due a lack of knowledge of the emotion word or by the "other" who does not allow the child to speak. Such a type of silence may be linked to social situations and interpersonal interactions. Regarding the experience of strategic silence, an adolescent may choose not to express a particular emotion or articulate a particular emotion label. This experience of strategic silence may be more personal in nature, and although the motivation to self-silence may be influenced by the interactions of others, the decision to remain silent remains at a more private level (Jack, 1991, 1999).

Given the importance of emotions in adolescents' lives, decisions regarding verbal expression are often value- and affect-laden. To name or label an emotion is to make a statement of value. Emotion understanding or knowledge refers to the ability to identify the expression on a peer's face or comprehend the emotions elicited by common social situations (Denham, 1998). As an integral part of emotional competence, Saarni's defines emotion understanding as the ability to discern one's own and others' emotional states and to use the vocabulary of emotion effectively (Saarni, 1999).

In the past 15 years, there has been a surge of interest in the development of emotion understanding among children and adolescents (Bloom, 2010; Saarni, 1999). Transcultural research shows that across the world, most children begin talking about emotions around two to three years of age (Denham, 1998). Recent research has shown that beginning in the preschool years, emotional lives become quite complex (see Denham, 1998). For example, research has shown that between the ages of two and four, children learn to label emotions accurately and begin to understand that certain situations are linked to certain emotions (see Denham, 1998; Harris, 1989). They show substantial ability to use emotion-descriptive adjectives, understand these terms in conversations with adults, and begin to employ emotion language to meet their own emotional needs. However, despite the increasing interest in children's and adolescents' emotional development, much remains to be learned about the complex processes involved.

Cognitive-developmental research has shown that across most cultures, children begin to first talk about the simple or basic emotions (e.g., happy, sad) (Denham, 1998). Accordingly, such emotions have been claimed to be innate and exist transculturally. Interestingly, the more complex emotions (social and moral), also sometimes referred to as secondary emotions, involve more complex reasoning and cognitive development. Emotions such as pride and embarrassment require the child to reflect upon her or his self-concept and to imagine the value judgment of others.

Despite the importance of emotions to language and social development, the complex or self-conscious emotions have remained somewhat neglected in the study of adolescents' emotion understanding. The majority of emotion research on children and adolescents has focused almost exclusively on the "simple" or primary and basic emotions (i.e., emotions linked to underlying physiology), such as happy and sad. In contrast, complex or secondary "self-conscious" emotions such as pride and embarrassment that involve the ability to self-evaluate against internalized standards of behaviour have received considerably less attention (Saarni, 1999). Thus, although a strong theoretical link exists among complex emotions, sense of self, and social relations, little is known about how such a nexus develops and differs in children and adolescents (Lewis et al., 1989).

As noted earlier, although strategic silence suggests a sense of personal agency in that it represents a speaker's decision to either refrain or withdraw from a conversation, the speaker's decision may be independent of any outside forces or, alternatively, the individual may feel pressured to comply with the silence and may therefore feel "silenced." Thus, the process of "silencing" is complex, and the decision to remain silent in a public forum may also have either positive or negative affect attached. For example, regarding academic learning, an adolescent who is called upon in class and chooses to remain silent may lead to a number of possible scenarios. One scenario could be that the silence either frustrates the teacher or challenges the teacher to encourage a response. A second scenario could involve the adolescent's peers, who then treat the silent adolescent differently. Thus, the decision to remain silent in the classroom has implications for both the teacher and the peers in that the reactions solicited from the audience (teacher and peer) may create a mainly negative emotional reaction such as increased self-consciousness and possible anxiety.

In contrast, adolescents asked to engage in structured class silence or "quiet time" such as silent reading may experience positive emotions. That is, this task provides the opportunity for adolescents to remain silent and to listen to themselves (exercise their imaginative and creative abilities by listening to both mental and physical messages from within). Both strategic and structural silence, as defined by an absence of verbal expression, provide an opportunity for an individual to listen to her or his thoughts, emotions, and physical sensations, which, in turn, may have either positive or negative influences on an adolescent's sense of self-worth and personal competence.

Similar to academic experiences, within the school context, social situations also entail experiences of silence, and such experiences may either ameliorate or exacerbate the adolescent's sense of social competence and confidence (Kessler, 2000). Given that a psychocultural approach to personal experiences of silence is founded on an interest in identifying what resources (experiential, cognitive, affective, linguistic, etc.) are most useful to the adolescent in a social world, we need to explore what the adolescent needs to know and feel to participate effectively in a variety of social contexts. Once these resources are acquired, how do adolescents apply these tools to social situations? Moreover, how does an adolescent's psychological and self-knowledge emerge out of experience in ambiguous pragmatic circumstances? The psychocultural approach assumes that the abstract knowledge construct is built out of experiential, pragmatic knowledge acquired in an interpreted, social world. This developmental view of psychological understanding agrees with various scholars' thinking on the connections between thought, language, and behaviour within the social world (Bruner, 1996; Dunn, 1988; Vygotsky, 1978).

SOCIAL AMBIGUITIES WITHIN THE ADOLESCENT CLASSROOM

To further illustrate the emotional and cognitive complexity of social ambiguity in the adolescent classroom, imagine the following scenario. In contrast to 'straight' talk such as the weather, could imply a question, a reproach, an injunction, an attribution about self and other, etc. In such straight talk, ambiguities are present, but implications can be taken up by other which may in turn be admitted or, or not intended, can be honestly disclaimed.

Frank and honest exchanges carry in them a great number of resonances, and the participants still 'know where they are' with each other. However, at the other end of the theoretical linguistic ambiguity scale, conversation can be characterized by the presence of numerous disclaimed, unavowed, contradictory, and paradoxical implications, or 'insinuendoes.' Such ambiguous social statements such as a teenage girl with her best friend may state to another girl who would like to join their twosome, "you can join us if you really want to." – holds multiple emotional meanings for the third or left out girl. The girls receives no clarification regarding her role in the other two girls' relationship as the statement is ambiguous and suggests, "You are being told not to do or be what you are big told to do or be." Thus, the girl, who may already have a fragile sense of self, and may be sensitive to such ambiguous encounters, may begin to puzzle or perhaps begin to ruminate about the meaning of the statement.

Socially ambiguous knots are illustrated by the example of the 'double bind' scenario which involves two or more persons of whom one is regarded as the 'victim.' Bateson et al., (1956) propose that it will be difficult for a person to be one who has been exposed to such a situation repeatedly. As Laing (1969) describes, one person conveys to the other that she or he should do something, and at the same time, conveys on another level such as nonverbally though the use of tone of voice, body language (e.g., posture, gestures), that she or he should not, or that he should do something else incompatible with it. The situation is sealed off for the 'victim' of a further injunction forbidding her to escape the situation or to dissolve it by commenting on it. The 'victim' is thus in an 'untenable' position, or a situation in which no matter how she feels or how she acts, or what meaning the situation has, her feelings are denuded of validity, her acts are stripped of her motives, intentions, and consequences, the situation is robbed of its meaning. Is these situations are repeated, she may learn that she will not be able to move without social catastrophe such as rejection and/or developing an unpopular social reputation.

Such social knots including double binds may play a role in many social settings within the adolescent's world, including the school context. For example, two popular or high social status girls may ask verbally another girl who is less popular to join them in an activity and simultaneously, combine this verbal invitation with contradictory messages such as negative nonverbal behaviour through the use of negative or flat emotional tone, turning their bodies and faces away or eye aversion while making the invitation, and setting up the invitation as a 'last minute' or 'over-thought' – in which the third girl has little or no chance to decide if this invitation conflicts with her schedule. Thus, if the less popular girl decides to join the other two, she may risk her relationship with both girls as they find her an annoyance to their activity as they may have not wished her to join them in the first place.

Interestingly, the lack of direct emotional feedback regarding an invitation may lead to more social and emotional confusion within the 'victim' or 'guest.' As past research has shown, the importance of direct social feedback regarding invitations must be applied immediately (or as soon as possible following a behaviour). For example, research in neurocognitivism (Harris, 2010 p. 224) explores how the brain responds to uncertainty or the mental state in which the truth value of a proposition (e.g, the popular girls would prefer to have the unpopular child join them) cannot be judged or not knowing what one believes to be true. Uncertainty prevents the link between thought and subsequent behaviour/emotion from developing. To help illustrate, when one believes what one sees and thus, she settles upon a specific, actionable representation of the world. However, applying belief to the social context, how can others be 'certain' of any social situation as we do not have access to all of the information necessary to lead to an informed social judgment.

Within the context of the adolescent classroom, different types of uncertainty exist including – expected uncertainty (where one knows that one's observations are unreliable), and unexpected uncertainty (where something indicates in the environment that things are not as they seem or appear to be). Ambiguous social situations within the school context are related to unexpected uncertainty such as described earlier, whether or not the look between the two popular girls are directed to the less popular girl, and what does this look or social message mean – acceptance? Rejection? For example, how does the less popular girl discern these ambiguous messages and to what extent will her interpretation influence her action to either decide to accept or decline the invitation.

As Harris (2010) describes, some researchers who explore behaviours within the context of economics found that expected uncertainty such as a situation where probably can be assessed is related to risk, whereas unexpected uncertainty is the uncertainty borne of missing information and relates to ambiguity. As I discussed in Chapter 1, research shows that one of the principal features of feedback is that it systematically removes uncertainty. Delgado, Frank, and Phelps' (2005) explored how our responses to feedback are influenced by prior expectations and how our ability to accept or reject linguistic representation of the world within a game context where the participant played a trust game with three adults assigned a hypothetical moral character – (good, bad, and neutral). Overall, participants responded the most strongly to violations of trust in the neutral character, followed by the bad character, and were most wiling to trust the 'good' adults irrespective of their feedback within the game.

Applying Delgado et al.,'s (2005) results to the three girl scenario outlined above, the less popular girl will be more likely to distrust the two popular girls if their nonverbal behaviours convey emotional ambiguity or remain emotionally neutral or flat. According to Delgado et al., socially ambiguous situations may be more likely to be interpreted as negative, especially within the social and moral domain. According to Laing (1969, p. 158), individual differences may occur in the social cognitive abilities to tie and untie social and personal knots. That is, some children may be more likely to excel at tying social knots around others, and/or personal knots within themselves, and some may excel at untying or unraveling the knots. In addition, some children may excel in detecting the knots and not necessarily excel in the ability to tie or untie. As research on children's interpretations of ambiguous social information suggests, when presented with ambiguous information, children are more likely to have a positive bias toward interpretation although this optimistic bias tends to decrease with age (Bjorklund, 2006; Boseovski, 2010; Boseovski & Lee, 2006; Dodge & Frame, 1982; Dodge & Tomlin, 1987; Grant & Mills, 2011), Thus, some children may not only have varied abilities to create and perhaps understand ambiguous social situations, they may also vary in their emotional biases that may help to colour their ability to decipher the ambiguous messages.

Researchers within the educational context exploring adolescents need to ask the question of why do some adolescents communicate in ambiguous terms, and is this intentional or unintentional and why? How are these choices related to power differentials within the classroom, and to what extent does ambiguity benefit or hinder social and personal relationships? What are the social and emotionnal implications of ambiguous communication? For example, why would an adolescent intentionally communicate in an ambiguous way if he or she are interested in meeting their personal and social goals? What is their reasoning in thinking about the function of ambiguity in social relationships? Why do some individuals use ambiguity as a tool in communication with others and how does this connect to research on emotions, deception, and persuasion (de Sousa, 2011; Larson, 2010)? How do some youth learn to become exceptional emotional and social detectives excelling in the ability to decipher the codes or ambiguous social messages exchanged between others and how does this connect to O'Sullivan's (2009) research with exceptional adult lie detectors known as 'truth wizards?' To answer the question of how youth can develop a feeling of safety that protects a fragile or vulnerable sense of self, researchers need to explore how adolescents perceive the thoughts and emotions of others and learn how youth learn to fear judgement or rejection of others. To address such questions, In Chapter 3, I will expand on future research possibilities and describe the ways in which educators can help to develop this ability to decipher meanings from ambiguous statements that may help adolescents cope with ambiguous social interactions.

SOCIAL AMBIGUITIES: IMPORTANCE OF PEER RELATIONSHIPS TO DEVELOPMENT

They are playing a game. They are playing at not playing a game. If I show them I see they are, I shall break the rules and they will punish me. I must play their game, of not seeing I see the game.

(Laing, 1970, p. 1)

Which particular cognitive skills enable adolescents to 'see the game' and more importantly, to let others know that you do not see the game that you know others are playing? What makes some adolescents more 'sensitive to meaning' as

Yuill (2009) mentions than others? Do these adolescents who excel in social deciphering and who serve as social emotional detectives have particular personality characteristics or cognitive abilities that distinguishes them from others? Which mode of thought do social detectives prefer – are they more likely to be verbalizers and choose the narrative mode of thinking and are they more likely to describe the situation verbally? In contrast, are they more likely to be imagers who choose the logico-scientific or paradigmatic mode of thinking and are thus more likely to depict the situation in images.

To help adolescents make sense of ambiguity, as I discussed earlier in this chapter, we can draw on Wiggenstein's (1953) notion of 'language games" in that language is expressed in terms of 'language games' which in turn represents forms of life or ways of being. Thus, by understanding language games, played by two or more players, the adolescent may learn how to understand the mental life of the characters including their thoughts and emotions. How can the ability to understand the language games of others help adolescents to make sense of the socially ambiguous situations within the classroom? For example, how does an adolescent learn how to make sense of silence and non-verbal communication such as gestures, facial expressions, emotional tone of voice, etc. Within the complex and multilayered social lives of the modern Canadian teenager, how do they learn to make sense of the emotional subtleties and meaning of social interactions.

Regarding the ability to understand language games in others, how does this ability influence one's own ability to play language games with oneself as through the use of private or inner speech? How does one's ability to understand the language game continue to feel about her or himself, and does she or he experience positive or negative emotions? Are these language games considered to be competitive or collaborative, or both? Does anyone have the goal of 'winning' a language game upon entering - and who creates the rules? Are the rules negotiable or are they fixed? Also, as have discussed previously within the context of adolescence (Bosacki, 2005; 2011), to what extent do adolescents learn how to make sense of silences and what do silence mean in terms of socially ambiguous situations, Given the complexity of this issue, I will return to the notion of language games in the final chapter when I discuss the implications such theoretical questions have for educational practice within the secondary school classroom.

Social Connections: Ambiguities of Perceived Popularity

It has become increasingly clear that children's school adjustment is inextricably tied to their ability to form positive relationships with peers. Although the facets of relationships and indices of school adjustment vary across studies, the overarching framework driving this research posits that stressful peer relationships impede healthy school adjustment and positive relationships promote school adaptation and academic achievement. Specifically, investigators propose that relational risks such as peer victimization, rejection, and exclusion interfere with children's ability to concentrate, heighten negative affect, and limit opportunities for class participation (Boulton, Trueman, & Murray, 2008; Buhs & Ladd, 2001; Hoglund,

2007). In contrast, social provisions (i.e., peer acceptance, friendship) are believed to facilitate school adjustment by providing children support, validation, and a sense of group belongingness and by motivating responsible classroom behaviors (Ladd, Kochenderfer, & Coleman, 1997; Wentzel & Caldwell, 1997). Consistent with this premise, peer difficulties are negatively related to, and social provisions are positively related to, children's school engagement, school attitudes, achievement motivation, and academic progress (e.g., Buhs & Ladd, 2001; Graham, Bellmore, & Mize, 2006; Wentzel & Caldwell, 1997).

Recently, there has been a resurgence of interest in the ambiguity surrounding children and adolescent's *perceived popularity*. Unlike peer acceptance and more traditional measures of popularity, which have their basis in how liked children are by their peers, *perceived popularity* refers to children's social status and prominence (Cillessen & Rose, 2005). Perceived-popular youth have power within the peer group, suffer few negative consequences as a result of engaging in socially aversive behaviors, and are sought after for companionship and friendship by peers (Cillessen & Mayeux, 2004; Lease, Kennedy, & Axelrod, 2002). Research also suggests that children's expectations play an important role in their interpretations of social outcomes. For example, 11 and 12-year olds expectations regarding liked, disliked, and or neutral peers relate to their expectations of each peer's behaviour in ambiguous situations (Peets, Hodges, & Salmivalli, 2008). It is not surprising then that achieving or maintaining perceived popularity is a salient goal for many youth (Eder, 1993; Hawley, Little, & Pasupathi, 2002; Sijtsema, Veenstra, Lindenberg, & Salmivalli, 2009).

Perceived popularity challenges traditional notions of the role of peer relationships in children's school adjustment. Although potentially a sign of healthy social development, perceived popularity is not strongly related to other measures of social adjustment, such as peer acceptance (Cillessen & Rose, 2005; Rose, Swenson, & Waller, 2004). In addition, although popularity has been linked to a number of characteristics valued by youth and adults, such as prosocial behavior, leadership skills, and athleticism, a number of popular youth also engage in hostile and aggressive behaviors aimed at hurting and manipulating peers (Lease et al., 2002; Parkhurst & Hopmeyer, 1998). Indeed, during early adolescence, boys increasingly rely on overt expressions of toughness (Adler & Adler, 1998) and girls rely on relational aggression (Rose et al., 2004) to obtain and protect social status. In accordance with these findings, researchers have distinguished between those popular youth whose social dispositions are predominantly prosocial in nature and those who exhibit a mix of prosocial and aggressive behaviors (Estell, Farmer, Pearl, Van Acker, & Rodkin, 2007). These two subsets of popular youth have been shown to vary in their school adjustment and academic achievement. Whereas popular, nonaggressive youth tend to be academically oriented, popular-aggressive children devalue school and show multiple indices of school maladjustment including absenteeism and poor academic progress (Farmer et al., 2003; Rodkin et al., 2000). It is unclear, however, whether high status itself contributes to the poor academic performance of popular-aggressive youth. Aggression is significantly associated with poor concentration, overactivity, and misconduct, putting aggressive youth at increased risk for school maladjustment (Ladd & Burgess, 2001). Indeed, early aggression is a significant predictor of later academic and school maladjustment (Cairns & Cairns, 1994; Chen, Rubin, & Li, 1995). Therefore, the school difficulties evidenced by popular-aggressive youth may be attributable to processes associated with their aggressive behavior and may be unrelated to their social status.

Alternatively, perceived popularity may make a unique and independent contribution to children's school adjustment. During adolescence, youth are motivated to engage in more adult-like behaviors in order to close what has been referred to as "the maturity gap," the discrepancy between adolescents' physical maturity and the limited amount of freedom and autonomy afforded to them (Moffitt, 1993). Investigators have proposed that in an effort to maintain their status, popular youth, particularly boys (Adler & Adler, 1998), move away from adult-sanctioned activities, including academic pursuits and partake in more risky and delinquent behaviors (Mayeux et al., 2008). In accordance with this proposition, perceived popularity has been associated with alcohol use and sexual activity in adolescence (Mayeux et al., 2008). In addition, more specific links to school adjustment can be gleaned from research showing that perceived popularity is related to poor academic functioning and disengagement from school (Adler & Adler, 1998; Hopmeyer, Kim, & Schimmelbusch, 2002).

However, a movement away from adult-sanctioned values and activities and toward greater delinquency may not characterize all popular youth. Children tend to affiliate with peers who share their behavioral and scholastic orientations (Kindermann, 1993; Ryan, 2001). Status within these peer groups may be maintained by exemplifying the values held by members of their social network. Among nonaggressive youth, an orientation toward school success may be reinforced and amplified (see Ryan, 2001; Steinberg, Dornbusch, & Brown, 1992), and popularity may be maintained through academic effort and success. Consequently, among nonaggressive youth, perceived popularity may function similarly to other relationship provisions, such as acceptance and friendship. Popularity may lead to validation of one's competencies and lower levels of anxiety in school contexts. Moreover, popular-nonaggressive youth may have greater opportunity and power to elicit peer support in the face of academic challenges.

Thus, perceived popularity may predict gains in school adjustment and performance among nonaggressive early adolescents. In contrast, aggressive children and their friends, who likely have greater difficulty achieving within academic domains, may minimize the importance of educational pursuits, allowing them to project competence and self-satisfaction despite academic failures. In order to maintain their status within their peer group, therefore, popular-aggressive children may disengage from school, leading to greater academic declines. Consistent with this premise, Schwartz, Gorman, Nakamoto, & McKay (2006) found that for aggressive youth, increases in perceived popularity predicted a rise in unexplained absences and declines in grade point average over a 2-year period. However, the investigators focused on high school students.

Ambiguity as to whether perceived popularity places children at risk for school maladjustment earlier in adolescence reflects a critical gap in our understanding of the role of status in children's development. For example, Mayeux et al., (2008) suggest that the link between perceived popularity and increased delinquency among high school students may be indicative of an adolescence-limited trajectory of risky behavior among high-status youth. Evidence of increasing school maladjustment at younger ages would suggest that the processes underlying the etiology of adolescent-limited delinquency have their onset in early adolescence (Moffitt, 1993). Accordingly, negative school attitudes and declines in academic progress among perceived-popular early adolescents may reflect a subtle shift away from adult-sanctioned behaviors and may precede involvement in more deviant forms of antisocial activities.

Moreover, as positive peer relationships are often associated with more positive academic development, declining school adjustment among perceived-popular youth may be overlooked or minimized by teachers and parents, resulting in lost opportunities to alter trajectories of decreasing academic progress before they become entrenched. Thus, the objective of a recent research study (Troop-Gordon, Visconte, & Kunt, 2010) was to examine whether perceived popularity is predictive of increased or decreased school adjustment during early adolescence and whether these associations differ for aggressive and nonaggressive youth. As future research continues in this area of ambiguity and peer popularity, researchers and educators need to explore how youth learn to make sense of the ambiguities of the judgements of others, and how to learn how to interpret such judgments and evaluations with a healthy, positive view. In Chapter 3, I will discuss programs aimed to help adolescent to view ambiguous situations from a meaningful and purposeful framework, with the goal of learning and growing from the uncertainty of the judgements of others.

Ambiguity of Play and Flow in Adolescence

Within the context of interpersonal relations and peer relationships, the paradoxical context of play as both Huizinga (1955) and Sutton-Smith (1997) note, is defined as an ambiguous event. Piaget (1962) also notes an ambivalent quality that represents the duality between tension/relaxation experienced by the child within the act of play. This complex combination of mixed valence and contradictory emotions also represents the child's dilemmas as s/he vacillates between attraction and withdrawal toward to the player. Similar to Empson (1947) claims that jokes have a moral component and depends on an ambiguity with both cases having contradictory meanings (e.g., naughty-nice/intellectual/instinctual), Sutton-Smith (1997) discusses the puzzle of play with the term ambiguity. Sutton-Smith agrees that there is little consensus regarding the definition of play, although there is an agreement that the concept of play remains ambiguous. Similarly, Mihail Spariosu (1989) refers to play as "amphibolous" which means it goes in two direction at once and is not clear.

Bateson (1955) suggests that play is a paradox because it both is and is not what it appears to be (e.g., animals play biting each other knowing that not only is a nip not a bite, but not a nip and represents what a bite represents)" For example, a youth who feels ambivalent or has mixed feelings toward a peer and unsure about the status of the peer as friend, may smile at her/his peer knowing that the smile is not a smile, but at the same time represents what the smile means to the person being smiled at, although this may not be the intent of the person smiling (see Ekman's work on facial deceit and smiles, 2009). Drawing on Duchenne's (1990/1862) work on smiling, and Ekman's (2009) research on the complexities regarding false or miserable smiles, as Sutton-Smith (1997) explains the process of play as illustrated by Empson's seven types of ambiguity, I would extend this framework of ambiguity to social play and the emotions of others including smiling among adolescents in that:

1) ambiguity of reference (is that a pretend or false smile?)
2) ambiguity of the referent (Is that an enemy or a friend?)
3) ambiguity of intent (do you mean it/authentic or is it pretend/artificial?)
4) ambiguity of sense (serious or nonsense?)
5) ambiguity of transition (you said you liked me)
6) ambiguity of contradiction (an enemy playing at being a friend)
7) ambiguity of meaning (is it affection or contempt?)

Within the context of adolescence, the definition of play becomes increasingly esoteric and complex connecting to concepts of leisure and recreation. As one example of research on an ambiguous psychological experience that is viewed as a positive growth experience that could be adapted into a holistic educational program, the concept of flow or flow episode is when an individual experiences an autotelic state of consciousness (Csikszentmihalyi, 1991). More specifically, an individual is said to be in a state of flow in which the activity becomes enjoyable in-and-of itself, to the point that individuals will engage in the activity to experience the resultant pleasure. This enjoyment comes about as a result of the satisfaction of the need for competence through the pursuit of challenge and mastery. The quality of the subjective experience is dependent upon a match between the perceived challenge and the perceived skill (Moneta and Csikszentmihaly 1996). If the subjective experience of satisfaction and pleasure is both the reason and outcome for "Flow is generally reported when a person is doing his or her favorite activity" (Csikszentmihalyi 1997, p. 33), and may not occur when one is doing something one would not want to do or feeling distracted. This suggests that flow is more likely to occur when individuals are engaging in an activity freely or autonomously, which is an inherent characteristic of intrinsic motivation (Deci & Ryan, 1985). Second, to be intrinsically motivated is to engage in an activity because the activity is inherently satisfying. Flow experiences are autotelic; the activities in which flow is experienced are undertaken because they are worthwhile in their own right (Csikszentmihalyi, 1991). As Humphrey (2011) notes in describing listening to music, "We say that you may 'lose yourself' in listening to music. Yet it might be closer to the truth to say that you lose the world and find more of your core self." (p. 106).

The link between intrinsic motivation and flow is an area of research that is just starting to be explored as although both concepts are multifaceted and ambiguous in the sense that they describe rich cognitive and affective experiences regarding the self. Recent research on adolescent Canadian males and their experiences regarding extracurricular activities involving skateboarding suggests that when the adolescent males were skateboarding they were experiencing a state of flow that was found to be related to their intrinsic motivation which was characterized by a sense of freedom, efficacy, euphoria, challenge and satisfaction (Seifert & Hedderson, 2009). Applying this finding to holistic educational programs to promote adolescent engagement and enchantment, as I discuss in Chapter 3, educators need to develop programs that create opportunities for youth to engage in activities that they experience flow. Participation in such activities could be used to promote feelings of self-determination and agency that may be connected to feelings of awe, wonder and enchantment, and help them to develop intrinsic motivation, peak performance, heightened concentration, positive affect and transcendence that may lead to a sense of purpose in the classroom.

AMBIGUITIES OF EXCLUSION: SILENCES, OSTRACISM, SOCIAL EXCLUSION

Adolescents' abilities to communicate effectively with others depends partly upon knowledge and skills that have little or nothing to do with language per se. Social conventions that govern appropriate verbal interaction are called sociolinguistic behaviours. For example, adolescents learn that they may have to greet others and to end a conversation with some form of a sign-off. Such behaviours fall within the broader domain of pragmatics, which includes not only rules of conversational etiquette—taking turns in conversations, saying good-bye when leaving, and so on—but also strategies for initiating conversations, changing the subject, telling stories, and arguing persuasively. According to White (1891), rules of etiquette have their allotted place amongst the forces of life and must be acknowledge as moral agents in refining and making more agreeable our daily intercourse with each other. They are agents for good. They teach us to be more lenient with the various elements which compose society (p. 10).

Building on this idea of learning social rules, children continue to refine their pragmatic skills and sociolinguistic conventions throughout the preschool years and elementary grades; however, this development is affected by cultural differences as different cultures often learn different conventions, particularly in the area of social etiquette. How do these cultural ways of treating others regarding social etiquette continue to develop during adolescence? For example, psycholinguistic research explores how cultural influences affect how youth learn effective communication through the subtleties regarding the rules of social language such as politeness and manners (Brown & Levinson, 1987; Cialdini, 2001; Grice, 1975). As White (1891) states, "the most exquisite and subtle quality necessary to a good talker, is tact. It is a fine gift to know just how to talk, to whom, and what is exactly the right thing to say on all occasions. It is people of the most delicate perceptions who possess this gift, but it can be cultivated." (p. 121). How can this delicate insight be cultivated in adolescence, and as I explore further in Chapter 3, how can we help youth to learn to speak with discretion, respect, and kindness, and interpret ambiguous contexts such as silence in conversation.

Regarding the role of silence in social communication and decorum, as I have discussed elsewhere in my research with adolescents and silence (Bosacki, 2005; Bosacki, 2008), silence remains an ambiguous concept as it may have multiple meanings, contingent upon the context, and the interpretation of the individual. For example, when two individuals experience the same silence, each person has their own interpretation of the lack of verbal content, including how they derive meaning from the silence, and how they feel about the silent experience. According to Prochnik (2010), the roots of our English term "silence" sink down through the language in multiple directions. Among the word's antecedents is the Gothic verb anasilan, a word that denotes the wind dying down, and the Latin word 'desinere,' a word meaning "stop." Both of these etymologies suggest the way that silence is bound up with the idea of interrupted action. As Prochnik (2010) notes in his conclusions about the importance of silence for our mental and emotional well being, he defines silence as a 'the particular equilibrium of sound and quiet that catalyzes our powers of perception." (p. 293). He warns us that the more we observe the distinction between things, the less mental space we have for our isolate selves and to take time for contemplation and inner peace. As White (1891) notes, "A good talker makes a good listener." (p. 124).

One situation commonly found among adolescents includes the case of social withdrawal and shyness (Rubin, Burgess, & Coplan, 2002). Within this framework, silence is often connected with negative social experiences and emotions, and silence may carry different psychological meanings that represent different motivations underlying the silence. These experiences of silence may be especially pronounced during social group situations, where verbal expression is often equated with confidence, popularity, and social status. Such situations occur frequently during childhood and adolescence, when an adolescent who holds psychological power over another adolescent in the social hierarchy chooses to harass or psychologically damage the adolescent with lower social status by choosing to not speak to the adolescent. That is, a popular adolescent may choose not to speak to another peer or to not respond to the adolescent's request. This "silent treatment" is often considered a form of psychological or emotional harassment if the adolescent receiving the silence is hurt emotionally, as the silence may be interpreted as a sign of rejection.

Alternatively, adolescents who find it stressful to join social groups or who are painfully shy may choose to remain silent in a group situation to avoid the negative feelings that may arise from possible rejection (Rubin et al., 2002). That is, adolescents may wish to say something to another peer, but the thought of rejection, social evaluation, and/or ridicule may prevent them from taking the risk to express their thoughts. If adolescents feel inhibited in a sense that they wish to contribute but cannot due to fear, some adolescents often decide to either remain silent or to withdraw from the social situation. In contrast to adolescents who choose to remain silent, those adolescents who are verbally and socially competent may experience feelings of control and powerfulness, as they may be aware of their ability to influence another adolescent's behaviour. Other adolescents may also choose to remain silent in that they are socially disinterested. They may lack the motivation to approach others while at the same time not necessarily have the motivation to avoid others. That is, when such individuals are approached by others, they will not remain reticent and retreat and may not experience wariness and anxiety (Rubin et al., 2002).

As I have discussed in my previous work on silences and social ambiguities (Bosacki, 1998; 2005; 2008), examples of social and personal ambiguity include social exclusion and ostracism which are often connected to discussions of silence as the experience of ostracism could also be referred to as "being silenced" by others. This ambiguous phenomenon of "feeling invisible," of being excluded from the social interactions of those around you, is discussed in more detail later on in the book, and is discussed in relation to forms of psychological and emotional harassment, bullying and teasing, in both virtual and real worlds.

The act of silencing someone else or performing the "silent treatment" has significant ramifications for adolescents sense of personal and social connection, when the peer group plays a large role in psychosocial, spiritual, and emotional health (Lightfoot, 1997; Twenge, 2006). As researchers on adolescents and the phenomenon of peer pressure have noted (Harter, 1999), engagement in some risk-taking behaviours may sometimes be due to the need to belong and to avoid ostracism and rejection (Williams, 2001).

As Williams and his colleagues note (2001; 2011), the act of ostracism is pervasive in that it transcends time and cultural differences (see Williams, 2001, for an extensive discussion). The term's definition is derived from the Greek word "ostrakismos," a practice which originated in Athens circa 488–487 BC to remove those individuals with dictatorial ambitions from the democratic state (Zippelius, 1986). In particular, Athenians would cast their vote to exile or banish the individual in question by writing their preference on shards of pottery (ostraca).

The ubiquity of ostracism is also reflected in the many terms used to describe it, including "avoiding," "shunning," "exile," "the silent treatment" and "silencing." Although ostracism is complex and has multiple causes and consequences, gleaned from the relevant literature, three main characteristics gleaned from the literature including ignoring, excluding, and rejecting create a workable definition (Gruter & Masters, 1986). Individuals who deviate from others' expectations are often the targets of ostracism, and existing research shows that ostracism is an aversive interpersonal behaviour to the targets. Given that silence plays a role in the ambiguous definition of ostracism, it is often considered a non-behaviour. As Messerschmidt (2010) research with adolescent males and females suggest, if adolescents realize that they are being intentionally excluded from a group, given that this may create a culture of cruelty in which the ambiguous social interactions are aimed at negative and harmful consequences for the victim, youth who are sensitive to such subtleties may question themselves, and as "Is this really happening, or is it my imagination?" Given that many adolescents experience increased self-consciousness and sensitivity, targeted adolescents may wonder why they are being excluded and how could they have provoked this treatment. For example, the private script of the sensitive adolescent may include statements like, "Why am I being left out?" What don't they like about me? Am I a bad person and that's why they don't want to be in my company? Educators need to work with such youth you appear sensitive to such subtle cues of social exclusion, as such harmful internal dialogue could lead to deleterious effects on one sense of self.

Such ambiguity surrounding ostracism may lead some adolescents to develop extreme social anxiety, self-doubt, and lowered self-esteem, etc. Developmental psychologists have documented the use of shunning and exclusion behaviours in children, used among other techniques as a form of peer rejection (e.g., Asher & Coie, 1990). For example, Barner-Barry (1986) describes a case where a preschool class systematically ostracized a bully (i.e., ignored him, excluded him from conversations and playing) without adult prompting, and apparent success. Such a case suggests that the use of ostracism as a means of controlling the behaviour of other is both adaptive and innate.

Regarding adolescence, research suggests that some teenage girls in particular favour ostracism as a strategy during conflicts or as a form of social aggression, described as "the manipulation of group acceptance through alienation, ostracism, or character defamation (Cairns, Cairns, Neckerman, Ferguson, & Gariepy, 1989, p. 323). In contrast to girls, Cairns et al., (1989) found that adolescent boys preferred to resort to physical violence as a means of resolving conflict. As outlined by Underwood (2002), ostracism may be viewed as another form of social aggression, That is, in contrast to direct aggression, to ostrasize someone, individuals direct aggression toward damaging another's self-esteem, social status, or both, and may take direct forms as negative facial expressions, body movements, and verbal rejections, and/or social rumours. Ostracism may also be considered a form of relational aggression, which includes behaviours aimed as harming others through the purposeful manipulation and damage of their peer relationships and self-worth.

Consistent with social exclusion and peer groups, related research on sociometric and social competence, including peer popularity and social acceptance have also examined the experiences of adolescents who have been silenced by their peers (e.g., Schuster, 1996). For example, Schuster found that rejected children, those disliked by their peers, and neglected children, those not noticed by their peers experienced victimization. In particular, rejected adolescents were more likely to experience victimization, whereas neglected children were not. Both types of adolescents claimed to have felt victimized, although in different ways in that rejected adolescents experienced more direct acts of rejection and social silencing. In the next section, I will discuss the role silence and ambiguity plays in instances of bullying, victimization, teasing and deception in adolescents.

AMBIGUITIES IN ADOLESCENT PLAY: DECEPTION, TEASING AND
PSYCHOLOGICAL BULLYING

Related literature on school bullying, peer harassment, teasing and aggression has
noted that the covert, indirect bullying acts such as social exclusion and the
spreading of rumors and insincere statements and actions or palters involving half
or partial truths may have greater emotional and psychological implications,
including lowered sense of self-worth, compared to more direct and physical types
of bullying such as punching and shoving (Crick, Grotpeter, & Bigbee, 2002;
Marini, Dane, Bosacki, & YLC-CURA, 2005; Keltner, 2009; Schauer &
Zeckhauser, 2009). As William James (1890) noted over one century ago, "A
man's Social Self is the recognition which he gets from his mates.... If no one
turned around when we entered, answered when we spoke, or minded what we did,
but if every person we met 'cut us dead,' and acted as if we were nonexisting
things, a kind of rage and impotent desire would ere long well up in us, from which
the cruelest bodily tortures would be a relief; for these would make us feel that,
however bad be our plight, we had not sunk to such a depth as to be unworthy of
attention at all" (pp. 293–294). As previously discussed, experience of being
socially silenced by others through ostracism, may include examples of both
silence and psychological bullying and/or teasing in that the situation may remain
ambiguous to the silencee.

In general, for some adolescents, silence may be viewed as a source of
inspiration and as a psychological and emotional venue for quiet reflection or
intense intellectual engagement. However, for others, silence may be accompanied
by loneliness and emotional pain. The latter vision of silence may thus bring
wariness in social company, victimization, and fear of rejection. In short, both
the antecedents and consequences of the behavioural expression of silence
remain contingent upon the individual and the context.

Early developmental theories and supportive data suggest that peer interaction
influences the development of social cognition, and ultimately, the expression of
competence social behaviour. Social interaction (with either peers or adults)
also influences children's understanding of the cultural and subcultural rules
and norms that guide social behaviours. This understanding of normative performance levels enables the child to evaluate her or his own competency against
the perceived standards of the peer group. Related to the social group and
being silenced or to the silencer, sometimes when silence is combined with
solitude, this may relate to spiritual awareness or a sense of meta-awareness in
which the individual becomes aware of "being aware." They are, as Buber (1970)
stated, "manifestations of relation," or moments of complete engagement with
what-is-there.

If social interaction plays a crucial role in the development of social
competencies and the understanding of the self in relation to others, researchers
need to consider the developmental consequences for those adolescents who,
for whatever reason, refrain from engaging in social interaction and avoid the
company of others. The question of why an adolescent would choose intentionally

to remain alone (either physically or psychologically), drives much of the current research on social withdrawal and the accompanying experiences of silence. For example, recent research suggests that the knowledge on the developmental consequences of social silence is constrained by cultural norms. Some studies suggest that in Western societies, shyness/social withdrawal may be less acceptable for boys than for girls (Coplan, Hughes, Rose-Krasnor & Bosacki, 2011; Sadker & Sadker, 1994). Furthermore, compared to Western countries, research suggests that shyness and social silence are more prevalent and carry more societal value in Eastern countries such as China (Chen, Rubin, & Li, 1995). Given the importance of the role shyness and social withdrawal have for social and personal relations, further research is required to elucidate these provocative findings.

As I will discuss further in the book when I explore the role of technology in self and social ambiguity - such research on social withdrawal and the need to be alone becomes further complicated technology and the virtual world is considered. What does it mean to choose to avoid social interaction regarding in-person only – such as face-to-face or private phone calls – and not a social call on a cell phone with multiple people around you. How does this differ from someone who avoids social contact both virtual and physical – and at what point does this become a concern for the healthy development of a sense of self and social connection during adolescence? What does it mean to prefer to *be* alone in contrast to *feel* alone – are the requests one an the same or different, and as educators and researchers, how do we know to discern the difference? How do these experiences differ according to either living in a virtual, electronic world, or a physical world?

The issue of virtual versus real life also complicates the experiences of ostracism and social exclusion during adolescence. To what extent do experiences of social exclusion on-line feel different from experiences of social exclusion in-person? Do both examples create the same level and intensity of emotions and how do we know this? Should we be concerned and why? As Williams (2001; 2011), Turkle (2011) and others explore examples of in-person and virtual ostracism they encourage us to become concerned about the role of technology in social relations as they state that given that Internet has the potential to be an effective and powerful communicative tool, some adolescents have chosen to use the Internet as a psychological weapon to hurt others.

Given the ambiguous, complex, and paradoxical context of the adolescent playground and classroom, adolescents learn how to hone their social cognitive abilities including ToM understanding to help them to navigate this sometimes perhaps tumultuous landscape of adolescence. As sophisticated social cognitive abilities may help adolescents to understand the social ambiguities among their peers, such sophistication may also help some adolescents to harm instead of help others within social situations. Research on deception and social interactions is wide and varied, occurring across the lifespan. Research on deception and young adults suggests that a form of lying or deception involves the ability to misrepresent reality in the absence of a literal falsity. This act of paltering or acting or talking insincerely according to Shauer and Zeckhauser

(2009) involves telling meaningless pieces of truth to create a false impression and is commonly understood to involve fabrications and manipulations of truth slanting, twisting, exaggerating, and selective reporting. Although the palter may be factually true as there is no literal falsity, the palterer has the intent to deceive, and the deceivee or victim believes the palterer's statement to be true. Thus, paltering involves creating a wrong impression through deliberate action or in other words, a deliberate attempt to create a misimpression in someone by means other than uttering a literal falsehood.

As outlined by Schauer and Zeckhauser (2009), The practice of paltering includes the ability to understand the mental state of the others in that you understand s/he holds a false belief – that the palterer intends to create – however, in contrast to a literal falsity – stating something that is false, the palterer will use alternative means to create a false sense of belief in the other (one being paltered too or palteree). To illustrate the process of paltering within an adolescent social context, imagine a scenario that involves a girl who wishes her friend to believe that she is also friends with a popular girl in class, although the girl (palterer) knows that she herself does not know this particular popular girl, she could refer to the popular girl by her first name to create the illusion to her friend that she knows this popular girl and that perhaps they are friends. Thus, this is a deliberate action to create a wrong impression in her friend other than uttering a literal falsehood. That is, the palterer does not state that she is friends with this popular girl as this would be a literal falsity and thus a lie. In contrast, by referring to the popular girl by her first name, the palterer deliberately leads her friend to believe that she (the palterer) is already friends with the popular girl.

As Shauer and Zeckhauser (2009) state, this process known as paltering, or acting or talking insincerely may be just as, or perhaps more harmful as lying. Because they involve literal falsities, lies are easier to detect than palters and as an adolescent who palters may be less likely to be identified or 'caught' by the authorities such as a teacher. In contrast, an adolescent that chooses to lie instead of palter may be more likely to be identified and be penalized by their teacher. Given this challenge to detect the subtle and ambiguous nature of such creative use of misrepresentation, little social cognitive research exists on paltering and various forms of deception in adolescence within social situations as higher order ToM abilities also remain difficult to assess (Hughes, 2011).

Future research could explore individual differences in adolescents' choices to deceive either through direct lying, or a version of paltering – and explore their reasoning why. An example of related recent research involves a current research study on deception and cognition in children and adolescence. Evans and Lee's (2011) studied verbal deception in late childhood and adolescents and found that the sophistication of 8- to 16-year olds lies' were significantly related to executive functioning skills including working memory, inhibitory control, and planning skills. Interestingly, Evans and Lee (2011) found that the participants' decisions to lie were not related to these cognitive skills and suggest that there is a need for future research on how to explore the ambiguity regarding adolescents' choices in deception, especially regarding socially ambiguous contexts, where the moral choice is not always clear.

Thus, building on Evans and Lee's study, future research needs to explore how adolescents understand social ambiguities regarding situations involving various levels of deception including ambiguous examples of indirect lying or paltering, and how does this connect with their ToM ability and self-concept? Also, to what extent are the adolescent's motivation to palter to others related to palter to oneself (and vice versa), and does this relation differ according to the level of deception? What are the emotional experiences and thoughts of the palterer before, during and after the event, and does this differ for individuals across age, cultural backgrounds, gender, etc. How does this compare to the experiences of liars and various levels of deception – as well across various modes of communication (e.g., virtual, face-to-face). I will return to such questions regarding the role of technology in deception later on in this chapter when I discuss the role the Internet plays in adolescents' understanding of ambiguity in social communication and self-representation.

The Ambiguities of Teasing in Adolescence

As paltering is a particular type or level of lying, teasing also falls on a moral continuum as it is defined more as a mode of play than a form of bullying (see Keltner, 2009; and Keltner et al., 2001 for a conceptual analysis of teasing). Similar to paltering, as compared to physical bullying that is easier to detect through overt behaviours, psychological bullying and relayed forms of teasing are more psychological and subtle and thus, more difficult for educators to identify as a harmful and possibly destructive behaviour. Regarding the ambiguous context of play in adolescence, teasing is sometimes referred to as an example of playful aggression as adolescents learn how to navigate the ambiguities of social living within the secondary school classroom such as social hierarchies, forming and establishing relationships (same and opposite gender), test commitment to social norms, negotiate conflicts over work, etc.). Thus, as Keltner (2009) notes, teasing is not a form of aggression, but a mode of play, with a sharp edge to which we use to provoke others. (p. 148).

Teasing occurs within the paradoxical context of adolescent relationships involving a continuum of friendships where teasing is situated somewhere on that emotional continuum ranging from a tease being a 'playful nip' to a tease being a full-fledged bullying statement or threat. As Boxer and Cortés-Conde (1997) suggest, "teasing runs along a continuum of bonding to nipping to biting" (p. 279). This ambiguity in the interaction may cause difficulty to the recipient or target in distinguishing which element of the interaction such as the verbal content of the comment as well as the facial expression/non-verbal communication which also deserves response. The element or component of the teasing interaction that the recipient chooses to focus on may help to determine the valence of the recipient's emotional response.

When an individual is engaged in the process of teasing, Shapiro, Baumeister, and Kessler (1991) explain that "the target must decode an ambiguous message in order to arrive at an attribution of the teaser's true intention" (p. 466). That is, the target needs to recognise whether "he or she is being insulted or is being engaged in play" (p. 466). According to Boxer and Cortés-Conde (1997) "as with all talk, much depends on the identification of context, and indeed the exact message cannot be interpreted without encoding/decoding the metamessage" (p. 279). Within the scope of contextual information, in addition to pre-existing relationships between those involved and linguistic and paralinguistic cues, it is important to be aware of the intent of the teaser and the interpretation by the target.

However, although there are cues to aid interpretation, a recipient cannot always be expected to see the funny side of teasing. That is, whether or not a comment or 'tease' which is meant to be 'funny' by the teaser is considered funny or hurtful is dependent upon the emotional response of the recipient. For instance, regarding Eder's (1993) research on teasing in adolescent females, Eder defines teasing as "any playful remark aimed at another person, which can include mock challenges, commands, and threats, as well as imitating and exaggerating someone's behaviour in a playful way" (Eder, 1993, p. 17).

Building on these cues to identify playful from harmful teasing, Keltner (2009) has gleaned from his research four lessons to draw from to help adolescents and those adults who work with youth to decipher the ambiguous emotional language of teasing, In other words, Keltner (2009) asks, what separates a productive tease from a damaging one? How do we measure others' emotional responses to teases? Drawing on his research with youth and teasing, the first lesson is the nature of the provocation in the tease. Harmful teasing is physically painful and hones in on vulnerable aspects of the individual's identity (e.g., an adolescent's appearance such as their weight, see Taylor, 2011). According to Keltner (2009), playful teasing is less hurtful physically, and thoughtfully targets less critical facets of the target's identity. For example, an adolescent's odd manner of laughing – although distinguishing between a harmful and playful tease is tricky as identity during adolescence is dangerous territory as an individual may be sensitive to this issue and any comment at all – despite the intention of the teaser willl be interpreted as negative and a criticism and thus may be perceived by the target as hurtful.

Keltner's second lesson pertains to the presence of the off-record markers or the exaggeration, shifts in vocalization patterns (i.e., chanting, singing), repetition, patterns, funny facial displays, etc. As Clark (1996) suggests in his linguistic analysis of teasing, when we tease, we frame the interaction as one that occurs within a playful, nonserious realm of social exchange. Keltner's (2009) research shows that the same provocation delivered with the ornate designs of nonliteral language produced little negative emotions and were more likely to produce feelings of amusement and affection. Keltner found that the same provocation delivered without these off-record markers mainly produced anger and affront. For example, a comment regarding a female adolescent's dress such as "nice dress – do you plan on meeting Prince Charming?" within a playful and positive tone will be more likely to be received by the target as a playful or funny comment as opposed to the same comment stated with a negative facial expression or sarcastic tone. Thus, a clue to detecting an effective tease from a hostile tease is to look and listen for those off-record markers that reflect the land of play and pretense.

Keltner's third lesson is that of the social context. A comment, action, look may have different meanings depending on the context, and if it is coming from a friend or foe, whether they occur in a formal/non-formal setting, alone in a room with another individual, or with a large group. As power is critical to the meaning of the tease, friends' power asymmetries, especially when the target cannot respond, may produce harmful teasing. As Keltner's (2009) research on teasing among young adult males at university fraternity parties suggests, bullies are known for teasing in domineering ways that prevent the target from reciprocating. Similarly, teasing in romantic bonds and friendships defined by power asymmetries take the shape of bullying. Thus, the art of the tease is to enable reciprocity and back-and-forth exchange. Thus, according to Keltner, an effective teaser invites being teased.

Keltner's fourth and final lesson reminds us to remember that the ability to tease improves with age or social-cognitive development. Beginning at age 10 or 11, children become more sophisticated in their abilities to endorse contradictory propositions about objects in the world as they move from either/or, black-or-white reasoning to a more interpretive and complex understanding of the world. Such an ability parallels children's ability to understand sarcasm and irony as described earlier, and also allows the child to learn how to palter or misrepresent the truth without stating a literal falsity (producing an insincere statement). Thus, given the connections between Keltner's work on teasing and literature on verbal deception, future research needs to explore how adolescents make sense of ambiguous contexts regarding teasing and deception and how they are able to manage and cope through both positive and negative experiences.

Ambiguities in Adolescent Play: The Role of the Bystander

Given the paradoxical context of play involving a complex concoction of negative and positive emotions and social interactions (Sutton-Smith, 1997), ambiguity plays a role regarding emergency situations, or situations that involve a psychological and emotional crisis. A major determinant of helplessness may be the characteristics of the stimulus for help. Research shows that ambiguous cues may result in fewer attempts to help, while distress cues that indicate greater rather than less need for assistance may lead to more help. Ambiguity may also give rise to concern that a helpful act would be inappropriate or appear foolish and thus may activate an approval goal. For example, as Latane and Darley (1970) emphasized, ambiguity often surrounds an emergency in that when a person faces a distressed other, the nature or source of the other's distress is often unknown or unclear.

Ambiguity and uncertainty about the need for help and about the type of action one should take may increase the observer's tension and discomfort, reducing the probability that she will approach the stimulus producing the discomfort. Ambiguity may also allow a person to interpret the distress cues in alternative ways. For example, within a bullying/victimization scenario involving four teenaged females, if two instigators or bullies are psychologically harassing or verbally assaulting another peer, perhaps as a means of how to cope by 'ignoring' the bullies' insults, the victim's distress cues may appear ambiguous such as the victim may remain silent or maintains an emotionally neutral facial expression, or flat affect. Thus, victim's decision to choose to 'ignore' the bullies' verbal assaults through means of ambiguous behaviour may lead the bystander to be less likely to help the victim in this situation.

A large amount of research has shown that a high frequency of helping behaviour perhaps in part because the stimulus for help minimized the ambiguity of the emergency. The distressed person's visibility of vulnerability have been found to minimize ambiguity and enhance the credibility of the need for help. Generally, information about eh sources of a person's distress may reduced ambiguity, and thus increase the likelihood that aid will be given , but this information also specifies the degree of her need for help, that is, the utility of help, how important it is for her to receive aid, and how much benefit the help may produced. The greater the need, the more motives to help may be activated. Social norms as well as personal values that prescribe help are presumably more imperative when someone's need is great, and both the social and personal costs of not helping would be greater. This concept of degree of need is similar to Berkowitz and Daniels' (1963) concept of dependency as their research showed that people extend more effort to aid another who is more rather than less dependent on them in acquiring rewards.

Thus, referring to the example of the psychological bullying with the four teenagers (two bullies, victim and bystander), in addition to ambiguity playing a role in the distress signals of the victim, it may also play a role in the bystander's relationships with the other players in the bullying scenario. That is, the bystander's behaviour may be contingent upon the relationship she has with the victim, or the bullies, and also if one of the players in the bullying scenario holds the dual role of bully/victim. If she is friends with one of the bullies, she would be less likely to help, whereas if she was the friend of the victim, she may be more likely to help.

More specifically, within the context of interpersonal relations including bullying and victimization, educational researchers have long investigated the role of bystanders in an emergency situation or one that includes violence or harm to another individual (Banyard, 2008; Nucci, 2008). This research has usually been experimental and has established important principles about the conditions under which individuals will choose to engage in prosocial bystander behaviors. More recently, interest has grown in applying this work to the important practical problem of preventing interpersonal violence in communities and bullying and victimization in schools. Yet, to date, remains little research on the role ambiguity plays in cases of interpersonal emotional and psychological violence such as teasing and hazing and how this influences bystanders' decisions to either help, join in, or leave the situation (Keltner, 2009; Waldron & Kowloski, 2009). Regarding the studies of the correlates of bystander behaviour, past research has shown that the level of ambiguity regarding whether or not someone is in distress may influence the extent to which bystanders help with the situation (Staub, 2003).

Within the adolescent bullying and victimization research, the bystander plays a role with this social process as she/he are witnesses to a particular distressing situation (Staub, 2003). However, the level of helping behaviour that may occur given a situation or bullying/victimization may differ according to the bystander's pre-existing (if any) relationship with the bully and vicitim. For example, if an adolescent female is witnessing two girls teasing another girl, at what point of the interaction will the bystander or witness chose to intervene the situation, and then if she decides to help, to what extent will her help be. That is, a girl who observes another girl being teased by two others has the opportunity to make some decisions. She could 1) ask the two girls to stop teasing the victim, 2) befriend the victim and ask her to join her and leave the situation, 3) leave the scene of the teasing and seek assistance from a guardian such as a teacher or older student. Alternatively, the girl could choose to join the two girls and tease the victim or target, or leave the scene without mentioning the incident to anyone. Thus, it is the ambiguity of the scene or situation provides the bystander with the opportunity to make sense and interpret the situation, and then decide which action to take (either for the better or worse).

Regarding ambiguity, the ambiguity of the quality or status of the relationship of the individuals involved in the bullying or paradoxical playing scene may also influence the bystander's behaviour (Faris & Felmlee, 2011; Taylor, 2011; Turkle, 2011). For example, if a boy who observes another boy being hazed or teased by two others is unsure of, or remains uncertain or ambiguous about his relationship with the boy regarding friendship, he may decide to either help or not help the victim of the teasing/hazing. Researchers have also started to explore the ambiguous role of the bystander within the virtual world, as researchers have started to explore the dynamics involved regarding on-line cyberteasing, bullying and the roles individuals play within the on-line culture (Beran, Ramirez-Serrano, Kuzk, Nugent & Fior, 2011; Wunmi Grigg, 2010). I will return to the topic of virtual social ambiguities later on in this chapter when discussing cyberbullying, as well as Chapter 3 when I discuss the educational implications for educators working with adolescents.

GENDERED AMBIGUITIES IN ADOLESCENTS: PERFECTIONIST PRINCESSES?

Gender is considered an integral factor in all aspects of human development, affecting both our mind and body. As Fine (2010) and Liben (2011) note, new models of gender witin the disciplines of neuroscience and cultural psychology question the notion that gender is attained as a secure status throughout life (see Fine, 2010 for further discussion of recent neuroscience and psychology research on gender-related difference). Such models are consistent with Maccoby's (1998) claim that gender is considered more of a "culture" or process than a fixed trait. That is, gender is now viewed by some theorists as a fluid construct, one that must be negotiated in social relationships and challenged by changing social, cultural, and historical contexts (Shields, 2003).

As noted by Miller and Scholnick (2000), most studies on social cognition and language tend to gloss over gender issues, or at least, have not specifically aimed to investigate gender-related differences and/or patterns. A psychocultural or "ethnopsychological" approach to ToM (Astington, 1996; Lillard, 1997) provides a valuable form of inquiry to investigate the effects of gender on social-cognitive development. As I noted in Chapter 1, a psychocultural approach to ToM asserts the notion that individuals' ability to understand mental states in others is largely relativistic and socially-constructed. In support of this view, cross-cultural research has shown that the development of social cognitive abilities including ToM may be dependent upon one's cultural experience (McCormick, 1994).

A psychocultural approach to development suggests that individual differences in the ability to understand mental states in others may indicate that this ability is acquired in different ways for women and men. Put differently, the process of learning to understand self and other within a social context may be contingent not on whether a child is female or male, but on the way in which a child's gender interacts with her/his environment. Thus, if an adolescent is viewed as a "cultural invention" (Kessen, cited in Cahan, 1997, p. 2), gender helps to create a separate culture for that particular adolescent. This conception of gender as a social category or particular culture suggests that acknowledging the contribution of cultural milieu to a ToM may prove to be a fruitful avenue for future research on development of gender-role conception and behaviour (Maccoby, 1998; Nelson, Henseler, & Plesa, 2000).

According to Thomas Cook and Kaiser (2004), age and gender ambiguity become pronounced in preadolescence as children engage in the transition from childhood to adolescence within an increasingly consumer and media infiltrated culture. Within such a cultural context, stereotypic gender-typed roles become increasingly pronounced, illustrating the increasing ambiguity and tension sur-rounding age and sexuality during early adolescence. Given the mixed messages received from our youth today regarding the gendered stereotypes of femininities and masculinities such that stereotypes of femininities are considered to be beautiful but competent, where as men are perceived to be sensitive but physically strong and infallible (Jackson & Chen, 2003; Orenstein, 2011). As Orenstein states, we need to question the consumer-driven stereotypes of modern and popular culture, and ask what is wrong with young girls and adolescent females aiming to be princesses waiting for their Prince Charming to appear? What is wrong with young boys and adolescent males aspiring to be a 'Prince Charming?' What type of messages do these princess and prince cultural narrative send? Messages that tell youth to value virtues of courage, compassion, honesty and integrity? Or aspire to be academically and socially competent? Physically attractive? More importantly, how do we encourage youth to critically question these paradoxical and ambiguous gendered stereotypes? In chapter 3, I will discuss holistic educational programs that aim to help youth develop the tools to question such ambiguous gendered messages.

A social-constructivist inquiry into the workings of the adolescent mind and its implications for social interactions would enable researchers to view gender in-context (e.g., Shields, 2002), as it operates within a social milieu such as the classroom. In opposition to the more traditional sex-differences model (i.e., gender differences not mentioned apriori, only post-hoc statistical tests to indicate differences), such a gendered approach to research is in line with Hill and Lynch's (1983) gender intensification hypothesis. This hypothesis claims that during preadolescence, gender differences increase among girls and boys due to the increased pressure to conform to traditional gender-role stereotypes. For example, research has shown that during preadolescence, traditional gender-role behaviour and ascription (i.e., femininity = sociality, submissiveness; masculinity = autonomy, aggression) become intensified (Hill & Lynch, 1983; Tavris, 1992).

In accordance with research that shows a link between traditional female stereotypic behaviour and depression among women (McGrath, Keita, Strickland, & Russo, 1990), intensification of gender identity among preadolescent girls may strengthen behavioural tendencies hypothesized to hold special relevance for vulnerability to depression such as interpersonal sensitivity, an eagerness to please and an increased concern for others (e.g., Zahn-Waxler et al., 1991). Thus, preadolescent girls who appear to be relatively competent in the ability to
understand and be sensitive to the needs of others may be more likely to read the emotional and social messages found in the complex and ambiguous social interactions that others may not be aware of. Thus, given this ability to read the positive and negative messages in social interactions (non-verbal, verbal), as some adolescent girls may be sensitive to negative comments as compared to boys, and thus be at risk for developing future self-concept disorders such as depression (Silverstein & Perlick, 1995).

In support of the gender-intensification hypothesis, many gender-related differences gleaned from research on social behaviour and social cognition in adolescence are usually consistent with traditional gender-role stereotypes. Concerning social behaviour, the majority of research findings show that compared to boys, girls are rated as more socially competent and popular by both their peers and teachers (e.g., see Fine, 2010). Similarly, research on teacher perceptions shows that girls are perceived by their teachers to be more compliant and prosocial than boys (Harter, 1999). Furthermore, studies on rejected and clinically depressed children have shown that compared to boys, girls tend to display more internalizing behaviours such as unhappy, withdrawn behavioural patterns. In contrast, boys have been found to display more externalizing behaviours such as aggressive, antisocial patterns (e.g., Hatzichristou & Hopf, 1996; La Greca, 1981).

According to teacher expectancy research (e.g., Jones & Gerig, 1994), perceptions and labels of teachers may play a role in how adolescents experience silence and interact within the classroom, particularly if adolescent is labeled as "quiet, shy," or "delinquent, troubled." Reflecting a self-fulfilling prophesy, this label may become integrated into the adolescent's identity. That is, once a teacher labels a student as quiet and shy, that adolescent may become to believe that they are quiet and shy and which in turn may cause the adolescent to exhibit quiet and shy behaviours. That is, to validate the teacher's label, the adolescent may choose to speak less or avoid and withdraw from conversation (either intentionally or unintentionally). Such behaviours may thus perpetuate the teacher's original label.of quiet and shy and given the complex relations between teacher' perceptions and students' behaviour, my colleagues and I continue to explore teachers' perceptions of gender in the classroom, particularly teachers' thoughts on gendered stereotypic notions of shyness and social withdrawal in the classroom (Coplan, et al., 2011).

Furthermore, the majority studies on teacher expectancies have shown that teachers' expectations of their students and subsequent student-teacher interactions have an effect on student behaviour and self-concept (e.g., Jones & Gerig, 1994). Given the crucial role teachers and peers play in both the gender-role social-lization and co-construction of sociocognitive and linguistic abilities of adolescents (Denham, 1998), it is surprising that few researchers have studied the links between teachers' and peers' perceptions of students social and academic beha-viour and children's self concept and how these perceptions shape silence experiences in the classroom.

Regarding teacher ratings and children's ToM ability, gender differences have been found in teachers' ratings of children's social behaviours with high ToM scores linked to mischievious behaviour for boys, whereas for girls high ToM scores were positively associated with prosocial behaviour (Walker, 2005). Gender-related differences were found in a recent study with 6 year olds where a stronger association was found between social understanding and sensitivity to teacher criticism for girls as compared to boys (Hughes, 2011), and related studies on young adolescents' bullying and victimization experiences have found girls with higher ToM to be more sensitive to social messages as well as more likely to engage in psychological bullying (Caravita, Di Biasio, & Salmivalli, 2010; Sutton, Smith, & Swettenham, 1999); such research remains to be explored with older children and adolescents. Similarly, given past findings that suggest a significant positive relation between younger children's higher ToM scores and their more negative interpretations and reactions to teachers' comments of criticism (Cutting & Dunn, 2002; Lecce, Caputi, & Hughes, 2011; Watson et al., 1999), and their peer conversations (Hughes & Dunn, 1998), it could be possible that gender-related links may also exist between ToM understanding and conversational experiences with peers and family among older school-aged children and adolescents.

During adolescence, as conversations with teachers and peers may increase in complexity and ambiguity with more references to non-literal language (Taylor, 2011), gender may continue to play a role in teachers' comments and peer conversations as they may often lead to multiple interpretations regarding the social and emotional messages (Tannen, 1994). Recent findings from our longitudinal research on young adolescents' ToM ability and their conversational experiences talking and listening with their peers and family showed that adolescent females (11–12 year olds) were more likely to refer to emotional and social situations in their conversations with their peers and families as compared to adolescent males who focused on physical activities (Bosacki, 2011). Regarding ToM and self-concept, we found that adolescents with higher ToM scores at Time 1 (8–9 year olds) were more likely to report lower feelings of self-worth and include references to psychological and emotional language in their perceptions of their conversational experiences with their peers and family two years later at Time 2 (11–12 years). We also asked adolescents their thoughts and emotions regarding listening and their experiences of silences in conversations and the majority of participants across both genders referred to negative or mixed emotions such as feeling bored or nervous. Given that this research project is ongoing, we will continue to explore the role gender plays in adolescent's experiences of social ambiguities in the classroom as future research should continue to explore gender-related differences and possible relations between adolescents' ToM ability and their sensitivity to comments of criticism including cynicism, sarcasm, irony, and teasing, as well as words of support and praise and from teachers and peers.

As I discussed earlier in this Chapter, research on children's interpretations of ambiguity shows that children may have a positive bias toward socially ambiguous information although this may decrease with age as children's perceptions become more realistic (Bjorklund, 2006; Boseovski & Lee, 2006), given the importance of these findings for education, future research needs to explore how gender will play a role in adolescents ability to make sense of ambiguous messages from teachers and peers within the classroom. Such research could also be expanded to explore gender-related differences in teachers' ToM ability as to date, there have been no studies that have explored gender-related differences in teachers' ToM ability and if this ability affects teachers' perceptions of adolescent students and gender-role expectations in the classroom.

Regarding social-cognitive abilities, research shows that boys score higher than girls on nonsocial spatial perspective-taking tasks (Coie & Dorval, 1973), whereas girls score higher than boys on social perspective-taking and empathy tasks (Jahnke & Blanchard-Fields, 1993; King, Akiyama & Elling, 1996). Likewise, Offer, Ostrov, Howard and Atkinson (1988) reported that across 10 countries, girls were more likely than boys to express a desire to help a friend when possible and thus gave evidence of a "more sociable and empathic stance" than did boys (p. 70). Gender-related differences have also been found in the social-cognitive area of person perception. In general, girls have been shown to emphasize such categories as interpersonal skills, psychological traits and social relationships (Honess, 1981, Sprague, Beauregard, & Voelker, 1987). In contrast, boys have been found to emphasize such categories as physical aggression, interests, and academic ability (Peevers & Secord, 1973).

Surprisingly, although social cognitive researchers investigate social-cognitive abilities like the ones mentioned above, to date, the exploration of gender-related differences among ToM abilities remains contradictory and inconclusive. Of the few ToM studies that explore gender-related difference, many report nonsignificant results (e.g., Jenkins & Astington, 1996). However, results obtained from preschool children, adolescents, and adults show that girls and women score significantly higher on ToM-type tasks including emotion and social and self understanding as compared to boys and men respectively (Bialecka-Pikul et al., 2010; Bosacki, 2000; Bosacki, 2008; Brown & Dunn, 1996; Cutting & Dunn, 1999). For example, regarding preschool children, Hughes and Dunn (1998), investigated theory of mind and emotion understanding in preschoolers. Hughes and Dunn found that compared to boys, girls referred to mental state verbs more frequently and their choice of verbs was more sophisticated or developmentally advanced. In contrast, the findings here are mixed, with some studies reporting that boys possess higher levels of ToM understanding than girls (Russell, Tchanturia, Rahman, & Schmidt, 2007). Thus, given the mixed findings and the growing complexity in the role gender plays in adolescents' social-cognitive development, future research needs to continue to explore the role gender plays in adolescent's ToM ability.

Although the research base in this area is thin, there is some correlational evidence that shows gender differences in the development of psychological understanding of self and others during adolescence. Despite the theoretical connection between ToM understanding and the self-concept (Wellman, 1990), few studies have investigated this link directly, particularly with respect to cultural context (Banerjee & Yuill, 1999; Johnson, 1997). For example, Hatcher et al., (1990) found that among 13-year-old girls, abstract reasoning was related to the understanding of others but not oneself, whereas the reverse was found for boys, abstract reasoning was positively related to self-understanding but not to the understanding of others. The authors claim that this finding suggests that girls are more likely to understand others than to understand themselves based on the tendency of modern Western culture to label interpersonal under-standing and empathetic sensitivity as "natural" personality traits for females. The implications of these findings for experiences of silence are interesting, given that silence could provides some time for reflection and deepening one's self-awareness.

With regard to ToM and self-understanding, findings have shown relatively sophisticated cognitive abilities such as the ability to understand recursive mental states in others (e.g., "She thinks that he thinks...") may be linked to feelings of negative self-worth (Farber, 1989; Veith, 1980). For instance, Veith (1980) found that preadolescents' ability to understand recursive mental states in others was related to a relatively negative view of the self. Similarly, preadolescent females who reported feelings of low self-worth and depressed mood were more likely to receive high scores on ToM tasks, particularly among highly academically competent preadolescent girls (e.g., Gjerde, 1995; Kerr, 1994). Past findings from our research study on ToM, self-concept, and social competence in children and adolescence revealed a positive relation between preadolescents' ToM ability and their ability to describe themselves as a person suggesting that preadolescents who have a more sophisticated ability to understand mental states in others were also more likely to provide more sophisticated self-descriptions (Bosacki, 2000). Regarding gender differences, we have also found stronger positive relations between self-concept and emotional understanding for preadolescent girls as compared to boys, and that girls were more likely to focus on their social relationships both through narrative and pictorial descriptions (Bosacki, 2007; Bosacki, Varnish, & Akseer, 2008).

In contrast to past research that suggests a positive link may exist between psychological understanding and self-concept (Selman, 1980; 2003), some investigators claim that the later correlates of ToM and feelings of self-worth may not be uniformly positive (Dunn, 2000; Hughes & Dunn, 1998). As mentioned earlier, there is some evidence to suggest that positive relations exist between high levels of children's ToM understanding and greater sensitivity to teacher criticism and lower self-esteem (Dunn, 1995; Cutting & Dunn,1999; Veith, 1980). In addition, studies have shown that children and adults with high levels of psychological understanding may experience diminished self-concept and emotional problems, given the time spent on self-reflection and imagining what others think of them (Hatcher & Hatcher, 1997). Also, given the finding that children who scored high on second-order ToM tasks were able to better understand self-presentation rules (Banerjee & Yuill, 1999), perhaps children who are adept at reading social cues are adept at pretending to be who they think people want them to be. Future researchers could continue to explore the areas of ToM and self-presentation in adolescents, particularly regarding gender-related differences.

Given Hatcher et al.'s (1980, 2007) findings, perhaps for adolescent girls, increased amounts of silence may promote the understanding of other's inner lives as compared to furthering one's private world. In contrast, perhaps for boys, experiences of silence may promote the development of self-awareness and self-knowledge. Given the ongoing discussions regarding the "boy turn" in research on gender and education (Fine, 2010; Weaver-Hightower, 2003), researchers will need to explore the gendered implications silence has for adolescents' self and other understanding.

Such self-presentation skills may suggest the ability to edit and/or perhaps silence particular aspects of the self and personal voice. Thus, investigations of links between ToM and self will illuminate the complex connections between understanding oneself and others. Taken together with other studies on adolescents that have shown links between social-cognitive abilities and self-concept (Bhatnager & Rastogi, 1986; Bosacki, 2008), these results support Farber's (1989) contention that high psychological mindedness or ToM may have deleterious consequences such as a negative self-concept. Overall, as discussed earlier in the chapter within the context of understanding ambiguous social relations, such findings suggest that social and emotional correlates of ToM need to be further examined in adolescents. In particular, researchers need to explore how such sophisticated mental capacities may enable adolescents to become highly proficient social detectives and editors as well as O'Sullivan's (2009) notion of truth wizards of ambiguous situations, especially concerning issues of identity and social relations (Park & Park, 1997).

Likewise, implicitly supportive evidence derived from investigations which suggest that for girls, a heightened awareness and understanding of the mental states and feelings of others may have negative consequences for later psycho-emotional functioning. For example, longitudinal studies investigating gender differences in developmental models of depression have found that as young girls, depressed adolescent females were more concerned with maintaining interpersonal relationships, more able to recognize the feelings of others and more likely to include moral issues in their play patterns than boys (Block, Gjerde, & Block, 1991; Gjerde & Block, 1991). Further supportive evidence derives from the literature on the socialization of empathy and guilt which suggests that high levels of empathy and guilt may serve as precursors for later depression in women (Bybee, 1998; Zahn-Waxler & Robinson, 1995). Similarly, in a study of 115 preadolescent girls and boys (8- to 12-years-old), Fraser and Strayer (1997) found that the most robust correlation between shame and sensitivity existed among the older girls (11- to 12-year olds). In sum, such studies support the view that individuals who are sensitive to interpersonal interactions may be preoccupied with the psychological needs of others to the detriment to their own, which may eventually lead to an ambiguous sense of self or lack of a coherent self-definition (Antonovsky, 1979; Bosacki, 2000; Park & Park, 1997; Silverstein & Perlick, 1995).

In sum, what do the past gendered findings on social cognition among adolescents tell us about their experiences of silences in the classroom? Based on the findings described above, compared to males, adolescent females may be more likely to engage in solitary, social-relational activities which may affect their silence experiences. Given Hatcher et al,'s (1990), compared to adolescent males, adolescent females may also be more likely to engage in thinking about the inner worlds of others rather than their own. Thus, researchers need to explore the implications of gendered social cognition for classroom silences among adolescents as the mental health of the adolescent is developing during this sensitive age.

Accordingly, connections between works on feminist epistemologies and psychoeducational research provides a valuable starting point for investigating the roles in which silence may play in the processes of understanding self and other in adolescence, and how this may influence their classroom behaviour (e.g., Belenky et al., 1986; Bosacki, 2005; 2008; Debold, Tolman, & Brown, 1996). The attempt to define and assess the processes that enable adolescents to understand social situations may offer some insight on gender-related research findings. Such a research agenda would help to shed some light on the wealth of findings from social-emotional studies that show around the age of 11 or 12, some girls (in comparison to boys) experience the following: a significant drop in feelings and thoughts of self-worth (Harter, 1999; Silverstein & Perlick, 1995), an increase in self-consciousness (Simmons, Rosenberg, & Rosenberg, 1973), and an increasingly negative sense of self worth despite high academic achievement, particularly among "gifted girls" (Cross, 2011; Freeman, 2010; Matthews & Smyth, 1997). Thus, research on the ability to understand mental states in others and its links to self-concept and social relations may help to further examine the related phenomenon of why girls may be more at risk than boys to lose their sense of self or "inner voice" during early adolescence (Brown & Gilligan, 1992; Harter, 1999). Finally, as Weaver-Hightower (2003) suggests, if we as educators aim to understand gendered silences and ambiguities within the classroom, we need the curriculum, pedagogy, and research programs that explore gender in complex and interrelated ways, by looking beyond issues of gender inequity and examine the ambiguous and co-constructed definitions of femininities and masculinities (Fine, 2010).

GENDER RELATED DIFFERENCES IN SOCIAL AMBIGUITIES

As noted above, given the complexity regarding the integral role gender plays in self and social development during adolescence, although a full discussion of gender and social and personal ambiguities is beyond the scope of this book, as many educators and researchers note, gender does matter, in education and in our human interactions, but we need to be cautious as we explore the issue of gender and adolescents (Eliot, 2009; Fine, 2010; Liben, 2011). As Fine (2010) and others note, given the recent research in neuroplasticity that suggest that biological differences between the sexes may be interpreted as minimal and that cultural context is key, the challenge for researchers and educators is to acknowledge and apply of understanding of sex differences to help adolescents, without turning this knowledge into self-fulfilling prophecies. As Eliot asserts, we need to embrace the uncertainty of the plasticity of gender differences, thus we need to be aware of gender, but also of the ambiguity of gender-roles and stereotypes.

Regarding the feminist approaches to viewing silence, drawing on the earlier works of Gilligan's (1982; 1993) and Perry's (1987) research on personal epistemologies, Belenky and colleagues (1996) framed the concept of silence within their theoretical framework of women's epistemological development. Goldberger and her colleagues (Goldberger, Tarule, Clinchy & Belenky, 1996) view silence as a position in which an individual feels as if he or she does not know something, as if she or he is missing out on an important piece of knowledge. This sense of uncertainty or incompleteness may lead the person to feel powerless, mindless, and voiceless. Given the ambiguous nature of experiencing silence as it has multiple interpretations, researchers have explored how culture and social factors may influence how adolescents interpret silence and how they respond such as becoming silent themselves. For example, is silence an obligation, social command, or personal choice? What are the functions and meanings of silence in adolescents' peer culture, and what role does silence play in their experiences of ambiguities regarding their identity and social conversations?

To describe this distinction between being silenced by others and choosing to be silent among others, or self-silencing, Goldberger (1996) suggested that structural silence (or societal rules that dictate when individuals should speak or be silent), may lead to particular individuals feeling "silenced." That is, such structural or societal silence may influence some people to a protective stance of silence and passivity that may stem from feelings of fear and threat which may be influenced by how the adolescent interprets the social exchanges.

In contrast to this structural silence in which an individual has either little or no control, Goldberger and colleagues (1996) refers to *strategic* silence. Situational and cultural factors could determine individual strategic silence in which the individual deliberately chooses to be silent and is still able to engage in conversations as an active contributing knower. Regarding social ambiguity, to what extent does the ambiguity of the social interaction influence the youth's interpretation of the social messages. For example, if an adolescent interprets a social exchange as negative and harmful, is she or he more likely to remain silent or to confront the issue verbally?

As I noted earlier, findings from our current research with adolescents and their experiences of silences with peers and family revealed mixed and negative emotions across both genders (Bosacki, 2011). We also asked adolescents of their perceptions of talking and listening with their peers with all adolescents stating that they experienced negative emotions such as anger and sadness when they felt as though they were not being listened to and thus silenced. In contrast, most female and male adolescents reported that they experienced mainly positive emotions such as happiness and excitement when they were talking with their peers and family. Thus, further research on gendered interpretations of socially ambiguous interactions is clearly needed as such research will help educators to understand the role gender plays in youth's ability to make sense of social situations.

Regarding adolescents' emotional experiences of social interactions, depressive symptoms have been found to be more prevalent among adolescent girls than boys (Brumberg, 2000; Compas, Orosan, & Grant, 1993; Gjerde, 1995; Gjerde & Block, 1991; Silverstein & Perlick, 1995). However, it is unknown whether this sex difference in prevalence of depressive symptoms also translates into sex-specific links between the complex and ambiguous experiences of clique isolation and depressive symptoms. Prior findings indicate that girls are more often members of a clique and place greater importance on clique membership than boys (Cohen 1977; Urberg et al., 1995). Therefore, depressive symptoms may be observed especially among girls who are outside cliques. However, the link between depressive symptoms and problematic peer relations, such as peer rejection and friendlessness, has often been reported to be sex-invariant (Ladd & Troop-Gordon, 2003; La Greca & Moore Harrison, 2005; Pedersen et al., 2007). Because these studies have not focused on clique isolation specifically, and given that Witvliet et al., (2010) that they did not find any significant gender differences, to date, it remains uncertain as to whether the link between clique isolation and depressive symptoms is different for boys and girls.

Studies on adolescence have found that boys are more often isolated from cliques than girls (Cohen 1977; Urberg et al., 1995), however, Witvliet et al.,'s (2010) study, which focused on clique membership in late childhood, sex differences were not found in clique membership status. This discrepancy in findings may have been the result of the difference in the investigated age periods. In adolescence, the concept of friendship changes and the emphasis on intimacy increases (Sullivan, 1953).

According to Maccoby (1998), intimacy is believed to play a larger role among girls than among boys, with sex differences in clique membership may become apparent particularly in adolescence when intimacy is a more important friendship goal.

Wityliet et al., (2010) that the association between clique isolation and perceived social acceptance was only true for boys and not for girls. More emphasis on group-oriented goals such as shared interests and activities in boys' friendships could explain why perceived social acceptance is more strongly related to problematic peer experiences at the group level for boys than for girls (Maccoby, 1998). Consistent with earlier findings about the association between. problematic peer relations and depression in childhood and adolescence (Ladd and Troop-Gordon 2003; La Greca & Moore Harrison, 2005; Pedersen et al., 2007, Witvliet et al., 2010) did not find sex differences in the association between clique isolation and subsequent depressive symptoms and also not in the mediating role of loneliness and social self perception. Thus, given the ambiguities and uncertainties surrounding adolescent's experiences of clique isolation, it remains to be a social risk factor for depressive symptoms in early adolescence for both boys and girls and needs to be studied in more detail in the future.

TECHNOLOGY AND AMBIGUITIES IN SOCIAL VIRTUAL WORLDS: EMOTIONAL IMPLICATIONS

"Winston turned round abruptly. He had set his features into the expression of quiet optimism which it was advisable to wear when facing the telescreeen." (Orwell, 1938, p. 21).

Increasingly, during the past decade, cyberbullying has become increasingly popular among adults and adolescents, using the Internet and e-mail as a way to psychologically harass others (e.g., sending an insulting or threatening e-mail; creating a website with derogatory, personal comments about a particular individual; posting unflattering photos without permission on websites, etc.). As noted earlier, examples of cyberostracism and cyberteasing are also on the increase, as practicing silence on the Internet as reflected by ignoring or not responding to e-mail correspondence or other social media technologies may have deleterious psychological and emotional ramifications (Beran et al., 2011; Williams, 2001; 2011; Turkle (2011). For example, Rintel and Pittman (1997) found that Internet users often perceive that they are being ignored. The researchers viewed chatters' responses to noninteraction as particularly difficult, because of the chatters' need to defuse carefully the "hostility of silence" (p. 510), while gaining the attention of another interactant. Rintel and Pittman acknowledged the particularly ambiguous nature of silence over the Internet relay channel, in that the silence can be interpreted on a spectrum from deliberate to nondeliberate. Therefore, depending upon how one uses her or his imaginative skills, chatters may perceive and thus feel that they are being ignored whether or not they really are.

As the processes of cyberbullying and cybervictimization occur within the virtual landscape of social networks, and create ambiguous messages, they are still in the process of being defined in fields of education and the social sciences. At the time or writing this book, there is not yet consensus among scholars as to what are the main characteristics of cyberbullying and whether this is an act of bullying at all. Bauman (2010) addresses this lack of consensus and suggests that we think of cyberbullying as the use of technology to intentionally harm or harass others (Bauman, 2010). Although research is nascent in this area, recent reviews illustrate that cyberbullying is increasing rapidly among youth globally, and has become a concern for educators and researchers and parents as they work together to try to develop ways in which to respond effectively.

Given the recent research in computer sciences artificial intelligence, the area of affective computing is a relatively new area of research that highlights the ambiguous nature between computers and humans sharing emotions and authentic social interactions. As Turkle (2011) states, the boundaries between human and machine are becoming blurred and to what extent do we need to main boundaries to remain human? To what extent does the possibility of developing emotions and affections for computers and social robots have for our moral lives – how does this help to clarify moral ambiguity?

As availability of electronic devices continues to increase, some researchers question the reason as to why the rates of cyberbullying and cyberostracism may also increase (Raskauskas & Stoltz, 2007; Turkle, 2011). At least 80% of adolescents own the technology (primarily computers and cell phones; David-Ferdon & Hertz, 2007) necessary to engage in cyberbullying, with even more youth having access at school, libraries, or after-school programs. What was once termed a *generation gap* has also been renamed by some scholars as the *digital divide*, to highlight the vast differences in the types, uses, and knowledge of technology between youth and adults (Bauman, 2010; Universal McCann, 2006). Initial studies have examined the prevalence of cyberbullying, the technology used, and gender and ethnic differences.

To add to the complexity, Nass and his colleagues (see Nass, 2010 for a review of his work on affective computing) claim that when we are confronted with an entity such as a robot or a computer that behaves in humanlike ways such as using language and respond on prior input, our brains respond and treat the entity as human. According to Nass and his colleagues (2010), humans use the same parts of the brain to interact with machines as they do to interact with humans. That is, talkers and listeners cannot suppress their natural responds to speech, regardless of sources. Technologies such as smart phones, technology-based voices activate all parts of the brain that are associated with social interaction. Such research has important implications for how adolescents respond emotionally to instances of cyberbullying and cyberostracism as I will outline below. Overall, although affective computer research does not appear to focus on emotions per se, the research by Nass and his colleagues and others at MIT with social robots and affective computers will have significant implications for research on self and social ambiguities in adolescence (Nass & Brave, 2005).

Regarding gender and cultural differences in cyberbullying and cyber-victimization, although few studies exist such as Smith et al.,'s (2008) research suggested that girls are more likely to serve as both cyberbullies and cybervictims compared to boys. However, according to Li (2006) junior high school boys were more involved in cyberbullying as both bullies and victims than girls, and that girls were more likely to inform adults than boys. As Bauman (2010) suggests, one explanation of these contradictory findings is that boys and girls may use different cyberbullying strategies, with girls preferring chats and instant messaging and boys making online threats and creating hate Web sites (Keith & Martin, 2005).

Although we have some information regarding the possible influence of age on cyberbullying such that it begins to appear in middle childhood and tends to peak during early adolescence approximately ages 11–13) and decline in later adolescence, much more research needs to explore possible intervening factors such as gender and cultural background. However, given the rapid increase in technology and the use of social media among youth in particular, the majority of research on cyberactivities and cyberbullying remains in the beginning stages, with gender studies resulting in contradictory findings and ethnic/cultural differences relatively unexamined. The role of ambiguities in technology, particularly regarding the implications for social and emotional development among youth have important significance for the development of holistic, inclusive educational programs that promote a sense of inner peace and social connection. The role technology may play in helping to develop such educational programs will be further discussed in Chapter 3.

AMBIGUITY OF DIVERSITY: SPIRITUAL/CULTURAL AMBIGUITY – DOES DIVERSITY PRECLUDE CONNECTIVITY?

"All animals are equal but some animals are more equal than other." (Orwell, 1945, p. 90).

As I noted in Chapter 1, as the Canadian cultural context becomes increasingly diverse and complex, researchers such as Costigan (2011; Yon, 2004), and Telzer (2011) note, revisions to the theories on the acculturation gap-distress models are necessary to address the complex cultural landscape. As a new area or research area neuroethics begins to explore questions of morality and diversity through the lens of philosophy and neuroscience (e.g, Churchland, 2011; Levy, 2007). This area of inquiry explores ambiguous and contradictory concepts such as the meaning of spiritual and emotional enhancement, mental privacy, and issues regarding moral relativism. Regarding the ambiguity of cultural diversity within Canada, what are the implications of Canadian acceptance of spiritual cultural, moral diversity? How does this influence an adolescent's ability develop a culturally coherent sense of identity that is unique to Canadian population. As the recent series in the National Canadian newspaper the Globe and Mail explored the moral and ethical issues regarding the concept of multiculturalism in Canada. As, Peritz and Friesen (2010) ask in the article entitled, "When multiculturalism doesn't work." How do we deal with the complexities of the culturally diverse workplace, especially regarding the diversity of values and faith orientations. To apply this question to the adolescent classroom, how do help our youth to makes sense of, and to effectively cope with the quandries of multiculturalism within the culturally ambiguous Canadian landscape? Do we want to encourage Canadian youth to question the concept of moral relativism and to try to make sense of the grey and ambiguous nature of cultural diversity?

Does tolerance and acceptance promote ambiguity and moral disengagement? (Bandura, 2001). For example, how do adolescents cope effectively with conflicting messages and increasing societal pressures that encourage youth to excel at all costs, while at the same time, care for others' needs first. That is, how do youth make sense of mixed cultural messages that encourage them to cater to one's individual needs first, while simultaneously, make sense of the cultural messages and increasing societal pressures to be tolerant, kind and compassionate towards diversity, and to strive to meet the needs of others toward social justices and human rights. As Harris (2010) notes, given the self-contradictory nature of moral relativism, we need to be tolerant of moral difference because no moral truth supersedes another. Thus, given the cyclic argument surrounding the concept of moral truth, the questions regarding human nature need to transcend culture and cultural norms. Such research has just started as illustrated by Hill, Lee and Jennway's (2010) to research reflexivity and to negotiate identity and ambiguity within a cross-cultural context.

SUMMARY

As I've discussed throughout this chapter, the secondary school context is a prime source for a host of multiple ambiguities and mixed messages regarding one's sense of self, social relations, and cultural issues. How do adolescents of both genders learn how to navigate and make sense of these ambiguities and to what extent can we provide effective educational tools to help adolescents negotiate these ambiguous landscapes. Our goal as educators and researchers needs to be promoting healthy and happy development in all areas of human growth. In the remaining chapters, I will focus on how educators and researchers can work together to create educational programs aimed to help adolescents grow emotionally well and manage effectively in an increasingly complicated and ambiguous world.

CHAPTER 3

HOW? APPLICATIONS (THEORY, EDUCATION, AND FUTURE RESEARCH)

HOW DO You INTERPRET Ambiguity and Silences?

"What I cannot build I cannot understand" - Richard Feynman – (cited in Damasio, 2011; p. 1)

"I confess that I have been as blind as a mole, but it is better to learn wisdom late than never learn it at all."

(Sherlock Holmes, Doyle, 1892, p. 507)

INTRODUCTION: WHO LEARNS FROM THIS RESEARCH?

This chapter builds on the previous chapters in that it will discuss how the current research findings help to further advance developmental theory regarding the personal and social lives of adolescents. That is, how do the theories and empirical evidence findings discussed in Chapters 1 and 2 further the discourse on current educational and developmental literature and help to develop programs that aim to foster the ability to interpret ambiguity and silences in adolescence? This chapter will describe the three main audiences that will benefit or learn from the findings including: 1) developmental neuro-social-cognitivitists, 2) educators, therapists, policy makers, and learners, and 3) future researchers. Each audience or community of learners will be discussed in turn.

RESEARCH ON ADOLESCENCE AND AMBIGUITY: APPLICATIONS TO PRACTICE?

As I've discussed earlier throughout this book, how do the findings on how infants and children understand ambiguities both perceptually and socially, further the discourse on current educational research literature regarding adolescents? How can such findings from developmental research by Tamis-LeMonda and Aldoph (2005) with infants and social referencing within the context of ambiguity and the virtual cliff further research on adolescents' experiences with risk-taking, resilience, and flow experiences (Seifert & Hedderson, 2009)? How can such findings from the theory of mind literature regarding children's interpretation of textual ambiguity such as Yuill's (2009) work with sarcasm and irony further researchers knowledge of adolescents' ability to understand the complexities involved with the social communications during conversations among peers?

Regarding the research on affective computing and how adults interpret ostracism regarding a computer program (Williams, 2001; Nass, 2010) help researchers to understand how adolescents make sense of ambiguous social situations involving teasing (Keltner, 2009), psychological bullying and victimization such as social exclusion and ostracism?

As researchers and educators investing in making positive changes within the educational system to promote youth's well being and social connections with others, I encourage researchers to collaborate from various fields and work together to create developmental research programs that aim to explore areas of emotional and psychological understanding and cultural competence in that they understand the complexities and ambiguities of understanding the personal worlds of others, as well as the ambiguous Canadian culturally diverse context. Given the increasingly complex Canadian cultural landscape involving diverse moral and faith orientations, we need to build and draw on research findings from multiple disciplines in the hopes that we help adolescents to make sense of such complexities as awareness and understanding must be developed before tolerance and acceptance can exist. For example, as Aydin, Fischer, and Frey (2010) suggest, researchers need to explore the multifaceted construct of religious experiences in the sense that they extend pre-existing measurements of religious and spiritual experiences and develop novel ways such of exploring such subjectivities to help researchers make sense of adolescents' spiritual and religious experiences. Longitudinal, multi-method approaches involving paper and pencil questionnaires as well as interviews and focus groups with groups of educators, youth, and their parents over time throughout adolescence and into early adulthood would provide a fruitful research program to help us understand the complex developmental trajectory of understanding such social ambiguities within the adolescent years.

EDUCATION ("SCHOOLING THE SENSITIVE") - EDUCATING FOR COPING WITH AMBIGUITIES AND UNCERTAINTIES IN THE 21ST CENTURY – BEYOND 2020...

How can educators concerned with promoting the emotional well being of the child work towards programs within the context of "Schooling Ambiguity?" How can relevant research findings from neuroscience, psychology and education help educators to learn how to encourage adolescents to navigate ambiguity regarding personal and social issues such as happiness, self-faith, and self-caring? Is it possible to school ambiguity? As Boorn, Hopkins Dunn and Page (2010) note, how can educators work together to develop programs that promote holistic grown and development for youth and adults by fostering relationships, emotional well-being and resilience?

As Miller (2010) and Suarez-Orozco and Satin-Bajaj (2010) among others note, how can we as developmental interventionists work towards building research-based educational programs that aim toward educating the whole, peaceful child for the whole, peaceful world? Such programs would help youth across the globe as we move together toward an increasingly technologically and socially and culturally ambiguous and complex exciting and challenging world of uncertainty and transition.

How can we create an engaging, inviting, and inclusive community of engaged scholars among youth? As Jerome Bruner (1990) stated, the key to understanding multiple perspectives remains in the ability to tolerate differences and diversity by remaining open-minded to other's values and beliefs. I also emphasize the importance of developing programs that foster the development of remaining open and accepting in a non-judgmental way of other's emotions, as well as one's own. This ability to develop open-mindedness and empathetic sensitivity is as Bruner (1990) claims, a way of living, a life choice as to how to lead one's life, and which values and beliefs will guide one's actions.

As we enter the second decade of the 21st century, I agree with other scholars within the psycocultural context such as Bruner (1996), Bronfebrenner, (2005), Damon, (2008), Keltner, (2009), Nucci, (2001) among many others that the challenge for educators and researchers during the next few decades will remain focused on creating a meaningful learning community that promotes a sense of personal well being and emotional health, as well as a genuine sense of compassion and care for ourselves and others. That is, how can we educate the whole child for the technologically interconnected but perhaps spiritually disconnected world, and how do we create a culture of care, kindness, compassion, respect, and purpose? That is, how do we develop educational programs that aim to connect our technological advancements with our moral and spiritual developments as humans such as our capacity for the radical acceptance of kindness, compassion, and loving kindness (Brach, 2009; Keltner, 2009; Miller, 2010; Neff, 2011).

How well equipped are schools and educators to help adolescents learn how to negotiate the ambiguous Canadian socio-cultural landscape and how does this translate to helping adolescents to negotiate the ambiguities both within the self, and with others in the classroom, home, and larger community? How can we build on existing models of holistic and inclusive models of education? For example, as recent research shows that resilient youth use humor to enhance socioemotional functioning during a day in the life of an adolescent (Cameron, Fox, Anderson & Cameron, 2010), researchers and educators need to explore how to incorporate aspect of humour into educational programs as this could have implications for emotional literacy and moral, inclusive education.

> Self - inner -peace ⟵⟶ Other - interpersonal peaceful relations ⟵⟶ World ⟵⟶ transcultural/global peace education ⟵⟶ Self (cyclic, dynamic structure)

Researchers need to work together with educators of youth to co-create holistic, inclusive programs aimed at promoting the emotional well being and socially adjustment of youth. Such programs could build on current models of holistic, Alternative Schools including the Montessori and Waldorf based Whole Child School that incorporates the principles of Montessori's and Steiner's thinking regarding holistic education. This model of education build on Montessori's notion of Cosmic Education that encourages children to think of themselves in relation to the universe, and thus promotes a reverence and respect for all living beings and the natural world including the universe. Thus, this program encourages children to develop a sense of meaning and purpose to help build a good and just society (see Miller, 2010 for a further description of this program).

Another example of a school that builds on similar holistic principles is the Ross School Model that focuses on educating whole child for the whole world that incorporates the use of art, music, video, and drama psychoeducational activities that promote the development of understanding ambiguity and the ability to understand multiple interpretations (see Suarez-Orozco & Sattin-Bajaj, 2010 for a further discussion). Thus, by drawing on such models of holistic education, we need to continue to develop programs that draw on religious and spirituality from multiple faith backgrounds to create and education for peace – both inner (self), interpersonal, and transcultural. That is, by drawing on models of peace and humane education (see Brantmeir, Lin, & Miller, 2010), education for peace needs to incorporate the spiritual and religious traditions of others in a way that suits the needs of the Canadian adolescent learning within our diverse learning environment. Such a developmentally and culturally appropriate educational agenda promotes the need for learners to build their strengths and the courage to challenge their own learning. As I discussed in Chapter 1, we can build on such existing educational programs to help adolescents to develop a sense of AWE in their everyday learning experiences. For example, in the application of the science of 'yen' to youth – how can we encourage youth to develop a positive 'yen' ratio (Keltner, 2009)? For example, how we encourage youth to see the good in others, to focus on the positive events in their life by helping them to develop the necessary cognitive and emotional tools to frame their experiences as meaningful and exciting opportunities to grow and learn? Such possibilities are exciting in that educators and researchers can work together to create such nurturing classroom environments (Boorn, Hopkins-Dunn, & Page, 2010).

Such holistic educational programs need to draw on current research findings regarding the interpretation of ambiguity such as Yuill's (2009) research on jokes and riddles. As I discussed in Chapter 2, Yuill's (2009) findings suggested that supporting children to articulate multiple meanings is associated with improvements in comprehension. Joking riddles provide an excellent example of how different contexts support or cue different meanings, and this point is underlined by the association between comprehension improvement and utterances expressing both meanings of an ambiguity. The ways in which children expressed such utterances combining cued and uncued meanings suggest an impressive facility with language, and this was shown across a variety of different ambiguities.

Drawing on research described in Chapter 2 (e.g., McGhee, 1984), the strength of a joke could be that it cues a particular context to give meaning to a phrase, but the answer requires a different context to be understood. As Casteel (1997) suggests, it may not be enough just for children to know 'different meanings of words': they have to be able to see how particular interpretations are required to fit different contexts. This requires a different context to be understood. As Casteel (1997) suggests, it may not be enough just for children to know 'different meanings of words': they have to be able to see how particular interpretations are required to fit different contexts. Thus, how can the findings help educators to learn how to encourage children to learn about ambiguous concepts such as happiness, faith, and caring for/in both self and other?

Continuing to build on related research exploring how we make sense of ambiguity, as discussed earlier in Chapter 2, Machnik and Martinex-Conde's (2010) research findings from their work in neuromagic could be integrated into all holistic educational programs to promote the development of divergent thinking and the ability to understand multiple perspectives. Future research could build on Machnik and Martinez-Conde's (2011) neuroscience research of understanding everyday deception findings with Wimmer and Doherty's (2011) work on the connections between children's ambiguous figure perception and theory of mind understanding. For example, graphic illustrations of ambigrams as I described earlier in Chapter 2 could be used to encourage youth to 'play' with and to make meaning of ambiguous drawings and text. Such activities could be applied all academic disciplines and encourage adolescents to work on creating their own ambigrams. Complex cognitive skills such as divergent thinking and perspective taking are necessary to help adolescents to develop a sense of understanding the mental and emotional worlds of others and themselves. As I've noted throughout this books, such cognitive competencies would be of great value to adolescents living with our culturally diverse Canadian context.

EMOTIONAL DIET: DAILY SERVINGS OF LOVINGKINDNESS, COMPASSION, MINDFUL-OPENMINDEDNESS

As our current educational research and programs are focused on cognitive and physical skills in that many are focused on our physical fitness and diet and aims for a healthy, well balanced diet of food and nutrients, how can we create a healthy diet of silence, mindfulness, and enchantment with the goal of becoming more open-minded, kind, caring, and compassionate to others and ourselves. That is, how can we develop programs that promote a sense of wonder, compassion, and mindful open-mindedness? As I have discussed elsewhere (Bosacki, 2005; 2008), similar to Miller, (2010), Prochnik, (2010), Damon (2008), and others, educational programs for adolescents need to integrate the benefits of silence into the school curriculum, which may lead to a greater focus on inner peace and mindfulness. Similar to holistic and inclusive programs for youth that focus on making healthy lifestyle choices regarding eating, drugs, smoking, sexual habits, we may wish to encourage healthy lifestyle choices regarding communication such as empathetic and respectful listening and dialogue, and choices regarding the use of technological tools such as the Internet, smartphones, etc. Building on holistic educational programs such as the Ross school mentioned earlier (Suarez-Orozco & Sattin-Bajaj, 2010), programs that incorporate various artistic mediums such as music, theatre, and psychodrama to name a few may help to encourage youth to develop a sense of enchantment and mindfulness of the world (Humphrey, 2011).

Thus, a healthy learning/communication (psychological) diet (listening and talking) well balanced with critical inquiry, dialogue, and silence may serve as an emotional and cognitive toolkit for adolescents to analyze social situations and to thus develop greater connection with oneself and others within our culture of uncertainty and ambiguity. I wil expand on this idea of a psychological toolkit for adolescents in Chapter 3 when I describe Burke's (1970) approach to persuasion as a strategy to help adolescents to understand self and social ambiguity. As this toolkit focuses not only on talking, but thoughtful observation as well as listening, as Prochnik (2010) contemplates, "Who knows, given enough quiet time, perhaps people may even find themselves tempted to become a little nicer.' (p. 293).

Regarding the importance of emotional health and well-being, a growing number of researchers (Brach, 2007; Germer, 2009; Gilbert, 2009; Neff, 2011) have started to explore the importance of being kind and compassionate not only toward others, but to also oneself. As Germer (2009) suggests, the notion of mindful, self-compassion draws on Buddhist religion and meditation to suggest that such a kind and loving approach to oneself provides the foundation of emotional health and healing. That is, the need to be aware in the present moment, mindful when we feel inadequate, upset, confused, and stress – which may occur when confronted by ambiguous situations, especially within the personal and social context. Once we become mindful of the situation, one must learn to response with kindness, love, and understanding toward to the self (self-compassion). As the Dali Lama suggests, we must learn to be compassionate with ourselves before we can experience compassion for others.

As Neff (2011) suggests, past research shows that self-compassion provides greater emotional resilience and stability over self-esteem as it focuses on non-judgemental approaches to self and others in a way that works towards connecting instead of comparing oneself to others. Such a positive, proactive approach to emotional well-being would be of great use to individuals of all ages, but especially for adolescents as they experience increasingly ambiguous contexts regarding developing identities and relationships with others. This kind and thoughtful approach would perhaps be valuable for adolescents to develop a mindful self-compassionate approach to dealing with silences and ambiguities in their relationships with themselves and others. For example, this Mindful Self-Compassion approach (MSC; Gilbert, 2009; Neff, 2011) could be incorporated into already existing positive education models and holistic education for the whole child that could benefit from this kind and loving approach to oneself. Thus, educational programs that adopt a holistic and inclusive approach to learning and development in adolescence could benefit by incorporating aspects of this mindful compassion framework to their curriculum with the goals of guiding adolescents through the tensions and ambiguities of the social and personal context of adolescence.

POSITIVE EDUCATIONAL PSYCHOLOGY

As an example of applying psychological research to education, various educators across globe are applying the principles of positive psychology to educational practices (e.g., see Dawson & Sing-Dhesi, 2010). As Seligman (2011) notes, building on his previous work in positive psychology and authentic happiness, his research explores how educators can help children to '*flourish*' and thus come to understand of happiness and well-being, Such positive education programs will help youth to make sense of the social and personal ambiguities within adolescents during the 21st century. In the following section, I will outline some holistic programs that apply positive psychology to secondary school classroom and list some suggestions for educators gleaned from common themes across such programs.

Building on Seligman and his colleagues' Penn Resiliency Program (2011) that works with adolescents at the Strath Haven Highschool outside of Philadelphia with the goal to increase students' ability to handle day-to-day challenges common during adolescence, educational programs across the globe are applying the concepts of positive psychology and holistic educational approaches to the classroom. For example, the movement in Australia applies positive psychology to programs such as the Geelong Grammar School Project (see www.ggs.uvic.edu.au for more information), and McGrath and Nobel's (2009) Bounce Back program reflect an interest in well being and resilience for schools, teachers, and students. Such holistic educational models include resilience educational programs help children to cooperate through learning flexibiity and coping skills. In contrast to reactive interventions, such programs focus on the need for prevention and well-being to drive the agenda. These programs promote the claim that if one is to build strong respectful relationships in school communities, educators need to emphasize the need for a long-term focus aimed to include the whole school context. Evaluative research on the Bounce back program shows that student well-being results in: positive relationships with peers and teachers; positive feelings and attitudes, resilience, self knowledge and self understanding, satisfaction with learning outcomes (McGrath & Noble, 2009)

As we aim to develop such schools that aim for purpose and meaning, we are encouraged to think about the broader social and cultural determinants of health, happiness and well-being. McGrath and Nobel (2009) and Seligman (2011) among others challenge us to go beyond individual well-being, and to address the broader social perspective and political determinants of adolescent well-being. As Dawson and Singh-Dhesi (2010) states, drawing on positive psychology in schools brings valuable benefits including reigniting teachers' passion for their work, enhancing student well-being and performance and improved coping skills, greater confidence and enhanced communication and interaction with families and the community, evaluative research on such programs also report that parents of youth involved in such holistic programs notice a positive difference in their children.

Building on the principles of positive psychology and mindfulness, the educational program "FRIENDS" aims to help youth to develop effective coping strategies to deal with negative and possibly anxiety producing situations (Stallard, 2009). The program builds on cognitive and behavioural therapeutic programs that combine the use of cognition, self-talk, and action to address the current situation the learner is experiencing. The program helps children to learn strategies to deal with stressful learning experiences through the following FRIENDS mental script: "Feel worried, relax, inner thought, explore ways to help, nice job, reward yourself, do not forget to practice, stay calm." This mental script encourages youth to deal with emotional issues such as anxiety in learning and would also be of use to help adolescents to make sense of emotionally ambiguous situations regarding social interactions and personal experiences. As Stallard (2009) notes, this program aims to adapt to all levels of learning exceptionalities, and would be of great use to all youth and their educators within the secondary school classroom.

SOCIAL DETECTIVE HANDBOOK: SEMIOTIC AND DRAMATIC TOOLS TO HELP
ADOLESCENTS DECODE THE SOCIAL AND PERSONAL AMBIGUITIES

How can we as educators help adolescents to detect and make sense of, or 'decode' ambiguous language – either from others in conversations, or in their private speech or self-talk. How are ambiguitites detected in their private language or self-talk as compared to their conversations with others? As Larson (2010) suggests, Drawing on advice from the semaniticist such as Korzybski (1947) among others who suggest to be aware of ambiguity in language by detecting any of language that is void of specific and concrete elaborations on any ambiguous term. The semioticians such as Buissac (1976) whose work on interpreting the codes found in the culture of circuses, advise us to see the full meanings in persuasive visual or verbal 'texts' by delving into various and on verbal 'signifiers' to determine what is really being 'signified.' Applying Buissac's (1976) approach to critically reading the chaotic and complex actions of the circus, such techniques of critical analysis of reading verbal and non-verbal messages could help adolescents to make sense of the ambiguous social codes used in the classroom. For example, adolescents could be encouraged to enact social scenarios found in the adolescent classroom such as watch films or enact through drama that involve complex and ambiguous social scenes such as ostracism, teasing, or watch films that depict complex, ambiguous social scenes that involve people and animals, as well as plays, film, dance, ballet, or operas. Such activities could be used to promote the critical analysis and dialogue to help interpret verbal and non-verbal modes of communication as well as the silences in conversations.

Thus, using both the semantic and semiotic approaches, adolescents could engage in activities that encourage them to decode ambiguity in language in examples of text, visual art, dramatic arts, etc. By encouraging adolescents to examine the denotations (do away with), and connotations (implied meaning) of persuasive symbols, educators could develop their ability to understand that many meanings are attached to various words. Such an approach could be applied to critical media analysis programs as noted by Larson (2010) as adolescents could view ambiguous texts in advertisements and engage in critical discussion as to which symbols have multiple meanings attached and how are the ambiguous messages interpreted including popular media, film, music (e.g., Bosacki, .Elliott, Bajovic, & Akseer 2009; Dyson, 2000)

Regarding the social and emotional lives of adolescents, what are the functions of ambiguity within social situations? As I noted in Chapter 1, drawing on the connections between strategic uses of ambiguity and persuasion (Larson, 2010), we could be viewed as our own social media advertisers. For instance, for popularity purposes, some adolescents may use ambiguous language intentionally to gain popularity and power. For example, similar to the common technique for advertisers to create ambiguous messages, language could be viewed as a means to encourage all responses to the advertisement, to what extent do adolescents use ambiguity for persuasion? Given the function of ambiguity as a possible tool for the semantic dimension, ambiguity may help to promote social and emotional functioning, in addition to avoiding specifity, ambiguity may have another function: to encourage persuadees to "fill in" their own private meaning for words. Thus, the ambiguity could provide a semantic "escape hatch" for the persuader who wants to please everyone. This may be relevant for a child with a low sense of self-worth who wishes to be liked by all her/his peers. For example, to gain popularity, a child may carefully chose her words that can be interpreted in numerous, contradictory ways, depending up on the receivers of the message, or her peers whom she wishes to accept her into their group.

Another linguistic tool to help adolescents to make sense of socially ambiguous messages found in the classroom involve Burke's device for decoding ambiguity is called the "dramatistic pentad" or a tool for analyzing ambiguous language usage and for developing a persuasive language strategy on the semantic level. As noted in Chapter 1, given Burke's (1960) emphasis on language as it is used to persuade people to action, Burke's (1960) notes that persuasion is a process of coming to identity with the persuader's position. Thus, the persuader, gets the audience (peers) to identify by achieving common ground, by adopting similar beliefs, appearance, behaviours, etc. Thus, given that Burke's dramatistic pentad involves the ability to understand the thoughts and emotion of self and other, the pentad could be used as an educative tool or Theory of Mind toolkit to help adolescents to make sense of socially ambiguous messages.

Burke (1970) thought of drama as a philosophy of language and capable of describing and analyzing human symbolic acts such as language use. Similar to Goffman (1959) who also focused on the connection between life and drama, Burkes' theory of dramatism maintained that the basic model used by humans to explain various situations is the narrative story of drama. The tool of analysis was a pentad as Burke viewed the world in terms of 5 universal elements of drama involving the scene, act, agent, agency, and purpose that play a role together and emerge from a common unified core or the drama itself. Further, this theory focused on the differences between action (motivated (e.g., smiling), and motion (not motivated, e.g., basic bodily functions such as digestion, breathing). Burke believed that when we communicate, we choose words because of their dramatic potential, and that different individuals find some elements in the drama more potent than others. That is, different people focus on different elements, depending on which elements seems to correspond most closely with their view of the world.

For example, some people are more sensitive to the persuasion based on the actor or agent, or child, other peoples may be more sensitive to the scene or setting.

According to Burke (1960), the most inclusive of the dramatic elements is scene and must be the "proper container" for the action that is occurring or that is about to occur. To describe tensions in relationships and to help identify the key term of the persuader, Burke created ratios (act-agent, scene-purpose). Thus, if there is a kind of imbalance between the scene and the act or the scene-act ratio – high emotional drama – tragic, comic, etc. is likely to occur.

Given the ambiguous social scenes found within adolescence, applying this device to adolescents' social worlds, adolescents can use these five key terms to develop a persuasive strategy such as trying to get a friend to invite you to a party. As this tool may help an adolescent understand the mind and emotions of the friend as they need to decide which persuasive strategy to use or which key element to focus on and which ratio (e.g. scene-act) is in balance to detect any emotional drama such as a tragedy, comedy, etc. For this example, the scene is the setting of the party, the act is the social action that will occur in the party, the agent is the girl trying to get the invitation to the party of the persuader, the agency could be the communication strategy that the agent is using to accomplish her goal of receiving a party invitation such as focusing on the persuadee's positive qualities such a being more popular or kind, and finally the purpose is the reason the agent is the agent acts in a scene using a particular agency or to receive the invitation. Thus, for the girl to persuade her friend to invite her to a party, she could focus on the scene if she thinks that the girl would like to create a larger more social party, she could focus on the act or the party itself – if by receiving an invitation she will be able to make the party more enjoyable, or she could focus on the agency as mentioned above- elaborating on the positive, helpful qualities the persuadee has that the persuader does not or would like to have.

In addition, within the adolescents' social and emotional worlds, there many exist great potential for an imbalanced scene-act ratio. This could occur with a psychological teasing example – for example, if two girls have just finished their friendship as one has decided to end the friendship to join a party, another girl may tease her friend by noting that the party could provide food for a celebratory or sad occasion. Thus, if the persuadee is able to identify the key term that the persuader is using it will help to predict future persuasion coming from them, thus preparing the persuadee to be critical of any future social messages coming from the persuader.

Overall, this cognitive and emotional analytic device could help adolescents to develop ToM skills such as understanding thoughts and emotions in others to predict their behaviours. Thus, holistic educational models that promote a positive sense of self and healthy social relationships could incorporate this educational toolkit into the curriculum to help adolescents to become critical readers of the social messages found within the complicated, socially ambiguous scenarios of the classroom. Further, they could learn to identify the five key elements of the pentad and apply these to any social situation in combination with ToM skills to learn how to become powerful persuaders and wise social detectives.

To help adolescents to make sense of social and personal ambigiuity in the classroom, another analytic tool similar to Burke's (1970) pentad device draws from Seligman's research technique refereed to as CAVE (Content Analysis fo Verbatum Explanations). This research technique is used to help analyze or make sense of the verbal and nonverbal messages exchanged during social interactions and to help us to learn how some some peoples' words predict subsequent behaviour. This method of assessing explanatory style or the habitual way in which a person explains an event or situation, allows researchers to analyze any naturally occuring verbatim materials for explanatory style or how a person explains a situation (Shulman, Casellon, & Seligman, 1989). For example, Seligman uses this device to analyze conversations and human interactions for understanding ambiguous emotional situations such as those experiencing emotional difficulties such as depression. Seligman found that the way a person explains an event frequently determines subsequent events such that a person who has a negative explanatory style or focus on the negative messages portrayed in an ambiguous social scenario, may also be more likely to engage in negative social interactions, which in turn, may lead to further negative perspectives. Seligman's theory places the learner, or the agent or persuader in Burkes's case is the center of explanation and motivation. This research tool could be applied to the adolescent classroom by encouraging students to view videos or films of ambiguous social situations such as a music video, movie, etc., and analyze or decode the verbal and nonverbal messages found in the interaction as well as the social action. Such an analytic research procedure also promote s the development of critical analysis skills as students must create meaning from an ambiguous social situation.

In addition to the analytic tools to help adolescents understand social and personal ambiguity in the classroom, gleaned from the Positive Psychology and Applied Developmental Research, I outline below key recommendations for educators to help co-create an inclusive and holistic educational program for adolescents that aim to address emotional well being and a positive sense of self. For example, how do we create a sense of awe and enchantment in youth regarding their learning and growth in their sense of self as well as their care and concern for others? As educators and researchers who work with youth, we need to go beyond individual well-being, and to address the broader social and cultural perspectives and political determinants of child well-being. Thus, as outlined below, the goals of such nurturing education programs are to help adolescents to learn how to become resilient, responsible, and caring learners as they navigate the ambiguous terrain of the social and personal worlds of adolescence.

- develop programs that require a whole-school focus including strong leadership for which support from the school, home, and community including government
- a long-term view is needed, and both teachers, parents, and community leaders who work with youth need to be fully involved and need to be role models as we need to broaden our work to consider the political and societal landscape
- create nurturing schools that incorporate a research-based, child-centred developmentally appropriate curriculum that promotes an "ethic of self and social relationships" situated within a co-created culture of purpose, kindness, caring and compassion for self and others aiming for personal

meaning and social justice (Damon, 2008; Larson, 2011; Selman, 2003; Seligman, 2011)

- adapt the Confucian principle of 'Jen' that refers to the teachings and learnings of Confucius and refers to a complex mixture of kindness, humanity, and respect that transpires between people to the secondary school classroom (see Keltner, 2009)
- help adolescents to create a positive jen ratio in that they interpret the positive, self-growth messages from their experiences as opposed to the negative and self-defeating
- help adolescents to develop the ability to be compassionate and understanding not only of others, but also themselves (Dachner, 2009; Neff, 2011), and to practice kind self-reflection and compassion through activities that promote reflective mindfulness and self-expression including drama, visual arts, music, dance, etc.
- foster adolescents' ability to understand others' perspectives and emotional worlds, as well as develop the ability or audience awareness, or the ability to understand the power of your words and persuasion given your audience through the use of critical media literacy programs that focus on socially ambiguous situations within the popular media (Selman, 2003; Semali, 2003; Larson, 2010)
- help students to develop a Theory of Mind Toolkit for adolescents to help them to decode socially and emotionally ambiguous messages and build healthy relationships with self and others
- encourage adolescents to apply analytic techniques such as Burke's (1970) dramatisist pentad, the CAVE method (Seligman et al., 1989), as well as ToM skills to critically read and decode ambiguous messages in the popular media and advertising, as well as electronic media and music (Turkle, 2011)
- incorporate educational activities to promote the development of adolescent learners who are caring, critical analyzers and compassionate persuaders to help them to develop the ability to understand social etiquette including politeness and manners (Brown & Levinson, 1987; Cialdini, 2001; Larson, 2010)
- to further promote emotional and social development, develop collaborative holistic programs that include connections with the community such as those involving global education that focuses on caring and respecting other humans but also nature and animal (Battro, 2010)
- to develop the ability to read others' emotions and understand other's perspectives in ambiguous situations, strengthen connections with humane educational programs that focuses on animal care and children's relationships with animals (Ascione, 2004)

In sum, as educators and researchers committed to promoting the emotional well being of youth, we need to think about the broader social and cultural determinants of health, happiness and well-being. Thus, we need to continually think, reflect, and act creatively and ask ourselves the question of how can promote the application of such holistic and nurturing programs to the secondary school classroom. As I noted in the introduction to this book, holistic educational programs aim to help youth to make sense of, and create personal meaning from the personal and social ambiguities.

FUTURE RESEARCH: TECHNOLOGICAL PROGRESS AND ONGOING AMBIGUITIES

As noted in Chapter 1, technology continues to progress into the twenty-first century, educators need to take a critical approach, and encourage adolescents to do the same to this the expansion of amateur production tools and Web access, particularly regarding electronic communication via the social network. As these advancements continue to develop, adolescents need to be encouraged to critically question through means of critical media literacy programs that provide opportunities for adolescents to consider both the benefits and consequences of the role technology plays in learning (Bosacki et al., 2009; 2008; Linn, 2005; Semali, 2003). As Terkle (2011) suggests, such advanced technology may afford many youth opportunities to adopt roles that have been traditionally assumed by adults and may begin to learn how to co-create and share their experiences globally. For example, the proliferation of peer-to-peer sharing and virtual community sites will play a key role in helping adolescents to connect socially and transculturally to collaborate and co-produce and communicate with others regarding text such as popular music. In turn, such advanced technologies provide learning opportunities and contexts to promote self-expression, creative control of music content, and the co-creation of material for adolescents.

However, as noted earlier in the previous chapters, many researchers and educators encourage us to remain skeptical and cautious regarding the role technology plays in the lives or adolescents today. We need to be aware and wiling to explore the complex web of the psychological implications that technology and cyberactivities hold for adolescents personal and social worlds. That is, we need to develop inclusive and developmentally appropriate educational programs that promote the development of healthy and effective relationships with ourselves and others. As mentioned in the introduction of this book, as Bruner (1990) suggests, a psychocultural approach to education and development will incorporate activities to develop a folk psychology of the ability to understand the culturally shaped notions of in terms of which people organize their view of themselves, of others, and of the world in which they live. Such a psychocultural approach will aim to provide the groundwork for the development of personal meaning and cultural cohesion among youth today. This approach will be of great use to adolescents given the mixed messages and ambiguous cultural context within modern-day Canada.

QUESTIONING THE PERSISTENT PARADOXICAL PUZZLES? 2020
AND BEYOND...

The way out is via the door. Why is it that no one will use this method?
Confucius (cited in Laing, correct citation is 1961; p. 1).

As a beginning, educators and researchers can work together to co-create programs
with the shared goals of aiming to help adolescents to develop a healthy sense of self,
personal meaning, and kindness and compassion toward others, educational
programs for youth need to incorporate the concepts of various holistic and inclusive
developmental and educational models. For example, as I discussed above, to help
adolescents navigate the ambiguous world of identity and relationships, educational
programs need to incorporate psychoeducational models that promote well being and
mindful self-compassion including positive self-talk or caring private speech
(Gibson, 2009; Neff, 2011). For example, Tara Brach's (2004) Radical Acceptance
that encourages individuals to embracing your life with the heart of Buddha. Brach's
psychotherapeutic model draws from the writing of Buddhism and dialectical therapy
with the focus on developing the ability to develop clear, inner vision, and aim
toward psychological mindfulness such as being in the moment, and practicing kind
and tender sensitive compassion with oneself and other. As we develop and grow a
nurturing classroom – one that integrates educational psychology to promote well
being, we need to develop programs that help adolescents to learn to make sense of
personal and social ambiguities in the classroom. Educators can be supportive by
creating a nurturing, psychological safe learning culture, one that cultivates a sense of
meaning and purpose. That is, adolescents need to feel psychologically safety to
share, discuss emotional and personal stories of growth.

Such programs will help to develop a culture of purpose in the classroom and to
help youth find their calling (Damon, 2008). Specifically, Damon (2008) suggests
that as educators aimed to create this learning community of caring, compassion,
and lovingkindness, we also must take into account some of Damon's (2008) work
on purpose, and aim to create holistic educational programs that focus on the why
in education. That is, as I noted Chapter 1, building on Bandura's (2001) work
regarding moral disengagement we need to encourage all youth and not only the
disengaged to question why we think, feel, and behave the way that we do and
consider our emotional and moral motives that guide our thinking. Thus, according
to Damon (2008) and Larson (2011) among others who work with youth, our
school systems would benefit from additional educational programs that aim to
develop a culture of purpose and include educators who help youth to make healthy
lifestyle choices that provide them with a lifelong sense of well-being and
emotional stability. Consistent with Damon (2008) and Humphrey (2011), I also
believe that we need to offer youth possibilities that spark their sense of awe,
enchantment, wonder, and imagination, provide guidance that encourages youth to
become aware of their highest aspiration, and co-develop an accepting,
collaborative cultural climate that inspires rather than demoralizes them.

Given the complexity of this task, educators and researchers need to work
collaboratively together in turns of working in collaborative learning teams with
parents, youth care works, and most importantly, the youth herself needs to be a

key creator in their learning journey. For example, as I have noted in part elsewhere (Bosacki, 2008; 2011), we need to further strengthen the connections between research within the discipline of positive psychology, holistic philosophies, affective computing, and applied social cognitive neuroscience, we need to further the connection between the research that shows youth are most likely to develop a personal sense of well being and happiness when they are engaged in learning activities that both challenge and inspire them to continue to grow and develop as lifelong learners in both their personal and social lives. Thus, growing a nurturing classroom will help youth to develop these abilities and to grow in meaningful and purposeful ways to achieve one' own full potential, as well as to inspire others to develop a sense of self (Boorn, Hopkins Dunn, & Page, 2010; Dawson, & Singh-Dhesi, 2010).

More specifically, research programs that combine neuroscience and education may continue to be a main avenue for future researchers. As I have described a selected few examples of research from neuroscience throughout this book (Machnik & Martinez-Conde, 2011; Wimmer & Doherty, 2011), a more thorough discussion regarding the role of neuroscience in understanding social and self ambiguity is beyond the scope of this book, Based on the multitude of researchers exploring the human mind, the field of applied neurcognitive science remains relatively new and burgeoning and will most likely be one of the main avenues for future research to explore the neuroboiology foundations of social and personal ambiguity in adolescence.

As Churchland (2011), Harris (2010), and DeWaal (2009) among others provide neurophilosophical and biological explanations of morality explores how brain-based science helps us to understand how our neuroboiology helps to guide our moral compasses. Similarly, Baron-Cohen (2010) discusses the role of neuroscience research plays in exploring how people learn how to be cruel and explores the origins of empathy and the concept of 'evil' among humanity. As various researchers and educators work together to make sense of self and social ambiguity in adolescence with the aim of promoting positive emotional and mental health, brain-based research on the neurobiology of social skills and the nature of the capacity to attribute mental states to others may help us to understand the emotional and social world of adolescent. Thus, such collaborations efforts among psychology, neuroscience, and education may help us to explore the complexities involved within the adolescent's emotional and social worlds. Perhaps it is the combined efforts of neuroscientists with educators who share the goal of understanding our inner worlds, will help to develop educational programs that encourage youth to become caring and compassionate learners.

CHALLENGES OF MODERN TECHNOLOGIES

The challenge for neuroscience researchers and educators for the next few decade will be for educators to adapt research findings on how modern technology influences developing minds. As Meece (2011) notes, we need to figure out how to cope and manage effectively with the current "technological tsunami." We need to find ways for ourselves to make sense of this in a healthy way, and to help adolescents make healthy choices regarding their use of technological tools to promote their learning, development within the current culture of personal and social ambiguity in adolescents. As many researchers discussed throughout this book (Turkle, 2011), a recent article in the New York Times entitled "Growing up digital: Wired for distraction" (Ritchel, 2010) states that "The constant stream of stimuli offered by new technology poses a profound new challenge to focusing and learning" (Nov 21, 2010). As wise and ethical researchers and educators, we need to ask the question of what is the effect of the abundant virtuality in the human brain and the mind?

Benefits of virtuality include diverse and wealth of educational materials, increased communication that eliminates travel costs (e.g, overseas communication), however, there are limitations to this technological progress re the speed of delivery of concerns and the multiplexing of contents within the same time windows affects the ability to multitasks and could be applied to faster problem-solving skills. For example, how does the speed of processing and divided attention affect memory retention, does it stifle creativity or enhance it? How do emotions play a role in this cognitive processing? Future research is needed to answer these and related questions re the expertise required to enhance the educational glue of the new technologies while minimizing the possible disadvantages.

Examples of negative influence regarding the use of technology in peer relationship involved the cyberactivities including the process of cyberbullying. As noted by an increasing number of researchers on the social, moral, and emotional implications of cyberactivities and the potential harms and benefits to one's social relationships and feelings of self-worth and identity (Bauman, 2010; Kowalski & Limber, 2007; Kowalski, Limber, & Agatston, 2008), researchers encourage educators and parents, and all adults who work with youth to create healthy, adaptive critical multimedia educational programs that foster students' abilities to think and reflect critically as they engage in social networks and communicate through the use of various technologies.

More specifically, in Jean Twenge's (2006) discussion of current North American youth as the "Me generation," supporting Turkle's (2011) caution regarding the use of electronic communication over physical, Twenge encourages youth to limit their time on the use of social technologies and exposure to cyberactivities, encouraging youth to engage in face to face social connections with their peers. Similar to Twenge (2006), as noted earlier, researchers involved in positive psychology also recommend that educators and researchers be cautious of the emphasis of promoting programs that focus only on maintaining positive self-worth and self-esteem among students (Baumeister, Cambell, Krueger, & Vohs, 2003; Neff, 2011; Seligman, 2011). As Seligman notes, programs such as Baumeister, Vohs, and Tice's (2007) that involve the development of self-discipline and self-monitoring encourage youth to develop a strong sense of self-agency and personal responsibility and accountability for their learning and self and social development.

Such social cognitive approaches that focus on self-control and discipline as well as educational programs including Neff's (2011) work that fosters self-compassion supports similar educational programs that promote resilience and developing competencies to create healthy and effective coping strategies to make healthy life-style changes (Damon, 2008; McGrath & Nobel, 2009; Seligman, 2011). Many educators suggest the need for further psychological and counseling support for youth in secondary school to help adolescents make healthy lifestyle choices, as well as increasing support for families to become active in youth's learning process. Such programs promote the need for collaborative and team-based approaches to a youth's learning journey by encouraging partnerships among the student, parent, peer, and educator within the larger community. As I discussed at the beginning of this book, support from significant others as well as developing a youth's sense of agency and competency will help youth to learn effective and adaptive ways to deal with personal, social, and cultural experiences of uncertainty and ambiguity with the goal of developing self, social, and cultural competence.

As Ryan (2011) suggests, an important direction for future research is to increase knowledge of what teachers can do to best support positive peer relationships that facilitate motivation, engagement, and achievement in school. To what extent do teacher behaviors affect peer relationships? From simpler issues, such as seating assignments to more complex issues, such as discipline style, classroom organization, and creation of a warm and supportive environment, teacher behavior is important to what transpires between peers around academic tasks. Future work that connects teacher behavior and features of the classroom context to aspects of peer relationships could provide important insights for educators regarding how to harness the power of peers to promote academic engagement.

This might be especially important during early adolescence when motivation, engagement, and achievement are vulnerable to declines. However, negative changes are not inevitable. Research from a stage–environment fit perspective has shown that the nature of change in students' engagement during early adolescence depends on the nature of the school and classroom environment. When students move into a favorable middle school environment, they do not show the same declines (Eccles et al., 1993). Less research has examined how aspects of the middle school or classroom context relate to peer relationships and interactions concerning learning. To this date, no studies have followed students' experiences of social and personal ambiguities across the transition from middle gradeschool to highschool. Given the great changes that take place in classroom contexts and peer groups during this transition, it provides a unique window to examine the interplay among context, peer relationships, and academic and social and emotional adjustment.

CONCLUSION

In conclusion, the research reported in this book represents a contribution to the literature on the role of ambiguity during early adolescence. Attention to peer dynamics should be considered in efforts to better support student success during this stage of life. Future work that explicates classroom and teacher effects on peer relationships as they relate to academic adjustment has much potential to assist educators help students navigate early adolescence and be successful in school. It is my hope that through the writing of this book, that my readers leave this book with a sense of hope in that they are able to see a positive ray of hope to lead them through the clouds of ambiguity within the 21st century.

How do we encourage the wise and caring critical adolescent listener within the Canadian cultural mosaic? How do teachers and parents help teenagers learn how to be emotionally and spiritually healthy within an increasingly ambiguous culture – including virtual and real worlds? How we do encourage youth to critically question what are the psychological and social, emotional, and cultural implications of role of diversity (moral, cultural, spiritual), technology, within an increasingly global learning community? How do educators help to immunize youth against the possible risk for emotional and spiritual alienation given the advancing technological progress, particularly expanding virtual realities? Similar to programs that focus on improving one's physically health and fitness, how do we aim to develop emotionally and psychologically 'fit' adolescents within our culture of ambiguity? Such questions remain intriguing puzzles and challenges for us to continue to work on, and I hope for other researchers, educators, parents, and youth themselves as we enter the second decade of the 21st century?

FINAL THOUGHTS (FOR NOW)

"I am not fond of the word psychological. There is no such thing as the psychological. Let us say that one can improve the biography of the person."

Jean-Paul Sartre (cited in Laing, 1969, p. 120)

During the writing this book, amidst the recent media flurry of the winning computer Watson on the television game show Jeopardy (Feb 16, 2011), there is currently an ongoing national 10-part series developed by the Canadian Broadcasting Company to "look at the plague of obesity that is overtaking North America by concentrating its vision on the small northern community of Taylor, B.C., where the entire population of the town has agreed to try to shed a collective ton of weight in just three months..." (Village on a diet project, www.CBC.ca, Jan. 4, 2011). Consistent with current national school programs that aim to focus on physical fitness and healthy diets, and as I have discussed throughout this book, given the emotional and social challenges faced by Canadian youth today, perhaps educators and researchers need to create programs that foster not only physical fitness, but also emotional health and mental well being. Such programs may help youth to develop social-cognitive and emotional skills to help them to make sense of and interpret ambiguity in ways that may promote identity development and social competence. As I reflect upon the complexities of our Canadian context regarding emotions, cultural values, and the role of social media and technology, I remain optimistic for the future of our youth. As long as we who work with youth maintain our commitment to collaborate with educators to co-create holistic and inclusive educational programs that promote emotional wellness and social competence, our youth will have guides and mentors to help them to feel safe on the virtual cliff of adolescent development.

REFERENCES

Abrahamsen, E. (2004). Linguistic humor comprehension in children with articulation impairments. *Perceptual and Motor Skills Research Exchange, 99* (1), 179–190.

Antonovsky, A. (1979). *Health, stress, and coping: New perspectives on mental and physical well-being.* San Francisco: Jossey-Bass.

Ascione, F. R. (2004). *Children and animals: Exploring the roots of kindness and cruelty.* West Lafayette, IN: Purdue University Press

Astington, J. (1993). *The child's discovery of the mind.* Cambridge, MA: Harvard University Press.

Aydin, N.,Fischer, P., & Frey, D. (2010). Turning to God in the face of ostracism: Effects of social exclusion on religiousness. *Personality and Social Psychology Bulletin, 36*, 742–753.

Baldwin, D., & Moses, L. (1996). The ontongeny of social information gathering. *Child Development, 67.* 1915–1939.

Banerjee, R. (2002). Children's understanding of self presentational behavior: Links with mental-state reasoning and the attribution of embarrassment. *Merrill-Palmer Quarterly, 48*, 378 403.

Bandura, A. (2001). Social cognitive theory: An agentic perspective. Annual *Review of Psychology, 52*, 1–26.

Banerjee, R., & Yuill, N. (1999). Children's understanding of self-presentational display rules: Associations with mental-state understanding. *British Journal of Developmental Psychology, 17*, 111–124.

Banyard, V. (2008). Measurement and correlates of prosocial bystander behavior: The case of interpersonal violence. *Violence and Victims, 23*, 83–97.

Barnett, M., Barlett, N., Livengood, J., Murphy, D., & Brewton, K. (2010). Factors associated with children's anticipated responses to ambiguous teases. *The Journal of Genetic Psychology, 17*, 54–72.

Baron-Cohen, S. (2010). *The science of evil: On empathy and the origins of cruelty.* New York: Basic Books.

Battro, A. (2010). The butterflies of the soul. In M. Suarez-Orozco & C. Sattin-Bajaj (Eds.), *Educating the whole child for the whole world: The Ross school model and education for the global era* (pp. 163–169).New York: New York University Press.

Bauman, S. (2010). Cyberbullying in a rural intermediate school: An exploratory study. *Journal of early adolescence. 30*, 803–833.

Bauman, Z. (1991). *Modernity and ambivalence.* Cambridge, UK: Polity Press.

Baumeister, R., Vohs, K., & Tice, D. (2007). The strength model of self-control. *Current Directions in Psychological Science, 16*, 351–355.

Baumeister, R. F., Campbell, J. D., Krueger, J. I., & Vohs, K. D. (2003). Does high self-esteem cause better performance, interpersonal success, happiness, or healthier lifestyles? *Psychological Science in the Public Interest, 4*, 1–44.

Bariaud, F. (1988). Age differences in children's humor. *Journal of Children in Contemporary Society, 20* (1–2), 15–45

Bateson, G., Jackson, D., Haley, J., & Weakland, J. (1956). Toward a theory of schizophrenia, *Behavioral Sciences, 1*, 251.

Belenky, M., Clinchy, B., Goldberger, N., & Tarule, J. (1986). *Women's ways of knowing.* New York: Basic Books.

Beran, T., Ramirez-Serrano, A., Kuzyk, R., Nugent, S., & Fior, M. (2011). Would children help a robot in need? *International Journal of Social Robotics, 3*, 83–93.

Berkowitz, L., & Daniels, L. (1963). Responsibilty and dependency. *Journal of Abnormal and Social Psychology, 66*, 429–436.

Bernstein, D. (1986). The development of humor. Implication for assessment and intervention. *Topics in Language Disorders, 6* (4), 65–71.

Bhatnager, P., & Rastogi, M. (1986). Cognitive style and basis ideal disparity in males and females. *Indian Journal of Current Psychological Research, 1*, 36–40.

REFERENCES

Bialecka-Pikul, M., Rynda, M., & Syrecka, D. (2010). Constructing a narrative in the standard unexpected transfer test in adolescence and adulthood. *Psychology of Language and Communication, 14,* 29–43. doi: 10.2478/v10057-010-0002-9

Bjorklund, D. F. (2007). *Why youth is not wasted on the young: Immaturity in human development.* Malden: Blackwell Publishing.

Bloom, P. (2010). *How pleasure works: The new science of why we like what we like.* New York: W.W. Norton & Company.

Bonitatibus G. J., & Beal C. R. (1996). Finding new meanings: Children's recognition of interpretive ambiguity in text. *Journal of Experimental Child Psychology, 62,* 131–150.

Boorn, C., Hopkins Dunn, P., & Page, C (2010). Growing a nurturing classroom. *Emotional and Behvioural Difficulties, 15,* 311–321.

Boxer, D., & Cortes-Conde, F. (1997). From bonding to biting: Conversational joking and identity display. *Journal of Pragmatics, 27,* 275–294

Bosacki, S. (2000). Theory of mind and self-concept in preadolescents: Links with gender and language. *Journal of Educational Psychology, 92*(4), 709–717.

Bosacki, S. (2003). Psychological pragmatics in preadolescents: Sociomoral understanding, self-worth, and school behavior. *Journal of Youth and Adolescence, 32*(2), 141–155. doi:10.1023/A:1021861902463

Bosacki, S. (2007). Children's understandings of emotions and self: Are there gender differences? *Journal of Research in Childhood Education, 22*(2), 155–172.

Bosacki, S. (2005). *Culture of classroom silence.* New York: Peter Lang.

Bosacki, S. (2008). *Children's emotional lives: Sensitive shadows in the classroom.* New York: Peter Lang.

Bosacki, S. (2011). *Theory of mind understanding and conversational patterns in early adolescence.* Manuscript submitted for publication.

Bosacki, S., & Moore, C. (2004). Preschoolers' understanding of simple and complex emotions: Links with gender and language. *Sex Roles: A Journal of Research, 50,* 659–675.

Bosacki, S., Varnish, A., & Akseer, S. (2008). Pictorial and narrative representations of children's sense of self and play. *Canadian Journal of School Psychology, 23,* 190–205.

Bosacki, .S, Elliott, A, Bajovic, M. & Akseer, S. (2009). Preadolescents' magazine reading habits and self-concept: Does gender play a role? *Journal of Research in Childhood Education, 23,* 240–250.

Boseovski, J. J. (2010). Evidence for "rose-colored glasses": An examination of the positivity bias in young children's personality judgments. *Child Development Perspectives, 4*(3), 212–218

Boseovski, J. J., & Lee, K. (2006). Seeing the world through rose-colored glasses? Neglect of consensus information in young children's personality judgments. *Social Development, 17*(2), 399–416.

Brach, T. (2003). *Radical Acceptance: Embracing your life with the heart of a Buddha.* New York: Bantam.

Bronfenbrenner, U. (2005). (Ed). *Making human beings human: Bioecological perspectives on human development.* Thousand Oaks, CA: Sage Publications.

Bronfenbrenner, U., & Morris, P. (1998). The ecology of development processes. In W. Damon & R. Lernre (Eds.), *Handbook of child psychology: Theoretical models of human development* (5th ed., Vl. 1, pp. 993–1028). New York: Wiley.

Brown, J. R., & Dunn, J. (1996). Continuities in emotion understanding from 3–6 yrs. *Child Development, 67*(3), 789–802.

Brown, L., & Gilligan, C. (1992). *Meeting at the crossroads.* New York: Ballantine.

Brown, P., & Levinson, S. (1987). Politeness: *Some universals in language usage.* Cambridge, UK: Cambridge Univeristy Press. Brumberg, J. (2000). *Fasting girls: The history of anorexia nervosa.* New York: Vintage Books.

Bruner, J. (1986). *Actual Minds, possible worlds.* Cambridge, MA: Harvard University Press.

Bruner, J. (1990). *Acts of meaning.* Cambridge, MA: Harvard University Press.

Bruner, J. (1996). *The culture of education.* Cambridge, MA: Harvard University Press.

Braun-Lewensohn, O., & Sagy, S. (2010). Sense of coherence, hope and values among adolescents under missile attacks: a longitudinal study. *International Journal of Children's Spirituality, 15,* 247–260.

Buissac, P. (1976). *Circus and culture: A semiotic approach*. Bloomington: IN: University Press.

Burke, K. (1970). *A grammar of motives*. Berkeley: University of California Press.

Bussey, K., & Bandura, A. (1999). Social cognitive theory of gender development and differentiation. *Psychological Review, 106*, 676–713.

Bybee, J. (1998). The emergence of gender differences in guilt during adolescence. In J. Bybee (Ed.), *Guilt and children* (pp. 114–122). San Diego, CA: Academic Press.

Cameron, A., Fox, J, Anderson, M., & Cameron, C. (2010). Resilient youths use humor to enhance socioemotional functioning during a day in the life. *Journal of Adolescent Research, 25*, 716–742.

Cameron, E.L., Kennedy, K.M., & Cameron, C.A. (2008). Let me show you a trick!: A toddler's use of humor to explore, interpret and negotiate her familial environment during a day in the life. *Journal of Research in Childhood Education, 23* (1), 5–18.

Capek, K. (1927). *The absolute at large*. London: Bradford & Dickens.

Capelli, C, Nakagas, N., & Madden, C. (1990). How children understand sarcasm: The role of context and intonation. *Child Development, 61*, 1824–1841.

Caravita, S., Di Biasio, P., & Salmivalli, C. (2010). Early adolescents' participation in bullying: Is ToM involved? *The Journal of Early Adolescence, 30*, 138–170.

Carpendale, J., & Chandler, M.J. (1996). On the distinction between false belief and subscribing to an interpretative theory of mind. *Child Development, 67*, 1686–1706.

Chen, H., Russell, R., Nakayama, K., & Livingstone, M. (2010). Crossing the 'uncanny valley': adaptation to cartoon faces can influence perception of human faces. *Perception, 39*, 378–386.

Churchland, P. (2011). *Braintrust: What neuroscience tells us about morality*. Princeton: Princeton University Press.

Cialdini, R. (2001). *Influence: Science and practice*. Boston: Allyn & Bacon.

Clark, H. (1996). *Using language*. Cambridge, UK: Cambridge University Press.

Compas, B. E., Orosan, P. G., & Grant, K. E. (1993). Adolescent stress and coping: implications for psychopathology during adolescence. *Journal of Adolescence, 16*, 331–349.

Coplan, R., Hughes, K., Rose-Krasnor, L., & Bosacki, S. (2011, in press). Is silence golden? Elementary school teachers' strategies and beliefs towards hypothetical shy-quiet and talkative-exuberant children. *Journal of Educational Psychology*.

Costigan, C. (2011). Embracing complexity in the study of acculturation gaps: Directions for future research. *Human Development, 53*, 341–349.

Craig, A. (2009). How do you feel – now? The anterior insula and human awareness. *Natural Review of Neuroscience, 10*, 59–70.

Crick, N., Grotpeter, J., & Bigbee, M. (2002). Relationally and physically aggressive children's intent attributions and feelings of distress for relational and instrumental peer provocations. *Child Development, 73*(4), 1134–1142.

Cross, T. (2011). *On the social and emotional lives of gifted children*. (4th Ed.). Waco, TX: Prufrock Press.

Csikszentmihalyi, M. (1991). *Flow: The psychology of optimal experience*. New York, NY: Harper Perennial.

Csikszentmihalyi, M. (1997). *Finding flow*. New York, NY: Basic Books.

Cutting, A., & Dunn, J. (1999). Theory of mind, emotion understanding, language, and family background: Individual differences and interrelations. *Child Development, 70*(4), 853–865.

Cutting, A., & Dunn, J. (2002). The costs of understanding other people: social cognition predicts young children's sensitivity to criticism. *Journal of Child Psychology and Psychiatry, 43*, 849–860.

Dabrowski, K. (1967). *Personality shaping through positive disintegration*. Boston: Little Brown.

Damasio, A. (2010). *Self comes to mind: Constructing the conscious brain*. New York: Pantheon Books.

Damon, W. (2008). *The path to purpose: How young people find their calling in life*. New York: Simon & Shuster.

Dawson, J., & Singh-Dhesi, D. (2010). Educational psychology working to improve psychological well-being: an example. *Emotional and Behavioural Difficulties, 15*, 295–310.

REFERENCES

Debold, E., Tolman, D., & Brown, L. (1996). Embodying knowledge, knowing desire: Authority and split subjectives in girls' epistemological development. In N. Goldberger J., Tarule, B., Clinchy & M. Belenky (Eds.), *Knowledge, difference and power* (pp. 85–125). New York: Basic Books.

Delgado, M, Frank, R., & Phelps, E. (2005). Perceptions of moral character modulate the neural systems of reward during the trust game. *Natural Neuroscience, 8,* 1611–1618.

Denham, S. (1998). *Emotional development in young children.* New York: Guilford Press.

DeSousa, R. (2011). *Emotional truth.* New York: Oxford University Press.

de Waal, F. (2009). *The age of empathy: Nature's lessons for a kinder society.* New York: Three Rivers Press.

Dodge, K. A., & Frame, C. L. (1982). Social cognitive biases and deficits in aggressive boys. *Child Development, 53,* 620–635.

Dodge, K. A., & Tomlin, A.M. (1987). Utilization of self-schemas as a mechanism of interpretational bias in aggressive children. *Social Cognition, 5,* 280–300.

Doherty, M., & Wimmer, M. (2005). Children's understanding of ambiguous figures: Which cognitive developments are necessary to experience reversal? *Cognitive Development, 20,* 407–421.

Doyle, A. (1892). *The adventures of sherlock holmes.* London: George Newnes.

Duchenne, G. (1990/1862). *The mechanism of human facial expression or an electro-physiological analysis of the expression of the emotions,* trans. A. Cutherbertson. New York: Cambridge University Press.

Dunn, J. (1995). Children as psychologists: The later correlates of individual differences in understanding of emotions and other minds. *Emotion and Cognition, 9,* 187-201.

Dunn, J. (2000). Mind-reading, emotion understanding, and relationships. *International Journal of Behavioral Development, 24,* 142-144.

Dyson, R. (2000). *Mind abuse: Media violence in the information age.* Montreal, Quebec: Black Rose Books.

Eder, D. (1993). "Go get ya a french!" Romantic and sexual teasing among adolescent girls. In D. Tannen (Ed.), *Gender and Conversational Interaction* (pp. 17–31). New York: Oxford University Press.

Ekman, P. (2009). *Telling lies: Clues to deceit in the marketplace, politics, and marriage.* New York: W. W. Norton & Norton & Company.

Eliot, L. (2009). *Pink brain, blue brain: how small differences grown into troublesome gaps.* New York: Houghton Mifflin Harcourt.

Empson, W. (1947). *Seven types of ambiguity.* New York: New Directions.

Evans, A., & Lee, K. (2011). Verbal deception from late childhood to middle adolescence and its relation to executive functioning skills. *Developmental Psychology,* advance on-line publication, May 9, 2011, no pagination specified.

Farber, B. (1989). Psychological mindedness: Can there be too much of a good thing? *Psychotherapy, 26,* 210–217.

Faris, R., & Felmlee, D. (2011). Status struggles: Network centrality and gender segregation and cross-gender aggression. *American Sociological Review, 76,* 48–73.

Filippova, E., & Astington, J.W. (2008). Further development in social reasoning revealed in discourse irony understanding. *Child Development, 79,* 126–138.

Fine, C. (2010). *Delusions of gender: How our minds, society, and neurosexism create difference.* New York: W. W. Norton & Company.

Fivush, R. (2008). Remembering and reminiscing: How individual lives are constructed in family narratives, *Memory Studies, 1,* 49–58.

Freeman, J. (2010). *Gifted lives: What happens when gifted children grown up.* New York: Routledge.

Fuhr, M. (2002). Coping humor in early adolescence. *Humor, 15* (3), 283–304.

Hoicka, E., & Gattis, M. (2008). Do the wrong thing: How toddlers tell a joke from a mistake *Cognitive Development, 23,* 180–190.

Germer, C. K. (2009). *The mindful path to self-compassion: Freeing yourself from destructive thoughts and emotions.* New York: Guilford Press.

Gilbert, P. (2009). *The compassionate mind.* London: Constable.

Gilligan, C. (1982). *In a different voice: Psychological theory and women's development.* Cambridge, MA: Harvard University Press.

Gilligan, C. (1993). Adolescent development rediscovered. In A. Garrod (Ed.), *Approaches to moral development* (pp. 103–132). New York: Teachers' College Press.

Gjerde, P. (1995). Alternative pathways to chronic depressive symptoms in young adults: Gender differences in developmental trajectories. *Child Development, 66,* 1277–1300.

Gjerde. P., & Block, J. (1991). Preadolescent antecedents of depressive symptomatology in late adolescence: A prospective study. *Journal of Youth and Adolescence, 20,* 215–230.

Goffman, I. (1959). *Presentation of self in everyday life.* New York: DoubleDay.

Gopnik, A., & Rosati, A. (2001). Duck or rabbit? Reversing ambiguous figures and understanding ambiguous reprsentations. *Developmetnal Science, 4,* 175–183.

Grant, M., & Mills, C. (2011). Children's explanations of the intentions underlying others' behaviour. *British Journal of Developmental Psychology,* Advance online publication. doi: 10.1348/026151010X521394

Grice, , P. (1975). *Logic and conversation.* New York: Academic Press.

Grinder, R, & Englund, D. (1966). Adolescents in other cultures. *Review of Educational Research, 36,* 450–462.

Habermas, T., & Bluck, S. (2000). Getting a life: The emergence of the life story in adolescence. *Psychological Bulletin, 126,* 748–769.

Habermas, T., & Diel, V. (2010). The emotional impact of loss narratives: Event severity and narrative perspectives. *Emotion, 10,* 312–323.

Habermas, T., & de Silveira, C. (2008). The development of global coherence in life narratives across adolescence: Temporal, causal, and thematic aspects. *Developmental Psychology, 44,* 707–721.

Hancock, J. (2009). Digital deception: The practice of lying in the digital age. In B. Harrington (Ed.), *Deception from ancient empires to internet dating* (pp. 109–120). Stanford: Stanford University Press.

Happe, F. (1994). An advanced test of theory of mind: Understanding of story characters' thoughts and feelings by able autistic, mentally handicapped, and normal children and adults. *Journal of Autism and Developmental Disorders, 24,* 129–154.

Harris, S. (2010). *The moral landscape: How science can determine human values* New York: Free Press.

Harter, S. (1999). *The construction of the self: A developmental perspective.* New York: Guilford Press.

Hatcher, R., & Hatcher, S. (1997). Assessing the psychological understanding of children and adolescents. In M. McCallum & W. Piper (Eds.), *Psychological understanding: A contemporary understanding* (pp. 59–75). Mahwah, NJ: Erlbaum.

Hatcher, R., Hatcher, S., Berlin, M., Okla, K., & Richards, J. (1990). Psychological understanding and abstract reasoning in late childhood and adolescence: An exploration using new instruments. *Journal of Youth and Adolescence, 19,* 307–325.

Hayward, E. (2011). *Theoretical and empirical support for the validity of an advanced Theory of Mind.* Paper presented at the 41st annual meeting of the Jean Piaget Society, Berkeley, CA.

Hill, P., Lee, V., & Jennaway, M. (2010). Researching reflexivity: Negotiating identity and ambiguity in a cross-cultural research project. *Field Methods, 22,* 319–339.

Homer, B. D., Halkitis, P. N., Moeller, R. W., & Solomon, T. M. (2011). *Assessing the effects of methamphetamine abuse and HIV on adult Theory of Mind.* Paper presented at the 41st annual meeting of Jean Piaget Society, Berkeley, CA.

Hughes, C. (2011). *Social understanding and social lives: From toddlerhood through to the transition to school.* New York: Psychology Press.

Hughes, C., & Dunn, J. (1998). Understanding mind and emotion: Longitudinal associations with mental-state talk between young friends. *Developmental Psychology, 34,* 1026–1037.

Huizinga, J. (1950). *Homo ludens: A study of the play element in culture.* Boston: Beacon Press.

Humphrey, N. (2011). *Soul dust: The magic of consciousness.* Princeton, NJ: Princeton University Press.

REFERENCES

Jack, D. (1991). *Silencing the self: Women and depression*. New York: Harper Collins.

Jack, D. (1999). *Behind the mask: Destruction and creativity in women's aggression*. Cambridge, MA: Harvard University Press.

Jackson, T., & Chen, H. (2008). Sociocultural influences on body image concerns of young Chinese males. *Journal of Adolescent Research, 23*, 154–171.

Jahnke, H., & Blanchard-Fields, F. (1993). A test of two models of adolescent egocentrism. *Journal of Youth and Adolescence, 22*, 313–327.

Jastrow, J. (1900). *Fact and fable in psychology*. Oxford, UK: Houghton, Mifflin.

Kahneman, D. (2003). A perspective on judgment and choice: Mapping bounded rationality. *American Psychologist, 58*, 697–720.

Kahneman, D, Slovic, P., & Tversky, A. (1982). *Judgment under uncertainty: Heuristics and biases*. New York: Cambridge University Press.

Keltner, D. (2009). *Born to be good: The science of a meaningful life*. New York: Norton.

Keltner, D., & Anderson, C. (2000). Saving face for Darwin: The functions and uses of embarrassment. *Current Directions in Psychological Science, 9*, 187–192.

Keltner, D., Capps, L., Kring, A. M., Young, R. C., & Heerey, E. A. (2001). Just teasing: A conceptual analysis and empirical review. *Psychological Bulletin, 127*(2), 229–248.

Kerr, B, & Kerr, B. (1994). *Smart girls two: A new psychology of girls, women and giftedness*. Dayton, OH: Ohio Psychology Press.

Kielar-Turska, M., & Bialecka-Pikul, M. (2009). Generating and understanding jokes by five-and nine-year-olds as an expression of theory of mind. *Polish Psychological Bulletin, 40*, 163–169.

King, C., Akiyama, M., & Elling, K. (1996). Self-perceived competencies and depression among middle school students in Japan and the United States. *Journal of Early Adolescence, 16*, 192–210.

Korzybski, A. (1947). *Science and sanity*. Lakeville, CT: Non-Aristotelian Library.

Kowalski, R., & Limber, S. P. (2007). Electronic bullying among middle school students. *Journal of Adolescent Health, 41*, S22-S30.

Kowalski, R., Limber, S. P., & Agatston, P. W. (2008). *Cyberbullying*. Malden, MA: Blackwell.

Kosslyn, S., Thompson, W., & Gangis, G. (2006). *The case for mental imagery*. New York: Oxford University Press.

Laing, R. D. (1961). *Self and others*. London: Penguin.

Laing, R. D. (1969). *The divided self*. London: Penguin.

Laing, R. D. (1970). *Knots*. London: Penguin.

Lalonde, C., & Chandler, J.M. (2002). Children's understanding of interpretation. *New Ideas in Psychology, 20 (2–3)*, 16–198.

Larson, R. (2011). Positive development in a disorderly world. *Journal of Research in Adolescence, 21*, 317–334.

Langdon, J. (1995). *Wordplay: The philosophy, art and science of ambigrams*. New York: Broadway Books.

Larson, C. (2010). (12th Ed.). *Persuasion: Reception and responsibility*. Boston, MA: Wadsworth.

Larson, R. (2011). Positive development in a disorderly world. *Journal of Research in Adolescence, 21*, 317-334.

Larson, R. W., & Richards, M. (1991). Boredom in the middle school years: Blaming schools versus blaming students. *American Journal of Education, 91*, 418 – 443.

Lecce, S., Caputi, M., & Hughes, C. (2010). *Does sensitivity to criticism mediate the relationship between theory of mind and academic competence?* Manuscript submitted for publication.

Lee, Y., Duchaine, B., Wilson, H.R., & Nakayama, K. (2010). Three cases of developmental prosopagnosia from one family: detailed neuropsychological and psychophysical investigation of face processing. *Cortex, 46*, 949–964.

Lee, E., Torrance, N., & Olson, D. (2001). Young children and the say/mean distinction: Verbatim and paraphrase recognition in narrative and nursery rhyme contexts. *Journal of Child Language, 28*, 531–543.

Levy, N. (2007). *Neuroethics*. New York: Cambridge University Press.

Liben, L. (2011). Sex differences in children: The continuing quest to understand and modify them. *Human Development, 53*, 356–360.

Lillard, A. (1997). Ethnopsychologies: Cultural variations in theory of mind. *Psychological Bulletin, 123*, 3–32.

Linn, S. (2005). *Consuming kids: Protecting our children from the onslaught of marketing and advertising.* New York: Anchor Books.

Long, G., & Toppino, T. (2004). Enduring interest in perceptual ambiguity: Alternating views of reversible figures. *Psychological Bulletin, 130*, 748–768.

Maccoby, E. (1998). *The two sexes: Growing up apart, coming together.* Cambridge, MA: Harvard University Press.

Machnik, S., & Martinez-Conde, S. (2010). *Sleights of mind: What the neuroscience of magic reveals about our everyday deceptions.* New York: Henry Holt and Company.

Machnik, S., & Martinez-Conde, S. (2011, January/February). The illusions of love: How do we fool thee? Let us count the ways that illusions play with our hearts and mind. *Scientific American Mind*, 18–20.

Marini, Z., Dane, A., & Bosacki, S., & YLC-CURA (2005). Direct and indirect bully-victims: Differential psychosocial risk factors associated with adolescents involved in bullying and victimization. *Aggressive Behavior, 32*, 1–19.

Matthews, K., & Keating, D. (1995). Domain specificity and habits of mind: An investigation of patterns of high-level development. *Journal of Early Adolescence, 15*, 319–343.

Markus, H., & Kitayama, S. (1994). The cultural construction of self and emotion: Implications for social behavior. In S. Kitayama & H. Markus (Eds.), *Emotion and culture: Empirical studies of mutual influence* (pp. 89–132). Washington, DC: APA.

Markus, H., & Wurf, E. (1987). The dynamic self-concept: A social psychological perspective. *Annual Review of Psychology, 38*, 299- 337.

McGhee P. (1984). Play, incongruity, and humor. In T. Yawkey & A. Pellegrini (Eds.) *Child's play: Developmental and applied* (pp. 219–236). Mahwah, NJ: Lawrence Erlbaum.

McGhee, P. (1977). Sex differences in children's humor. *Journal of Communication, 10*, 176–189.

Mc Ghee, P.E., & Goldstein, J.H (Eds.) (1983). *Handbook of Humor Research.* New York: Springer.

McGrath, E., Keita, G., Strickland, B., & Russo, N. (1990). *Women and depression.* Washington, DC: American Psychological Association.

McGrath, H., & Noble, T. (2009, May). *Applying positive psychology in education: A seven-year journey from 2002 to 2009.* Paper presented at the Positive Psychology in Education Symposium, Sydney Australia University, Sydney Australia.

Meece, M. (2011). Who's the boss, you or your gadget. New York Times, cited in the *Toronto Sunday Star*, p. 13, Feb. 27, 2011.

Messerschmidt, J. (2010). The struggle for recognition: Embodied masculinity and the victim-violence cycle of bullying in secondary schools. In M. Kehler & M. Atkinson M. (Eds.), *Boys' bodies: Speaking the unspoken* (pp. 113–131). New York: Peter Lang.

Miller, S. (2009). Children's understanding of second-order mental states. *Psychological Bulletin, 135*, 749–773.

Miller, J. (2010). *Whole child education.* Toronto: University of Toronto Press.

Mills, C. M., & Keil, F. C. (2005). The development of cynicism. *Psychological Science, 16*(5), 385–390.

Moore C. (2006). *The development of commonsense psychology.* Mahwah, NJ: Lawrence Erlbaum Associates.

Nass, C. (2010). *The man who lied to his laptop.* New York: Current.

Nass, C., & Brave, S. (2005). *Wired for speech: How voice activates and enhances the human-computer relationship.* Cambridge, MA: MIT Press.

Neff, K. (2011). Self-compassion, self-esteem, and well-being. *Social and Personality Compass, 5*, 1–12.

Nelson, K. (2007). *Young minds in social worlds: Experience, meaning, and memory.* Cambridge, MA: Harvard University Press.

Nucci, L. (2001). *Education in the moral domain.* New York: Cambridge University Press.

Nucci, L (2009). *Nice is not enough.* Upper Saddle, NJ: Pearson.

REFERENCES

O'Sullivan, M. (2009). Why most people parse palters, fibs, lies, whoppers, and other deceptions poorly In B. Harrington (Ed.), *Deception from ancient empires to internet dating* (pp. 74–91) Stanford: Stanford University Press.

Olson, D. (1994). *The world on paper.* New York: Cambridge University Press.

Olson, D. (1996). Toward a psychology of literacy: On the relations between speech and writing. *Cognition, 60,* 83–104.

Olson, D. (2007). Self-ascription of intention: responsibility, obligation and self-control. *Synthese, 159,* 297–314.

Orenstein, P. (2011). *Cinderella ate my daughter: Dispatches from the front lines of the new girlie-girl culture.* New York: Harper Collins.

Orwell, G. (1938). *1984.* London: Penguin Books.

Orwell, G. (1945). *Animal farm.* London: Penguin Books.

Park, L., & Park, T. (1997). Personal intelligence. In M. McCallum & W. Pipher (Eds.), *Psychological mindedness: A contemporary understanding* (pp. 133–168). Mahwah, NJ: Lawrence Erlbaum Associates.

Paulos, J. (1980). *Mathematics and humor.* Chilcago, Ill: University of Chicago Press.

Peets, K., Hodges, E., & Salmivalli, C. (2008). Affect-congruent social-cognitive evaluations and behavior. *Child Development, 79,* 170–185.

Peritz, I., & Friesen, J. (2010, Oct. 1). Part 1: When multiculturalism doesn't work. *Globe and Mail.*

Perry, W. (1970). *Forms of intellectual and ethical development in the college years.* New York: Holt, Rinehart & Winston.

Pexman, P. M., Glenwright, M., Krol, A., & James, T. (2005). An acquired taste: Children's perceptions of humour and teasing in verbal irony. *Discourse Processes, 40*(3), 259–288.

Phinney, J. (2011). Increasing our understanding of the acculturation gap: A way forward. *Human Development, 53,* 350–355.

Piaget, J. (1962). *Plays, dreams and imitation in childhood.* New York: W.W. Norton & Co.

Piaget, J. (1981). *Intelligence and affectivity. Their relationship during children development.* Palto Alto, CA: Annual Reviews.

Poldrack, R. (2006). Can cognitive processes be inferred from neuroimaging data? *Trends in Cognitive Science, 10,* 59–63.

Radomska, A. (2007). Understanding and appreciating humor in late childhood and adolescence. *Polish Psychological Bulletin, 38* (4), 189–197.

Ramon y Caja., Santiago (1923/1981). *Recuerdos de mi vida: HIstoria de mi labor cientifica.* Madrid: Alianza.

Recchia, H., Howe, N., Ross, H., & Alexander, S. (2010). Children's understanding and production of verbal irony in family conversations. *British Journal of Developmental Psychology, 28*(1), doi: 10.1348/026151008X401903

Reddy, V. (1991). Playing with the other's expectations: Teasing and mucking about in the first year. In A. Whiten (Ed.), *Natural theories of mind* (pp. 143–158). Oxford, England: Blackwell.

Ritchell, M. (2010). Growing up digital: wired for distraction. New York Times, Nov. 21, 2010.

Robinson, E. J., & Robinson, W. P. (1983). Children's uncertainty about the interpretation of ambiguous messages. *Journal of Experimental Child Psychology, 36,* 81–96.

Rock, I., Gopnik, A., & Hall, S. (1994). Do young children reverse ambiguous figures? *Perception, 23,* 635–644.

Russell,T., Tchanturia, K., Rahman, Q., & Schmidt, U. (2007). Sex differences in theory of mind: A male advantage on Happe's "cartoon" task. *Cognition and Emotion, 21*(7), 1554–1564.

Ryan, A. (2011). Peer relationships and academic adjustment during early adolescence. *Journal of Early Adolescence, 31,* 5–12.

Sacks, O. (2010). *The mind's eye.* New York: Knopf.

Saarni, C. (1999).*The development of emotional competence.* New York: Guilford Press.

Schauer, F., & Zeckhauser, R. (2009). Paltering. In B. Harrington (Ed.), *Deception from ancient empires to internet dating* (pp. 38–73). Stanford: Stanford University Press.

Shulman, P., Castelllon, C., & Seligman, M. (1989). Assessing explanatory style: The content analysis of verbatim explanations and the attributional style questionnaire. *Behaviour Research and Therapy, 27,* 505–509.

Simmons, E., & Blyth, D. (1987*). Moving into adolescence: The impact of pubertal change and the school context.* Hawthorn, NY: Aldine de Gruyter.

Simmons, R., Rosenberg, F., & Rosenberg, H. (1973). Disturbance in the self-image at adolescence. *American Sociological Review, 38,* 535–568.

Schultz. T. (1972). The role of Incongruity and resolution in children's appreciation of cartoon humor. *Journal of Experimental Child Psychology, 13,* 456–477.

Schultz, T. R. (1974). Development of the appreciation of riddles. *Child Development, 45,* 100–105.

Seifert, T., & Hedderson, C. (2009). Intrinsic motivation and flow in skateboarding: An ethnographic study. *Journal of Happiness Studies, 11,* 277–292.

Schultz, T., & Horibe, F. (1974). Development of the appreciation of verbal *jokes. Developmental Psychology, 10,* 13–20

Selman, R. (1980). *The growth of interpersonal understanding.* New York: Academic Press.

Selman, R. (2003). *The promotion of social awareness: Powerful lessons from the partnership of developmental theory and classroom practice.* New York: Russell Sage Foundation.

Semali, L. (2003). Ways with visual languages: Making the case for critical media literacy. *Clearing House, 76(6),* 271–277.

Semrud-Clikeman, M., & Glass, K. (2010). The relation of humor and child development: Social, adaptive, and emotional aspects. *Journal of Child Neurology, 25*(10), 1248–1260,.

Shapiro, J. P., Baumeister, R. G., & Kessler, J. W. (1991). A three component model of children's teasing: Aggression, humor, and ambiguity. *Journal of Social and Clinical Psychology, 10*(4), 459–472.

Silverstein, B., & Perlick, D. (1995). *The cost of competence: Why inequality causes depression, eating disorders, and illness in women.* New York: Oxford University Press.

Slonje, R., & Smith, P. K. (2008). Cyberbullying: Another main type of bullying? *Scandinavian Journal of Psychology, 49,* 147–154.

Smith, P. K., Mahdavi, J., Carvalho, M., Fisher, S., Russell, S., & Tippett, N. (2008). Cyberbullying: Its nature and impact in secondary schools. *Journal of Child Psychology and Psychiatry, 49,* 376–385.

Sorce, J. Emde, R., Campos, J., & Klinnert, M. (1985). Maternal emotional signaling: Its effects on the visual cliff behavior of 1-year-ods. *Developmental Psychology, 21,* 195–200.

Stallard, P. (2010). Mental health prevention in UK classrooms: The friends anxiety prevention program. *Emotional and Behavioural Difficulties, 15,* 23–25.

Staub, E. (2003). *The psychology of good and evil: Why children, adults, and groups help and harm others.* Boston, MA: Cambridge University Press.

Suarez-Orozco, M., & Sattin-Bajaj, C. (2010). (Eds.). *Educating the whole child for the whole world: The Ross school model and education for the global era.* New York: New York University Press.

Sullivan, H. (1953). *The interpersonal theory of psychiatry.* New York: Norton.

Sutton-Smith, B. (1997). *The ambiguity of play.* Cambridge, MA: Harvard University Press.

Sutton, J., Smith, P., & Swettenham, J. (1999). Bullying and 'theory of mind'; a critique of the 'social skills deficit' view of anti-social *behaviour. Social Development, 8,* 117–127.

Tamis-LeMonda, C., & Adolph, K. (2005). Social referencing in infant motor action. In B. Homer & C. Tamis-Le Monda (Eds)., *The development of social cognition and communication* (pp. 145–164). Matwah, NJ: Lawrence Earlbaum Associates.

Tannen, D. (1994). *Gender and discourse.* New York: Oxford University Press.

Tayler, N. (2011). "Guys, she's humongous!": Gender and weight-based teasing in adolescence. *Journal of Adolescent Research, 26,* 178–199.

Telzer, T. (2011). Expanding the acculturaion gap-distress model: An integrative review of research. *Human Development, 53,* 313–340.

Thomas Cook, D., & Kaiser, S. (2004). Betwixt and be Tween: age, Ambiguity, and the sexualization of the female consuming subject. *Journal of Consumer Culture, 4,* 203–227.

Tomasello, M. (1999). *The cultural origins of human cognition.* Cambridge, MA: Harvard University Press.

REFERENCES

Turkle, S. (2011). *Alone together: Why we expect more from technology and less from each other.* New York: Basic Books.

Twenge, J. (2006). *Generation me: Why today's young Americans are more confident, assertive, entitled – and more miserable than ever before.* New York: Simon & Schuster.

Veith, D. (1980). Recursive thinking and the self-concepts of preadolescents. *The Journal of Genetic Psychology, 137*, 233–246.

Village on a diet, (2011). Retrieved January 4, 2011 from http://www.cbc.ca/liverightnow/village/blog_archives.html

Waldron, J., & Kowalski, C. (2009). Crossing the line: Rites of passage, team aspect, and ambiguity of hazing. *Research Quarterly for Exercise and Sport, 80*, 291–302.

Walker, S. (2005). Gender differences in the relationship between young children's peer-related social competence and individual differences in theory of mind. *Journal of Genetic Psychology, 166*, 297–312.

Watson, A., Nixon, C., Wilson, A., & Capage, L. (1999). Social interaction skills and theory of mind in young children. *Developmental Psychology, 35*, 386–391.

Weaver-Hightower, M. (2003). The "boy turn" in research on gender and education. *Review of Educational Research, 73*, 471–498.

West's *Encyclopedia of American Law.* (2008). (2nd Ed.). The Gale Group, Inc.

White, A. (1891). *Polite society at home and abroad: A complete compendium of information upon all topics classified under the head of etiquette.* Monarch Book Company: Chicago, Ill.

Whitney, I., & Smith, P. K. (1993). A survey of the nature and extent of bullying in junior/middle and secondary schools. *Educational Research, 35*, 3–25.

Wicker, B., Keysers, C., Plailly, J., Royet, J., Gallese, V., & Rizzolatti, G. (2003). Both of us disgusted in my insula: The common neural basis of seeing and feeling disgust. *Neuron, 40*, 655–664.

Wiggenstein, L. (1953). *Philosophical investigations.* Oxford: Basil Blackwell.

Wimmer, M., & Doherty, M. (2011). The development of ambiguous figure perception. *Mongraphs of the Society for Research in Child Development, 76*, 1.

Winner, E. (1988). *The point of words: Children's understanding of metaphor and irony.* Cambridge, MA: Harvard University Press.

Witvliet, M., Brendgen, van Lier, P., Koot, H., & Vitaro, F. (2010). Early adolescent depressive symptoms: Prediction from clique isolation, loneliness, and perceived social acceptance. *Journal of Abnormal Child Psychology, 38*, 1045–1056.

Wnumi Grigg, D. (2010). Cyber-Aggression: Definition and concept of cyberbullying. *Australian Journal of Guidance and Counselling, 20*, 143–156.

Yuill, N. (2009). The relation between ambiguity understanding and metalinguistic discussion of joking riddles in good and poor comprehenders: Potential for intervention and possible process of change. *First Language, 29*, 65–79.

Zahn-Waxler, C., & Robinson, J. (1995). Empathy and guild: Early origins of feelings of responsibility. In J. Tangney & K. Fischer (Eds.), *Self-consciousness emotions: The psychology of shame, guilt, embarrassment, and pride* (pp. 143–173). New York: Guilford Press.

Zhang, N., & von der Heydt, R. (2010). Analysis of the context integration mechanisms underlying figure-ground organization in the visual cortex. *Journal of Neuroscience, 30*, 6482–96.

Żygulski, K. (1976). *Wspólnota śmiechu (The community of laughter).* Warszawa: PIW.

GIORGIO PRESSBURGER

THE LAW OF
WHITE SPACES

Giorgio Pressburger was born in 1937 in Budapest. He left
Hungary in 1956 and now lives in Italy, where he works as
a film and theater director. This is his first book to be
translated into English.

INTERNATIONAL

ALSO BY GIORGIO PRESSBURGER

Homage to the Eighth District
(with Nicola Pressburger)

The Law of White Spaces

GIORGIO PRESSBURGER

THE LAW OF
WHITE SPACES

TRANSLATED FROM THE ITALIAN
BY PIERS SPENCE

VINTAGE INTERNATIONAL

Vintage Books

A Division of Random House, Inc.

New York

FIRST VINTAGE INTERNATIONAL EDITION, JUNE 1994

Translation copyright © 1992 by Piers Spence

All rights reserved under International and Pan-American Copyright
Conventions. Published in the United States by Vintage Books, a
division of Random House, Inc., New York. Originally published in
Italy as *La legge degli spazi bianchi* by Marietti SpA, Genoa, in 1989,
copyright © 1989 by Giorgio Pressburger. This translation
originally published in Great Britain by Granta Books, London,
in association with Penguin Books, in 1992. First published in
the United States by Pantheon Books, a division of
Random House, Inc., New York, in 1993.

The Library of Congress has cataloged the Pantheon hardcover
edition as follows:
Pressburger, Giorgio, 1937–
[Legge degli spazi bianchi. English]
The law of white spaces/Giorgio Pressburger; translated
from the Italian by Piers Spence.
p.   cm.
ISBN 0-679-42048-7
I. Title.
PQ4876.R387L4413   1993
853'.914—dc20   92-50470
CIP

Vintage ISBN: 0-679-75246-3

Manufactured in the United States of America
10   9   8   7   6   5   4   3   2   1

CONTENTS

PREFACE

Some years ago I resolved to research the lives and careers of a number of doctors I had known when I was a child and had never forgotten. I was in relatively good health at the time, and that fact enabled me to view the individuals with a certain distance, far removed from the terror with which I had regarded them as a boy. (Even for many years afterwards, every visit to the doctor would reawaken in me the old feeling of coming face to face with someone who could determine my fate at his whim.)

My fears were partly dispelled as I studied the contents of the personal archives of Professor S, a history scholar and a man of great intellectual and moral honesty. He had decided, a long time before, to conduct research along the same lines as mine, but with quite a different aim. During our brief conversation seven years ago I was able to establish that for Professor S, medicine, and indeed science in general—notwithstanding the huge advances made in the last few decades—represented 'the darkness born of the light.' I well remember his exact

11

words, as I remember his hasty correction: 'or rather, the light which feeds on the darkness.'

Professor S's voice was very hoarse at the time and I had to strain to hear him. But my discomfort was nothing against the compassion he showed towards those modest doctors who, in the course of their careers, had been forced to try their strength against 'mysteries bigger than themselves.' He had a kind word for all of them, but not for himself. 'They're deciding on my destiny in the Fourth Palace*,' he said with a smile. 'Let's hope they get it over with quickly. What a lot of red tape!'

He lent me the papers relating to the five cases described in this volume. I have summarized them as best I could.

* See 'Treatise on the Palaces', *The Book of Splendours*

THE LAW OF WHITE SPACES

One winter morning Doctor Abraham Fleischmann realized that he could no longer remember the name of his best friend. He was alone in the house; his housekeeper only came in on week-days, and his old friend Lea was confined to her bed with a severe migraine. In the night the doctor had dreamed about an earthquake, and after that about a meeting with a curious individual whose hair shone with brilliantine and whom everyone referred to as the Spirit of the Times. In the morning when he awoke his thoughts turned to his friend, a television announcer and a master of chess.

He had never written down his friend's telephone number in his leather-bound address book, nor stored it in the memory of the personal computer that was a present from his cousin in Connecticut. He phoned his friend every day: it seemed quite unnecessary to commit to paper or to an electronic circuit a series of digits that he had to recall with such frequency. But in November

15

the friend had left for a four-week holiday, and between then and now his telephone number had erased itself from Doctor Fleischmann's memory.

He went to look it up in the telephone directory—but under what name? For more than ten minutes the doctor was unable to recall either the first or the last name of Isaac Rosenwasser. 'I'll just see if I'm still asleep,' he said, pinching his arm. 'Of course, this might be only a dream too,' he went on, aloud. 'Dreaming of pinching oneself—what nonsense,' he thought.

Fleischmann set great store by the discipline, by the almost stately formality of his own thought processes. He was the sort of person who always manages to find a brilliantly appropriate saying for every occasion, and his patients, as well as praising him as a great doctor, considered him a veritable master of life.

In his personal computer he kept a record of every house-call, together with the case history of each and every one of his patients. His emotional life was kept at a safe distance from this attempt to impose a perfect order on the world: neither his mother nor his children, his wife nor his friends had a file on the screen of his computer.

'What is his name?' he persisted to himself that cold morning. 'It's here on the tip of my tongue, and yet I can't remember it. This is ridiculous—we grew up together!'

Before long his indignation turned to fear, timidly at

first, then more violently. 'What if it's the beginning of a disease?' He banished the thought. 'Don't go assuming the worst just because of a simple memory lapse. The synapses of two neurones got a bit mixed up. An ion of sodium or potassium missed the boat between two cells in the cerebral cortex.'

He got out of bed and did a few gymnastic exercises. At fifty-five he was in the prime of life, fit enough on the ski slopes to leave many younger men behind. He had more than one lover among the forward women of the Eighth District, even among the young girls. He telephoned one of them, and during their afternoon encounter in a tiny apartment in Acacia Avenue he was able to forget his disagreeable case of amnesia.

But five days later Doctor Fleischmann was surprised to find himself searching at length and in vain for the word 'injection': the sounds escaped him. He stood speechless before his patient. The word's meaning was circulating in the convolutions of his brain but its sound would not come out. After twenty long seconds the doctor located it again in his acoustic memory. He wrote the patient a prescription for injections of vitamin B12 to be taken once a day for a week.

'I'm so tired!' Fleischmann exclaimed loudly, as soon as the patient had closed the door behind him. 'Perhaps I too ought to take a cure for my nerves. And I must try and put my life back in order. I have too many commitments. I

need to sort things out.' At that stage it hadn't occurred
to him that he might possibly be dealing with an organic
illness. He was sure in himself of the machinery of his
body; his daily performances, at sport and in bed,
convinced him that it was functioning perfectly.

He wasted no time in attempting to reassure himself
that all was well: in an exercise that, while a little childish,
was entirely typical of him, he repeated over to himself a
hundred times the word 'injection', each time
scrutinizing every thought and mental association that
passed through his head. In this way he alighted on the
thought of death, and beyond it, of nothing. For an
instant he felt like he was dying. 'It's obviously a case of
an irreversible deterioration of the brain cells,' he thought
on the subject of his unexpected amnesia, something that
had never occurred to him before then. He began to
sweat, and felt an emptiness in his stomach. So, he
thought, the pencil was poised over his name; soon it was
to be scored off the list of the living. He would end up,
limbs rigid, on the marble slab of some dissecting room.
And then dissolution, sewage, earth. Was that all there
was? Was that what life was about?

Without thinking he made an appointment at a clinic
for the next day, and at seven in the morning he went to
have blood and urine samples taken. Soon he would
know if the machine really was condemned to the
scrapyard.

'It's not as if I'm waiting to be sentenced,' he thought as he came out of the clinic. 'The judgement was pronounced long ago, the moment I was cast among the living. It won't matter if one day I can no longer pronounce the word "I", because the "I" will no longer exist, or it will be unable to speak. I won't care.'

He went straight away to see the patients waiting for him. During his visits he noticed with triumphant bitterness and a growing sense of the ridiculous that the number of words disappearing from his vocabulary for seconds, for hours at a time was increasing. It was no longer just words with complicated sounds, like 'plantigrade' or 'clepsydra'; even everyday terms, like 'toothpaste' or 'sand', were beginning to obstruct momentarily the flow of thought in the labyrinth of his brain. 'I'm worse, and deteriorating by the minute,' thought Fleischmann. 'But it will pass. I'll get used to it.'

He went to his wife's house and spent a long time talking with her about trivial, everyday things. He was astonished at how sharp and alert he felt. It was as if he had only begun to live from the moment his life had been put in danger. Before, he'd always seemed to be living in a memory, never in the present, as if he'd been in a larval state, a blind thing, completely bereft of intelligence and consciousness. Now, even his astonishment struck him as an emotion he had never experienced before.

Two days passed in this way. On the third day he went

to get the results of his tests. These revealed a significant alteration in his blood analysis. Three or four values were quite a bit above their normal limits and, in the absence of external intervention, would soon have caused Doctor Fleischmann to have what his colleagues called a Turn. In fact, as he was giving him the results of the tests Flebus asked him, 'Have you had a Turn yet? Do you stammer now and again? Get a bit tongue-tied? Have difficulty getting the words out?' Fleischmann denied that he had. He went home, shut himself in his study and cried.

That evening, in the circle of his former family, with his elbows resting on the clean table-cloth, he looked long and hard at his son, his mother, his wife, all of whom had remained living together after he had moved out. 'Does any of this make sense?' He was coming to realize with a sense of horror that everything he cared most about—love, affection, responsibility for the lives of his dear ones—was deserting him, leaving him in mocking conversation with a world that was a stranger.

'You look pale, Papa,' said his son Benjamin. 'You're taking on too many patients. Perhaps if you wrote fewer prescriptions for purgatives and tried to enjoy life a bit more . . . ' Fleischmann knocked over his bowl of soup and stormed out. As he went he saw a terrified, hunted look on the faces of his wife and son.

Outside in the street near the People's Theatre the evening was cool and full of sounds. The drunks were coming out of the wine cellars on all fours. Fleischmann did not know how to escape his self-inflicted torture. He tried talking some courage into himself. 'Who said the suppositions of science were absolute truths? The human brain is immense: the size of two continents, two planets, two universes. I'll find some way out of this. My time has not yet come.'

He enrolled in a speed reading and memory course that was being held in a dark two-roomed apartment on Joseph II Street.

On the first evening, climbing the blackened staircase of the five-storey building, he met a group of unshaven young people and some fastidious office workers determined to get on in life, all dressed in more or less the same fashion in rough and shoddy clothes. Inside the apartment, on its creaky and worn-out wooden floor, twenty or so chairs and a table were set out in a manner intended to lend a serious and traditional air to the proceedings. This was one of the first private enterprises allowed by the State. 'So the State permits the use of memory!' he thought. 'Quite. The State is all memory. And like all other memories it is destined to destroy itself.'

A few weeks into the course he noticed a significant improvement in his ability to remember names, faces and places of recent acquaintance (remote events had been preserved intact in his memory and in his forgetfulness).

21

The atmosphere that reigned in the class made him feel as if they were initiates of some sect whose duty was to continue life on earth after the Catastrophe. Reading at speed, across the page, backwards and forwards, up and down, techniques based on the combined use of the senses and on hypnosis; to Fleischmann these were what would sustain him for the rest of his life, what would make it liveable and free from the shame of physical decay. The three weeks of the course were the last bearable moments of the illustrious doctor's existence.

When the course ended he received a diploma and the professor—a small, fair, insignificant-looking man who had learned the techniques of memory in England—heaped praise upon him. Never had he come across a pupil so diligent and at the same time blessed with so much intelligence.

Fleischmann took up his work again full of optimism. He criss-crossed the back streets of the Eighth District, visiting dark apartments and making calls on pensioners with bad hearts and on ninety-year-old women resigned to loneliness. He was full of the conviction that he had something important to offer them: a few minutes of life.

One day returning from his rounds he heard the telephone ring while he was still at the bottom of the stairs. He ran up the remaining steps. He was not in the habit of hurrying, and indeed he hated the phone for the way it enabled the most unforeseen cases of life and death

22

to reach him, of all people, at any time of the day or night. He hadn't considered that when he had decided to pursue a career in medicine. When he opened the door he found his housekeeper—a thin, deaf eighty-year-old—already holding out the receiver to him with tears in her eyes. 'Come in, come in, Doctor,' whispered the little old lady. 'It's for you.'

This is how Abraham Fleischmann learned of his brother's death. Like him, a doctor, professor of comparative anatomy and a surgeon of international repute, his brother had always had something of a delicate constitution. But his death was a surprise. 'A stroke, or a heart-attack . . . ' Fleischmann murmured to himself with professional objectivity. A moment later he burst into tears, letting out such a painful wail that the old maid fled. The doctor left the house and ran down Kun Street, sobbing loudly and choking on his own tears. A few passers-by turned to stare at him, but left him alone.

Abraham Fleischmann had loved and admired his brother in adulthood. When they were children, however, he had found his brother's melancholy and introspective manner irritating. At that age he wasn't capable of recognizing what gentleness and depth of feeling lay hidden behind his apparent listlessness. Now his brother lay in hospital, wrapped in a sheet like some kind of mummy. He had been dead for half an hour and under the folds of linen Fleischmann could just make out his features, the protrusion of his nose, the shape of his mouth. And though Fleischmann was used to attending to the dead and the dying, the sight had the same effect on him as it has on other men. A cry rose to his lips: 'Why? Why? Why?'

The doctor sobbed and moaned, his face running with tears, while inside he was accusing his brother of being in some way improvident, of having consented to death, of having wanted it. And yet he already knew that, within a few days, he would have yielded to the superior wisdom and mildness of his late brother, whose wish for death— for why else should one so young and so wise have fallen ill?—was simply another expression of his great good sense. To Fleischmann, staying alive now seemed an act of unparalleled foolishness, and the whole of existence nothing more than a huge, filthy, slaughterhouse. He didn't yet know that this single event would within a few days have completely changed the meaning of his life.

The process began suddenly, from the moment he spotted his sister-in-law hiding in a window bay in the hospital corridor. From her he learned that his brother had been ill for a long time, a number of years, and that purely out of regard for his mother—herself suffering from the infirmities of old age—he had hidden the full extent of his illness from everyone, including her.

The day before he died he had summoned all his

strength and telephoned his mother, and when she had asked him how he was, he had told her without hesitation and in a steady voice that he was fine. Then, in the same voice, he had said his goodbyes to her, saying that he was off on a long journey but would be back in a few months. There wasn't a hint of self-pity in his tone. Hanging up the receiver he stared long and hard at the wall before whispering, 'In five or six months' time, once she's got used to my absence, tell her everything. Look after her.'

As he listened to this story, Fleischmann was overcome by a feeling of radiant emotion, as if he were present at some great and solemn event. Then came the moment of truth. First his sister-in-law asked him to go to her house and fetch the clothes to dress the corpse in, telling him in which chest he would find them. There was a short silence. 'Do you still remember the prayer for the dead?' she asked, timidly. 'You have to recite it. If you don't remember it, learn it tonight. It's about twenty lines long. You have to do it. For him. I'm sure you'll manage.'

Doctor Fleischmann left the hospital in great agitation. It was beginning to look as if his brother's fate depended on him, on his ability to learn the prayer for the dead. 'Just now that my memory's in ruins!' he laughed in desperation. 'What nonsense. He's gone and that's that.'

He went to his brother's house, fetched the clothes and took them back to the hospital; then he went to his wife's and mother's house, saying nothing about his brother's death to them, according to the wishes of the deceased, and finally he returned home. He asked his housemaid to find him the old ivory-bound prayer book, its title page covered with the scrawled names of his ancestors and the dates on which they had died.

That evening he didn't eat. He sat down in his dark and dusty study and placed the prayer book in front of him on the writing desk. How long had it been since he had held that book in his hands? Thirty years? Forty? Why did he have to pretend to subscribe to rituals which he had always found childish and incomprehensible? Life and death, the doctor realized, made no more sense to him than those prayers.

He began to wonder what did make sense. The senselessness, the incomprehensibility of everything gripped him like a fever. He felt his ears go red. An almost erotic excitement was taking hold of him. 'No, I won't question it. I know, in the middle of all this uncertainty, that I have to make this small effort, I have to learn these words, these sounds that mean nothing to me. It is the last gift I can give my brother, or my sister-in-law. I, who always held so much back from them.'

He opened the book. At first the square-shaped characters appeared completely unfamiliar to him. The whole system seemed stupidly complicated and arbitrary. 'Still, I don't suppose there's much point in starting to pick holes in the alphabet now that I've made up my mind to go through with it. It's archaic, I know, but right now there's not much of an alternative.'

With the help of a transcription into the Roman alphabet, Fleischmann began to decipher the prayer word by word. But then he decided to memorize the text using the old square characters. Through all this, the meaning of the words remained completely obscure to him. 'It doesn't matter,' he thought, 'even my father who could recite all the prayers so fluently didn't know the meaning of a single word he pronounced. I'll pretend I'm learning a musical score.'

The doctor's thoughts returned to his brother's motionless body, as incontrovertible now in mute self-affirmation as it had ever been in life. And it struck him that the meaning was there, in the self-evidence of a corpse, of an event, the event of death. All the rest—the words, the sounds—merely complicated the significance of such simplicity. But all the same he began to repeat the words over to himself, those useless and necessary sounds, slowly at first, in brief snatches, and then with growing confidence more and more rapidly, lengthening his phrases from three words at a time to seven or eight.

By one in the morning he had said the entire prayer one hundred times over, but still he could remember only the first line. Try as he might, both with the old square characters and with the Roman ones, he was unable to conjure up the remainder before his eyes, nor hear the sounds reverberate in his head. Fleischmann knew from experience how difficult it was to remember sounds for more than a few seconds. His father had been dead only eight years, yet already he had forgotten the sound of his voice. It had become a mere phrase for him, 'a deep, strong voice', no longer a reality. The same would happen with his brother's voice. Even listening to recordings of their voices he would no longer recognize them.

Fleischmann was horrified at the prospect. Following these thoughts, he felt instinctively but obscurely that it was up to him to determine his brother's destiny, even in his present state, deprived of the faculties of memory which sustain the intellect. He began again to repeat the words of the prayer but the telephone rang. It was his sister-in-law asking him to make her something to eat. She had been keeping watch by her husband's bedside and was by now completely exhausted. Her sister had just relieved her. It wasn't right to leave him alone, poor man. She needed a bath and a bite to eat. She would be around in twenty minutes.

'Twenty minutes . . . twenty minutes . . . ' he repeated to himself. Perhaps if they'd left him alone he might have succeeded in learning the rest of the prayer in the remaining hours of the night, but if it went on like this . . . But then how could he deny his sister-in-law the comfort she needed?

'Fine, come on round,' he said, and went to wake the housekeeper. Then, before going to help her prepare a hot meal, he shut himself in his study and tried to see whether the interruption had helped to clear his head and make room in it for a few words of an unknown language. He attempted a quick self-hypnosis, but he was too agitated to use it to help him remember. So he transcribed the text of the prayer into the memory of his personal computer. 'Perhaps tomorrow, reading it over and over on the screen in front of my eyes, I'll learn it. I'll get up at five. No, at half past four.'

His sister-in-law wept copiously, her head bowed over the table. Instead of eating the soup she filled the bowl with the salt tears of her own glands. Long after she had locked herself in the bathroom, Dr Fleischmann could hear her cries. She seemed to be talking to someone, shouting and railing at him, but in the words of a child, blubbered in the sort of secret language that schoolchildren use. It frightened him.

As a child he too used to have conversations, before going to sleep, with someone to whom he only spoke in rhyming verse; and he would ask him every night to let him die together with the rest of his family, all at exactly the same moment, so that none would suffer pain at the death of the others. How long was it since those conversations had ceased? And was it a good thing or a

29

bad thing that they had? 'What a mess we get ourselves into!' he exclaimed, before locking himself in his study.

He spent hours in front of his computer. Until dawn the low hum of the screen was accompanied by a quiet muttering. Then with first light there was silence. At seven in the morning his housekeeper saw him leave the room. 'I've learned it,' the doctor said. He woke his sister-in-law, huddled up on the sofa, with a kiss on the forehead; he took her home for a change of clothes, and together they set out in a taxi for the old cemetery in Kozma Street.

His brother had been washed and dressed and was lying in the simplest of coffins in the House of Purification. His face was a luminous yellow. The terracotta shards placed on his eyes and on his lips made Fleischmann think of a newborn child.

The Purifier of Bodies Goldstein whispered in the cold of the room: 'It took four of us to get him ready. There are four of us. Four, do you understand?' He was looking for an appropriate reward. And as if to demonstrate his own honesty he pulled a wrist-watch out of his pocket. 'Take it. And this was his ring.'

The sheer practicality of this piece of theatre quite distracted Fleischmann from his spasmodic repetition of the prayer for the dead. He gave Goldstein some money, took the objects rescued from an untimely burial, and gave them to his sister-in-law. He unbuttoned his coat, then buttoned it up again; he rubbed his frozen hands together. The Purifier asked him to go outside. 'I bought the grave for both of us,' murmured Fleischmann to his brother as he left, knowing that what he was saying had been heard many times before. 'Goodbye.'

After the speeches, the tears, the brief, thundering prayers, the congregation moved towards the grave. Fleischmann had managed, by paying an appropriate sum, to secure a site near the entrance, away from the older and more overgrown area. A small crowd had gathered, around two hundred people.

The coffin was resting on two planks of wood over the grave. Doctor Fleischmann's heart was beating fast. The time had come for him to recite the prayer for the dead. Someone gently took hold of his arm. He felt a great tension in his chest and in his throat. With a huge effort of will he spoke the first part of the prayer, at the top of his voice, almost shouting it. He had won. The words emerged clearly and distinctly from his mouth, even though for him they were simply sounds without meaning. He, Abraham Fleischmann, was affirming the meaning of the world, of life, beyond all doubt and bitterness. He had to do it for his brother.

He opened his mouth to shout, even louder than before, the second phrase of the prayer for the dead. But with a feeling of terror he realized that he could no longer remember the sounds. The letters themselves had

31

been erased from his memory. He stood gawping, his mouth wide open. The graveyard was silent. Everyone was looking at him. Fleischmann was sure that even his brother was watching him from the coffin. But the second phrase would not come to him. He could only remember one word, one that contained all the vowels, and the mysterious sound of that single word howled around inside his head. Someone understood his embarrassment and spoke the second phrase in his place.

'There, now for the third,' he thought, 'yes, there's that word that reminds me of a dog, yes, like the command to attack. But what might it mean? What is the meaning of that word? I must have someone translate the prayer for me. Maybe then I'll remember it. But no, the meaning doesn't count. It is so vague, so difficult to grasp. It's the form that matters. And it's that—the sounds—that I don't remember any more.'

Someone, meanwhile, was finishing the prayer in a monotonous, sing-song voice, speaking quickly and without reverence. Fleischmann wanted to cling to this word or that as they surfaced from the threatening waves which rose in the lungs of the speaker and headed inexorably towards him.

And then suddenly there was silence. 'Can the prayer have been that short? And I couldn't learn it!'

Someone passed him a shovel. He had to throw the first clod of earth. He bent over, scooped up some earth in the shovel, and threw it on the coffin which had been lowered on ropes into the grave. He heard a thud. It was the sound of the only good deed he had managed to do for his brother.

As some of the crowd scattered and others gathered round him (including his wife and son, alerted by goodness-knows-whom, fortunately without his mother finding out), as he felt himself being shaken by the hand and kissed on the cheeks, Doctor Fleischmann was still trying to evoke the words that he'd found and then lost again.

He returned to work without a period of mourning. What was the point? He had to think of his patients, of his sick, he had to try and help the living since he was unable to help the dead.

And yet every morning after shaving he spent a quarter of an hour repeating the prayer to himself. He brought to bear all the techniques he had learned in the course of the preceding weeks. He used every mental trick he knew, exploited all his psychological skills. He tried to imagine idyllic countryside scenes; he concentrated on regular breathing; he repeated words that were supposed to be able to overcome the guard of what we call consciousness. When he missed a word, he would look at the book. In the evening before going to bed he would switch on the screen, plug in the keyboard and start up the computer for a couple of runs through his act of faith, the prayer for the dead.

After two weeks of this he put himself to the test. Everything went well up to half way through, but his memory of the second part was very poor. He was missing words crucial for their sound or for their graphic impression—their meaning still remained unknown to him. Doctor Fleischmann was taking ten minutes over a prayer which could be spoken in forty seconds.

He continued his efforts, however. 'I won't give up,' he thought. 'I won't give in so easily to illness and degradation.' Fleischmann was convinced that by a supreme exertion of will-power and a faith in his own abilities he would be able to overcome his illness and its symptoms, the loss of short-term memory. Neither techniques nor hypnoses nor computers were of any use; the only thing that could help him was the affirmation of his own existence: 'I am here, I exist!'

His thoughts returned to his brother, silent and motionless in that hospital bed, and to the many sick people he had treated without success. 'They are dead. So they must have been alive. Death is the greatest proof of existence. Forward. I mustn't give up.'

Then one night he had a wonderful dream. He was a king, he was in a golden room, church bells were ringing. He girded on his sword and announced to the people the birth of his son and heir.

He awoke with the same feeling of solemnity in his

34

veins, in his heart. He went to the hospital and started to work with a will. His patients seemed on their way to recovery, he saw hope for all of them. He continued to repeat to himself the prayer for the dead, but each time he got stuck at the same point, after which he could remember no more. Still he felt he was making progress.

One evening he went to bed exhausted after a long series of visits. He fell asleep and immediately began to dream. In one sense it was the sequel to the dream of a few days before; there was the solemn air of a momentous event.

He was in a beautiful room; his brother entered, looking healthy, elegant, a little awkward the way he had always been, and stopped in front of him. He reached out towards the doctor, incredibly happy and benevolent; then laid his hand on his shoulder and began to recite word for word the prayer for the dead. He smiled as he pronounced the meaningless syllables. But this time it seemed to the doctor, quite unexpectedly, that he understood their meaning. There was no need to translate the words, the sounds, into this or that language; they had a sense—inexplicable, unrepeatable—in themselves.

Fleischmann kissed his brother's hands as he continued his serene psalmody. And then something else became clear: all the childish meanings that the doctor had attributed to the words—because of the resemblance of some sounds to those of words he knew—really were there; they seemed to coexist happily with the real and solemn meanings and they cheered his spirits. From time to time an obscenity would jump out of that dance of syllables and sounds, and it too would be joyful, not offensive.

When his brother had finished saying the last word of the prayer, Doctor Fleischmann said to himself in his dream: 'At last I've learned the whole thing. For it was I who was reciting the prayer. My brother was just a figure in my dream. So I can't be ill. The worst of the sentences that nature can pass, the biochemical disturbances by which fats paralyse and obscure our blood vessels, count for nothing. For man exists beyond memory, beyond language and meaning.' He was already half awake before he had finished this sentence.

He opened his eyes and saw the grey light of early morning. His feeling of joy evaporated instantly. 'What if it really was my brother who said the prayer from start to finish? Perhaps he really did visit me, who knows how, who knows from where?'

He was deeply moved and began to cry. 'I can't do a good deed for my dead brother, but he, dead as he is, can do one for me! We're not alone on the earth, we're not alone. There is an infinite host of beings who love us, as my brother knew how to love, and who intervene for our sake inside us. I would never have believed it was possible.' And in his turn he thought of his brother with that feeling of belated love that can remain a torment a whole life long.

The telephone rang and the doctor was called to help a poor old woman of seventy-five who had had a heart attack. He dressed in a hurry saying only to his maid: 'She won't die. I'm sure of it.'

He went out and ran all the way from Karfenstein Street to Danko Street. He tried, breathless from running, to recite the prayer just to be sure. He was unable to remember a single syllable. He stopped. He wanted to batter his head against the wall. 'No. I mustn't give up. My brother will help me again. He'll help me every time I need him.'

When he arrived at Mrs Wolf's house she had been dead for a few minutes. The doctor stood looking at the corpse as he had looked at many before in his long experience in medicine. 'With her last words she thanked you, Doctor,' a relative said. 'This corpse thanked me,' Fleischmann thought. He stared at it for a while, then left the house without signing the death certificate.

After those of the prayer, other words began to disappear little by little from Doctor Fleischmann's vocabulary. Faces and shapes disappeared from his sight, melodies from his hearing. Towards the end his memory had almost completely deserted him. When they took him in to St John's Hospital, he didn't remember ever having had a brother. To Isaac Rosenwasser, who together with a nurse helped him into the ambulance, he said: 'Everything is written in the white spaces between one letter and the next. The rest doesn't count.' Among his notebook pages of appointments and scientific observations, on the back of an instruction sheet for the use of his computer, was the following scrawl: 'The louder you shout, the better he'll hear you.'

For the complete works of A. Fleischmann, see *New Life*, nos 1, 2, 3, 4, 1970

A.R. Luria, *A Prodigious Memory*, Moscow, 1968

A.R. Luria, *A World Lost and Found*, Moscow, 1971

THE CLOCK OF LIFE

Don't be shocked, dear brother, by the case I'm about to lay before you; don't be ashamed or disgusted or scandalized, I beg you, by what you are about to learn. You know me as well as you know yourself; and though things can turn out an infinite number of different ways, and the natural order has been taking knocks ever since man appeared on the earth, you know what to expect of me.

Your research into what you call the 'biological clock' has convinced you that life is made up of a string of physical processes and chemical reactions whose sequence is rigidly fixed—within certain more or less predictable limits—in time and space and follows predetermined patterns. I'm sorry to say that my own experience, much as it may disgust you, stands in absolute contradiction to your conception of existence. I say all this ironically, in self-doubt and desperation, and with the distressing vagueness that accompanies a state of alcoholic delirium.

I know exactly how you see it: we are simply machines made of matter, with all the attendant faults one would expect. But there is another possibility, one we hear so little about. If we take it into consideration it can give our lives meaning, or make them incomprehensible. And that's why I'm writing to you, to tell you about this possibility, and about my own case. From here, where I've been living in hiding for three years, from this miserable refuge I can bear witness with my own life to the strangeness of an existence which—whether seen from the vicinity of someone who is involved, or from an infinite distance—gives the lie to every one of nature's laws, known or merely guessed at.

What of me? Some years ago my destiny took such a strange and unexpected turn for the worse that I've thought it better to break off all contact with friends and acquaintances of old, with professional colleagues and even with those closest to me, such as you, dear brother. But today I've decided to let you know I'm alive and to confront you with the difficult subject of my existence. If you want you can seek me out. Otherwise I'll live out the rest of my days in happy degradation—but who can judge these things?—without ever again attempting to rejoin the society of other people.

You know how committed I was to my vocation as a doctor, with what patience and perseverance I tried to keep faith with my charges in our derelict neighbourhood, where I've always worked, a neighbourhood of abandoned old people and hopeless drunks. These specimens of humanity demand the most care and the greatest understanding from a doctor with a conscience. It is here that the cry is weakest and the heartbeat is most faint. My story must begin with one of these pitiful cases. Of course I want to take a little time before telling you about me, but I also want to try and make you understand how much I was influenced by your research.

I was on my way to Danko Street one day to visit an old woman of ninety. Crossing the market I was struck by the sound of the calls of the hawkers and street-traders. I listened more closely: I wanted to hear all the individual voices; to take pleasure in them all at once, and in each distinct from the others. And at the same time it occurred to me how much invisible activity—of molecules, of chains of acids and proteins—went to make up the organisms running around and making all this noise. If only one were capable of hearing those sounds, the consonances and dissonances of chemical compounds as they bonded, broke apart and transformed themselves! I'm telling you this because the old lady I was on my way to see, a tiny woman but quite alert and full of energy, had a very strong heart—I had known this for years and years—which affirmed with every beat all the will to live of an organism that was not yet ready to break down into its constituent elements.

Each time I went to see her I was filled with a sense of happiness. I would check her blood pressure, her appetite and her digestive function; that was all she needed. And on every visit I was reminded of your own fascinating field of study: the clock that regulates all our lives and also—should a chain of fats obstruct some chemical reaction, a poison destroy some vital function, or simply if the clockwork runs down—leads inexorably to death. But why is it that the clockwork, for want of another word, has to run down? This was the question that occurred to me that day as I arrived at the house of my elderly patient, Mrs Hirsch.

Climbing the dirty, blackened stairs of the three storey building on the corner of Danko Street and Wednesday Street I took out of my case the little bag of toffees I always brought the old lady. Thirty years before her only son had gone to live in a distant continent and she had no other surviving relatives. Her son did come to visit her once a year however. For a week he would drag her along to cafés and theatres, buy her dresses and shoes— which she never wore—then leave again. Mrs Hirsch lived for that week, and had been doing so now for thirty years. She had never been to visit her son, 'so as not to be a burden on him.'

Arriving on the landing I found the door of my patient's apartment slightly ajar. I knocked, pushed the door open and went in. The only window in the small single room was shut, the curtains drawn. Seated in her armchair in those darkened surroundings, Mrs Hirsch seemed to give off a certain luminosity. She was dead. I could tell that she must have passed away some time in the night. The pain I felt at the death of my charge was redoubled by a tremendous pang of guilty remorse. Out of sheer carelessness I had not been to see her for nearly a fortnight, and I felt that this omission might somehow have been the cause of the old lady's death.

I asked myself again and again why it was that her small light, without which the world now seemed so dark, had had to go out. Was it because I had not fed her with the love that her delicate state demanded of me? Or was it for some other reason? I was filled with self-reproach. I was even on the point of resigning my post as district doctor and retiring to some position in the office of public health.

I was the one who paid the funeral expenses—the old dear had left me all her possessions and savings in her will—and who bought the grave. And this was how the death of Mrs Hirsch took on for me all the aspects of a prodigious event of rare and solemn justice. For as I was arranging transport for the coffin, I came across a telegram which had arrived from Canada on the very day of her death, informing Mrs Hirsch of the 'tragic loss' of her son Benjamin two days before. I found out later, in a letter from an acquaintance of the deceased, that he had died without warning, of a heart attack.

And now perhaps you will begin to understand the strange fascination your research has for me: the way in which the clock of life sometimes stops for reasons that are as mysterious as they are impartial, and often informed by a unique sense of mercy. For you must know that by comparing the precise times of death I was able to ascertain that Mrs Hirsch preceded her son to the grave. Chance—if that's what you like to call it—had been extraordinarily kind to that old lady, deserted and alone in her old age. The heart attack, the 'kiss of death', had spared my patient terrible suffering. Or else the spring which regulated the clockwork of the son in exile led beyond his body to a bond which not even the distance between two continents could break. What is this bond? The workings of some hormone secreted by the hypothalamus? Are these chains of acids so potent that they can cross mountains and oceans and deserts?

And it was during that period, while I was still troubled by these momentous events, that I had the encounter which would bring about a sea-change in my life. I was still overwhelmed by intense feelings of excitement and despondency when I was called out on a visit to the old apartment building where we used to live. Do you remember it? The yellow tiles in the courtyard, the black enamelled wrought iron railings, the ramshackle old elevator all welcomed me with the same harsh indifference that I felt every day on my way home from school. I had been very unhappy in that building. Now, with a scientist's detachment, I can ascribe my oppressed childhood and my unhappy adolescence to various factors: genetic, psychological, environmental, and so on. But the unhappiness that I felt there seemed greater than even the sum of all these various internal and external factors. Having said that, I don't feel particularly depressed about it today; on the contrary, I feel strangely light-headed. And of course I should add that there was always the sight of Adele Polak to lighten up those dark days I spoke of.

Every afternoon from June to September she would sit down on her doorstep to sunbathe. Our house was deserted; we used to watch her secretly, pushing aside the net curtain on the kitchen door which opened onto the railed courtyard. Do you remember Mrs Polak? She would have been about thirty or thirty-five then. She nearly always appeared in shorts, lying in a deck-chair, her legs stretched out in front of her. Her skin was smooth and shiny, and the sun seemed to join in her splendour. I think I might even have written a poem about her one time. Every day I waited, my heart in my mouth, for her to appear. She lived on the other side of the courtyard, one floor higher than us.

When the nurse gave me the address it didn't occur to me to think of her, nor was I particularly surprised or moved when she came to the door. 'Help me, Doctor, please. I've heard so many good things about you. It's such a long time since we've seen each other. I watched you grow up. Please help me. My husband is so ill.' A door opened in the dark hall and the husband came towards me. It all seemed perfectly natural, as if everything had continued exactly as it had once been, without interruption; as if no time had passed. I had no trouble recognizing the man I had last seen thirty years before; he looked almost exactly as I remembered him, even though he was now nearly eighty years old. Only his voice turned out to be quite foreign to me; it was raw and cracked, inhuman somehow. Compared to the wrinkles which had invaded the features of his face, the distortion of his voice seemed to owe more to some cruel and distant cause. He muttered something incomprehensible then turned and opened the door he had just closed behind him. Only then did I become aware of the stench in the place. I could see into a darkened room lit only by a red lamp on a little table covered with old lace. I was shown in, Mrs Polak was leaning lightly on my arm. I looked her in the face for the first time since I had entered that awful place. I immediately noticed her teeth: they were intact, a little yellowed, but still with that gap between the two central incisors that gave her, even as a grown woman, the look of a little girl. And although almost seventy years old, she still had the smile that had entranced me thirty years before.

'He doesn't remember a thing,' Adele Polak whispered, leading me into the room. 'Not even what he told me a minute ago. It's terrible.' We took our seats. Adam Polak sat down opposite me in a velvet-covered armchair. He stared at me with eyes that had lost none of their melanin content; they were darker than those of a young man, but lifeless. I realized that it was extremely difficult to communicate with him. Whatever I said to him he would have forgotten a moment later, and I would be lost for an explanation.

I opened the old bag father gave me on my graduation and took out the stethoscope to listen to his breathing and his heartbeat. His lungs fluttered timidly. After a little I stopped listening and looked at him. His hair, smooth, shining and dyed black, gave him the look of a waxwork. I took out my sphygmomanometer to take his blood pressure, a routine measure. 'Put it away!' yelled the old man. 'Put it away or I'll break it! You're not going to kill me with your machines! Just watch out!'

I was dealing with a hopeless case. I should have had him hospitalized there and then, and for good. His wife's large brown eyes were begging me to. She was blushing, something you encounter only rarely in someone of that age: she was red-faced with shame. But we know, dear brother, what really lies behind feeling shy, feeling ashamed, blushing, do we not? It hides something which cannot be confessed in words: not repentance, reluctance or the wish to remain hidden, but rather the opposite.

I rose, disturbed, to take my leave, giving Adele a prescription for a mild sedative. 'Who are you?' asked the old man, this time without aggression.

'I am a doctor. I'm here to make you well again.'

'Impossible,' he shouted. Then, calm once again, he turned to his wife: 'Is he here with my death certificate?'

I fled from the room, from that ruined life. Adele came with me, closed the door behind her, and suddenly in the darkened hallway burst into stifled sobs.

'Rescue me, rescue me, I beg you. I've always been fond of you. It's so difficult to find someone you can trust, someone to confide in. Men always die on you. Won't you help me?' She leaned on my shoulders and kissed my cheeks. She was wearing perfume. Even her dress, red with white flowers, gave out a faint, girlish scent. 'I've nobody left, all my relations are dead. Illness is a terrible thing; all the evil, all the spite comes out. Save me!'

I promised her that the very next day I would make arrangements for her husband to be admitted to a psychiatric ward. 'There's no remission from his illness, at least from what we know today.' The old man's brain was obviously riddled with disease.

'I'm afraid that he'll attack me in the night. I've found him twice with a knife hidden under the pillow. Can I call you if he gets worse during the night?' I promised her that

I would certainly come if it was necessary, she only had to telephone. 'He doesn't seem dangerous to me. He hasn't reached that stage. Try to do as he says,' I suggested to her. I pulled myself from her embrace and ran off.

That night I didn't shut my eyes. I kept thinking of Adele Polak and her husband. I fell asleep with the image of them in the prime of life, not yet grown old and driven insane by illness. How had such a change in fortunes come about? With their business as second-hand dealers they had amassed great wealth. I lay thinking, half-awake and half-asleep, of all the old people, helpless and half-mad as they were now, that they must have swindled out of furniture, clothes, shoes, the last tokens of their existence, in exchange for next to nothing. That was when they hadn't actually been paid for clearing a house of all its junk, leaving it as empty as a shell. Now it was their turn. But perhaps Adele Polak had not been quite as cruel as her husband, I thought. I was reluctant to accept the idea that the woman of my youth was capable of taking part in such exploitation. Sinking into sleep I saw her again in her shorts. She was in the courtyard, crying in heart-rending sobs.

I awoke with a start and without thinking began to dress. It was two in the morning. I was terrified by the thought of finding her already dead. I ran to the corner of Strand Road and rang for the concierge. I had been called by the Polaks, I stammered. Taking the old elevator, I

caught a glimpse of the concierge's vacant look as I closed
the door. As I arrived at the fifth floor I saw a door
opening slowly. Mrs Polak was waiting for me.

'Thank you, thank you, I was sure you'd come. It is
really kind of you. I was so frightened. He's had a terrible
attack. He's sleeping now. I don't know what I'd have
done without you.'

She showed me into the kitchen, switched on the light,
put the cafetière on the stove and switched the light out
again, leaving only the gas flame to illuminate the room.
'This way they won't see us through the curtains. They
could see our shadows.' She stayed by the stove, but
turned towards me. 'When you were a boy you really
loved me and wanted me. But I knew you'd soon forget
me, and that's why I didn't return your feelings. You
could have had me easily you know. Now you've become
a man, your greying hair makes you even more attractive.
I love you. You see the clock of our lives has always run
fast or slow, but never kept time for us. And now here we
are, brought together by suffering.'

What did she know of me, of my feelings, of time, and
of its measure? 'I don't know what you mean, Mrs Polak.
I only came to . . . '

'Don't say anything! That's a lot of lies.' She sat down
next to me, on the same seat, and took my hands. 'We can
still live together, we can try. I know you still want me. It
wouldn't be the first time in history. I've always thought

of you, all these years. Time isn't really like I said it was just now . . . fast or slow, it doesn't matter. We have to find each other.'

There was something provocative in her look, in her expression. I thought then that the agent of whatever illness had destroyed her husband's mind might also exist in her. I promised her that I would think about what she had said and that to be on the safe side I would call the ambulance in the morning to take Mr Polak away. She calmed down, moved away from me and poured the coffee made with yesterday's grounds. I recalled the neighbourhood gossip that her husband had accumulated a considerable fortune thanks as much to his legendary meanness as to his professional abilities.

'We could be happy. Think about it. Everything I have will be yours. We'll go and live in another part of town where nobody knows us. Please . . . please.' She kissed me on the lips. I was aware of her warmth and her perfume, and something so lewd that I drew back in alarm. I made my excuses, saying that I had another call to make.

'I know that isn't true. But go anyway. Think of it till tomorrow, I beg you. Look at me. Promise you'll come back. I'll make you come back anyhow, like I made you come tonight.'

Was I simply acting according to her plan? I became angry. But Adele's eyes filled with tears, and at the same time she smiled a bitter smile, her lips creased, the smile of

53

a passionate, disillusioned woman. She kissed my hands, and I caressed the back of her neck. I felt sorry for her. She opened the door without another word. The concierge asked after Mr Polak and I told him all was well.

Two days later I learned from a patient that Adam Polak and his wife had died that night, suffocated by gas. A neighbour, alerted by the smell, had smashed the glass in the door and discovered their two bodies locked in an embrace. For many nights I dreamed of those two unhappy people, the petrified face of old Adam Polak and the cheerful expression, the sensual mouth, the pretty hands of his wife. I was seized by an overwhelming longing for her: for her bitter-sweet voice, for her hands as they caressed me that night, for the scent of her dyed hair, for her silk dress. My desire tormented me no less than my remorse. What had happened to the molecules of my body? Had my olfactory receptors and my centres of vision undergone some structural change that they were now reliving the stimuli they had first perceived thirty years ago, rather than those of the present? Had my entire central nervous system turned itself upside-down? Or does the clock of life run in such a way that defies understanding? I knew I could easily have accepted the love that poor Adele Polak proffered that night, and in doing so would either have confirmed or corrected a fault in the mechanism. But perhaps the mechanism is capable of producing only errors, and these have been perpetuated in the combining and recombining of acids since the formation of the first living molecule. Life itself might be due to such an error.

Faced with those two deaths, faced with total uncertainty about the meaning of it all, I found no better resort than that most ancient expression of desolation: drunkenness. Naturally after a short time I had to give up my job; I began to steal, I ended up in prison a few times, and in the asylum. Now I'm an alcoholic.

You can meet me in the market where you'll find me sweeping up the dirt, moving boxes and wooden cases around. I often talk to myself. I often hear whispering behind my back: 'He used to be a doctor, well-bred, a man of culture. Ending up like this. What a shame!' Every evening as I throw myself down on my bed of cardboard boxes I think of my love and of the injustice of it all. It hurts terribly. I hope it will end soon.

(This was Dr Spitzer's last letter. Don't ask what happened before or after, if you don't want the 'before' and 'after' to collide in your head.)

K. Spitzer, *The Operon Circuit in the Control of Gene Action*, Colorado, 1970

J. Monod and F. Jacob, 'Teleonomic Mechanisms in Cellular Metabolism', *Cold Spring Harbour Symposia*, 1961

VERA

Schekkinah is what our holy sages call that part of God's being in which the light has grown weak in order to allow the angels and the souls to exist.

J. d. P.

And for that reason Schekkinah would sooner permit invading demons to injure her with sharp spears than obstruct man's everlasting happiness.

The Book of Splendours

I'll never forget the case I came across recently in a little country in Central Europe where I was stationed from the first days of the armistice. My duty was to organize aid to the starving population of one of the tiny states in the area, in Hungary, and I was sent from Berlin with a cargo of food, medicine, blankets and toothbrushes.

The aid parcels were distributed in old cinemas, ruined school halls and bombed theatres to silent crowds of evil-smelling people who tore them from our hands. One day about a month ago, from the stage of an old theatre, I spotted a woman coming towards us. She was not alone . . .

They came towards the doctor slowly, the woman holding the child from behind. With each step the woman took, the child's legs moved like a marionette's. She walked as if pushed along by the belly of her older companion who was holding her under the arms. A blue

59

handkerchief covered her hair, emphasizing the perfect regularity of her features and the innocence of her expression. The woman standing behind her had olive skin and large eyes set in deep sockets; she looked like a model for what the child would become three decades later.

'How old is the little one?' asked the doctor, as the exaggeratedly swaying steps came to a stop in front of him. He placed his hand gently on the sick child's neck.

The woman did not reply. A smile broke out between her large, irregular teeth.

'Six or seven, I suppose,' the doctor continued, smiling back. The child nuzzled him in the stomach, rubbing her nose in his coat. He moved away without appearing to be shocked.

'Dear child, you mustn't do that,' he murmured, his smile widening.

'The child is sixteen years old,' her mother said suddenly, more as if she wanted to clarify matters than to contradict him.

Doctor Friedmann took a step back. 'Good God,' he thought, 'sixteen! That's impossible. The woman's mad. The child's obviously not a dwarf. Still there's no way she can be sixteen and look like that. But what if the mother—it must be her mother—what if she isn't mad? How could she joke about something so serious? How could a mother's heart be so indifferent? But the child is clearly having great difficulty in walking. Perhaps she's suffered the scourge of polio?'

All of this happened a long time ago, when the planet was still plagued by awful diseases, by now all but eradicated.

'Would you let her go for a minute?' said the doctor, and the woman, after a moment's hesitation, removed her arms encircling the child's chest. But she didn't move far away, standing ready to catch her if she fell. The tiny body began to sway, but the head remained straight and erect. And at that moment the child's eyes, which until then had been firmly closed, flew open wide. She stared at the doctor with a look completely devoid of intention and significance, irresistible in its neutrality. The man felt himself being sucked into her gaze. Again he took a step backwards.

'What lies behind those eyes?' he wondered, lowering his head, unable to withstand the force of a stare which drew everything towards a single point—the centre of her consciousness—where nothing seemed to exist.

'She has had three operations on her brain. She was treated by Professor Olivecrona in Sweden. That's where our inheritance went—the rest was taken by the war. My husband, my parents, my brothers and sisters, they're all dead. There are only the two of us left alive.'

The woman said all of this quietly but without reticence. A long silence followed. The child closed her eyes and the doctor, sensing the force of her stare fade, worked up the courage to look at her again.

The blue handkerchief hinted at a beautifully shaped head, fine and gracefully rounded. Her face, devoid of sharp angles and tinged with pink around the cheek bones, seemed perfectly complete in itself. Her small straight nose, her soft pink lips, fleshy without being aggressive and with a soft but precise outline, could not have been other than they were.

'I've never seen anything more beautiful,' thought the doctor. Looking at this small creature, the picture of innocence, he was deeply moved. She was wearing a red dress with white flowers, and little red canvas shoes. Her breathing was but the slightest murmur, gentle and perfumed, and so unobtrusive that it excited admiration rather than pity.

'What's your name?' the doctor asked, almost whispering so as not to break the spell.

The child neither moved nor opened her eyes.

'Her name is Vera,' her mother answered for her. 'She hasn't spoken a single word for three years.'

Vera. The name sounded so false, so deliberate, that the doctor began to doubt the whole thing.

'Is she really as old as you said before?' The woman nodded her head in confirmation, her eyes fixed on the doctor. A succession of differing expressions passed rapidly across her face, in complete contrast to her daughter's. The doctor took note of the relatively young appearance of the mother. He guessed she was about thirty-five. Her slim, supple body showed off its well formed curves under a light and elegant dress of shiny green silk.

'What can they possibly want from us?' the doctor asked himself again. 'They are not reduced to misery, like these others. The war seems barely to have touched them. Perhaps they've simply come for the aid packages.'

Looking up, he saw the ragged crowd, the inhabitants of that ruined district who had survived the slaughter of war. They stood there in the empty stalls of a theatre whose stage was piled up with parcels from all over the world. The theatre seats had probably ended up as fuel in the neighbours' stoves. The end-of-May sun filtered through the wide open doors.

'Does she have the medicines she needs? Might I be able to help find them?' the doctor asked.

'I don't need medicine. The child is perfectly healthy. We came for the aid parcels. What is in them?'

The man signalled to two soldiers who were wearing white silk armbands bearing the symbol of the red cross. The soldiers took from the pile two small parcels made of rough packing cardboard. They gave them to the woman.

'There. Have a look for yourself,' the doctor murmured, not lifting his gaze from two of the strangest

individuals he had ever met. The woman opened one of
the packs, glanced indifferently at the contents and said:
'Wonderful. I'm sure it will all be very good.'

She put the parcels in a string bag she carried on her
arm.

'For all eventualities, since your case is so out of the
ordinary, would you like to leave us your address?
Perhaps later we might be able to be of some help to
you.'

'My address?' The woman looked blank for a moment
as she repeated the word. Finally she whispered: 'Grand
Transport Street, number 24.'

The doctor took down the address in the margin of the
list of names he was holding. Then the woman and the
child did an about-turn pivoting on the little girl's left leg.
Darkness and the silent crowd of starving people soon hid
the two figures from the doctor's sight.

That night Friedmann could get no peace. He tossed
and turned from side to side, prey to an inexplicable
anxiety. Sudden wild racings of his heart alternated with
long bouts of feeling faint. Around five in the morning
the doctor finally fell asleep, exhausted, lying flat on his
back.

The next day he didn't go to the Communal Theatre.
He brushed his uniform, took his doctor's bag and set out
to look for Grand Transport Street.

He had difficulty finding it, despite the accuracy of the

map headquarters had supplied. Many of the houses had been destroyed and in some places the street signs—small white painted metal plates bearing the names of the streets in black—were missing. Majestic buildings stood exposed, disintegrating quietly.

Doctor Friedmann looked up with a start. One storey up, from the mullioned window of a neo-Gothic apartment building, the child's mother was waving at him, beckoning him up.

He skirted around what looked like a bomb crater, crossed the road and went into the greenish-stuccoed five-storey building.

He found himself in a long low passage. A gold-lacquered plaster statue of a boy admiring himself in the mirror graced the stairwell. At the top of the first flight he came face to face with the woman, who was smiling behind her deep-set eyes.

'It was quite by chance I saw you,' she said, waiting on the stairs. 'I rarely look out of the window.'

'I was lucky,' replied the doctor.

'Lucky?'

'Yes. I really wanted to see you. In any case I had your address.'

How had he let such a compromising admission slip out? The doctor was shocked to find himself standing there like a beggar, no longer the just father handing out rewards and punishments, cures and illnesses, even death itself.

'I thought you were just passing; I wanted you to have a look at the child. She has a bit of a cough. I'm the one who is in luck: it's so hard to find a doctor these days, and I would have had to take the child with me. You know how difficult it is. The telephone lines are still not working.'

But in spite of what she had just said the woman did not move from her position, as if to prevent the doctor coming any further up the stairs.

'I have to confess that I came here with the sole purpose of seeing you. It was no accident that you saw me from your window.' As he was saying this, Friedmann was aware that he was obeying a strange uncontrollable impulse.

A faint, hoarse cry sounded unmistakably from the landing: 'Mama, ma-ma.' The child was wearing a pink cotton dress and a pale red headscarf decorated with white butterflies. The doctor leaned back against the wall.

'Good God, the child can talk!'

'She says one word every five or six days. Always the same: mama. She doesn't know any others. She might not even know that I am her mother, that I gave birth to her. Perhaps she just repeats the sound because it corresponds to something she's heard, maybe from me,' the woman muttered, half to herself. 'Come on, let's not leave her alone. She might fall over. Every so often she has a fit.'

'Epilepsy?'

'Yes. She just collapses without any warning, and hurts herself. One of her teeth is loose. The next time she might knock it out.'

'Don't let her fall,' yelled the doctor. 'Don't leave her for an instant.'

Inside the house everything was immaculate, as if the war had passed the rooms by. The walls, decorated with great purple flowers outlined in gold on a silver background, were perfectly intact. The living room was filled with elegant bentwood furniture. Glass-fronted cabinets displayed porcelain figurines. The woman sat the child down in an armchair upholstered in red velvet and indicated a sofa to the doctor.

'We would rather have suffered the cold of winter than sell a single stool, a single chair. My father collected examples of Viennese furniture. My family were all very sensitive, they loved Vera so much. Do you remember, little one, how grandmother would take your hand and sing to you? You know, don't you, that grandmother is gone?'

The child's mouth and eyes took on a hardly perceptible expression, the merest hint of a smile.

'You see how she smiles?' said her mother. 'If you can see that, it means you understand her, you understand people, life. If you can't . . . '

The man looked hard at the child and he imagined he

could see what the woman was describing.

'I knew immediately that you were a good person, gentle and caring. I noticed from the start your concern for the child. That's why I called you here.'

'You called me here?'

'Yes, with my thoughts.' As she was saying this the woman sat down next to the doctor. 'It always works like this!'

I've fallen into the clutches of a madwoman, he thought.

He felt something brush against the back of his hand, light and somewhat irritating, like the legs of an insect. The instant he pulled back his arm he became aware of Vera's tiny form standing in front of him, her arm stretched out towards him as if to stroke him. But he knew almost immediately that he must have imagined this, since all he could actually see was the brusque withdrawal of his own arm, an absurd twitch, and the effect his violent movement had on the child. All of a sudden her expression changed to one of blank, ashen-faced stupor; he caught a flash of white teeth between her lips before her small body crowned with white butterflies fell to the floor with a dull thud.

'Good God, her tooth!' Seizing the child by the wrist and supporting the nape of her neck with her other hand, the mother began to wail. The child's body was stretched rigid, jerking and twitching to the electric impulses of the epileptic convulsions.

'Help me, please. We must carry her over there. Please.'

The doctor leaped to his feet, pressed the child's hand in his own, and held it till the convulsions became less violent and finally stopped altogether. Then stroking Vera's smooth round face he began to murmur words of tenderness, the most tender words he could find in himself to say. He hadn't spoken like that for decades. He picked the child up, one arm behind her knees, the other supporting her shoulders and waited for her mother to show him where to take her.

They came into a darkened room where a huge white bed blotted out nearly all of his field of vision. Beyond, a door opened into another room lit by the reddish light of an oil lamp.

'Come in,' said the woman, returning with the lamp and lighting the way to the smaller room. Once inside, Friedmann noticed that it was filled with dolls and toys of every sort. 'Be careful you don't trip up.' The woman's voice was still thick with tears. He felt paralysed with trepidation.

He walked towards that tabernacle carrying the child's body with all the respect due to the Scrolls of the Law. He remembered carrying his own son like that after he had twisted his ankle on a trip—how time had flown by!—through the Rocky Mountains.

The seven-year-old boy, jumping down on to the path, had dared to defy nature and the limits of his own body. Now, at twenty-five, he could boast a real talent for mathematics, for music, and his marks in theology were evidence of a rare depth of intellect.

'Put her down here, gently. Gently, I beg you.' The woman was nearly invisible in her dark blue dress. She smoothed the pillow and waited for the doctor to lay the tiny body down in the white child's cot. She began to take off the child's clothes and the man instinctively turned to withdraw to the adjoining room.

'Don't go . . . ' said the woman, drawing one corner of her mouth into a half-smile. Vera's snow-white skin was revealed, her breasts half the size of a fist, the swelling of her belly, her sparse covering of pubic hair, her straight, tapering legs.

'Have you ever seen such a perfect body? Who knows who she takes it from. Not from me, as you yourself can see.'

The mother smiled again and with great difficulty helped the child into her nightdress. The next moment Vera fell back on to the pillow and closed her eyes as if she wanted to sleep.

He was suddenly aware of a strong perfume which seemed to emanate from the mother and the child. 'Rêve d'Or,' he thought, 'I'd know it anywhere. The girls at school used to wear it.'

'It's always like that,' said the mother. 'She reacts to any strong external stimulus by having a fit. It is probably not your fault, Doctor, that she fell over just now. I don't think you had anything to do with it. You just gave her a little push and the child reacted badly to it.'

'How can I make amends? I was too brusque with her. One has to be so careful in a case like this.'

'Don't blame yourself. I'd rather you gave me a hand.' The woman's face tightened. 'I'm going to open her mouth. You will see her broken tooth. Help me pull it out.'

He started. 'No, please. Let's wait till tomorrow and find a dentist.'

'Out of the question. Can't you see it's bleeding?'

A thin trickle of blood oozed from the left corner of Vera's mouth.

'Come,' she said, in a tone which brooked no argument. 'You hold her arms and legs and I'll pull out the tooth.'

He did as he was told, powerless to resist. He approached the bed and held the child down, using his hands and the weight of his body. The woman took hold of the scarf which covered Vera's head and with a sharp tug pulled it away. Her small head, like a new-born child's crowned with a few very fine hairs, brought home to the doctor the fragility of her condition.

'Her hair has stopped growing. Three years ago we had

a wig made for her, but I haven't made her wear it for a few months. What's the point? Now hold tight . . . '

The mother parted Vera's bloody lips with her finger and took hold of the broken incisor which hung wretchedly from her gum. She wound one corner of the scarf around it. A hoarse cry emerged from the girl's throat. The mother yanked hard on the free corner of the scarf and pulled out the tooth.

The next moment she was sitting on the sofa, sobbing miserably. 'Why, why does it have to be like this? What will become of the poor child?'

The man was filled with a terrible sense of despair. He let the child go, wiped the blood from her mouth and turned to her mother. He sat down beside her and put his arm around her shoulders.

'You have to hope for the best,' he murmured, kissing her tear-stained cheeks. 'Hope for the best.' The woman pressed against him.

That night Abraham Friedmann had a strange dream, from which he awoke with a start at four in the morning. He felt the need to get in touch immediately with the woman he had dreamed about. He dressed in haste and went out into the street, convinced that the dream had revealed to him the future course of his existence. He felt unusually happy and surprised himself by skipping through the moonlit ruins. But he could also see the first grey light of dawn.

The people he met on the way depressed him. Tramps and vagrants stretched out on the ground, immersed in an unjust sleep; some old man raving; the elderly prostitutes clicking their heels as they walked up and down with their net bags in their hands; all gave him the impression that nothing had changed with the new day.

'I was coming to see you,' murmured the woman, appearing out of nowhere just two steps away from him.

'What are you doing here?' Friedmann asked, almost breathless with shock.

'I was coming to see you. I couldn't stand the idea of not seeing you for so long.'

'And what about the child, did you leave her alone?'

'Yes, I tucked her in so she can't get out of bed.'

The doctor's good mood changed to one of panic. 'You can't do that—it's dangerous! Have you ever done it before?'

'No, this is the first time. But I just couldn't bear the idea of you being so far away. They might transfer you tomorrow to another city and then what would become of us?'

The doctor didn't dare ask who she meant by 'us', whether it was her and him or her and the child. He took her arm and they set off in a hurry for Grand Transport Street.

'Who knows where this might lead?' he thought. 'It's a dangerous business, getting involved with a woman. After the first time they want your soul. I don't even know whether I should tell her about my dream.' But he hadn't gone five hundred yards with her along the way before he was seized by an irresistible impulse to tell her everything. Against his better judgement, and becoming more breathless by the second, he began to recount his dream.

The woman might not have been listening. She opened the heavy outer door, left unlocked so that the concierge wouldn't hear them come in, or perhaps so that she wouldn't be obliged to wake him by ringing the bell. Under the golden statue she embraced the doctor.

From that day on, Doctor Friedmann went to the house on Grand Transport Street every afternoon. The two hours that he spent there became the most important part of his day: more important than work, more important than attending his clinic, more important even than keeping in touch with his family. This is how the letter from his wife sent to his address at headquarters lay unread for four days. In it was the news that his elderly mother, already dangerously ill with coronary ischaemia, had worsened noticeably. The tersely-worded note from his colleague who was looking after the old lady left little room for hope, and anyone reading the letter would have set out immediately to be at her side. But on hearing the news Doctor Friedmann found himself facing a terrible dilemma.

'What shall I do with that poor child?' he asked himself, his hands pressed to his temples and his elbows on his knees. This was the thought in his mind that he was able to give voice to; the precarious state of his mother's health he felt only as a great emptiness in the cavities of his body. For two hours he stayed like this, immobilized. Then he got up, took the medicines he had smuggled out of the store cupboard and headed for Vera's house.

He felt that he was saying goodbye for ever to something that for the whole of his life had protected him from the inevitable knocks of fate and the facts of existence. From that minute on it would be a struggle to make it alive from one day to the next.

With every step he was coming closer to committing some offence he couldn't yet define precisely. But he was already aware of its awfulness and the corresponding demand for punishment. He was ashamed to be alive.

On the way to Grand Transport Street he stopped at the post office and sent two telegrams, one to his brother's address and one to his own, for his wife. Then he almost ran to the green house. Vera's mother opened the door the instant he arrived: she had obviously been waiting for him, peering out from behind the curtains.

'At last you've arrived,' said the woman, pressing her body close to his.

It was only after doing what they had done every afternoon for over two months with all the precision of a ritual that Friedmann had the courage to tell her he was leaving.

'I understand,' she sighed. She was in the habit of talking to herself in a whisper, so that now whenever she lowered her voice she seemed to be talking to herself. 'I understand perfectly.' There followed a long silence punctuated by the gentle breathing of the child.

'She's much better. She's getting up on her own. She's walking about. You just have to watch that she doesn't bump into the furniture. She is getting over her fits. I can't imagine life without her, it wouldn't make sense. Look, I have her medicine ready. If I should ever fall ill and no longer be capable of looking after her . . . You know I wash her twice a day, from head to feet. Sometimes I have to wash myself afterwards. Her dirt, her diarrhoea even gets into my hair, the poor thing.'

'Why are you telling me all this?' he said, trying to sound cutting.

'I don't know. But I believe she still has all the words in her head. Thoughts we can't even guess at. One day I'll tell you everything. But now go. You have to leave.'

Friedmann took the packet of medicines out of his pocket; he wore the look of a thief caught in the act of stealing. But not because of the stolen medicines. He was robbing himself of two people. He turned to go.

A ridiculous wail rose into the air of that wretched morning, almost like the boo-hoo-hoo of a mechanical doll. Vera's mother stood there in front of him in her nightdress, overwhelmed by despair.

'She's faking it,' thought Friedmann, 'there's not a tear in her eyes. And if she's not faking it, then so much the worse, for that means her emotions are ice-cold.'

'Boo-hoo-hoo,' came the cry from the mechanical doll, 'who will think of us?'

'What a difficult situation,' the doctor reflected, 'just my luck to have to make such a weighty choice. But I have to go. I can't leave my mother to die alone. I have to go.'

He thought it over at length; he even went as far as denying the priority of erotic over filial love. Finally he was able to wriggle out of the woman's embrace. Without so much as looking at Vera he turned and went. As he closed the door behind him he caught a glimpse of her little head raising itself from the pillow and he heard a quiet voice whisper his name.

Or was it just an illusion, a product of his guilty conscience?

'Choices, choices,' he repeated to himself as he walked along the streets, now full of people all of whom seemed to be celebrating something. 'Too many choices. I don't like it. There must be more to life than choices. It would be ridiculous otherwise. But it seems to be the rule.'

It was with a great sense of relief that, a couple of hours later, he was able to climb aboard the light aircraft that in various stages would take him back home. During the trip he jotted down some of his thoughts in a diary: 'Every evening, from the age of five, I have prayed that I would die together with all those I love and all those who love me. Now I have to watch my mother . . . But why should I complain? Perhaps it is better to live the torment of a life without laws than to die in a split second, with a split second of terrible pain. I suppose it must be like the pain of giving birth: one's whole life force gathers its strength in the belly, and then lungs and blood and muscles and bones all work together to expel the new individual. Except that in death one is expelling life itself from the body. A split second . . . it would be better.'

His mind would not leave this slow procession of thought for the length of the journey. He felt strangely guilty about living on if his mother died; he couldn't even imagine her dead. He didn't notice the sunset. The day's torture forced him to think and to reflect.

Arriving at his destination he found his mother unexpectedly well. 'You're the reason they let me stay,' she said openly with a smile. 'If you go, I'll go too, for ever.' She seemed a little shy, as if she felt her illness was somehow her fault, and she spoke to her eldest son with an affection that she'd never before thought appropriate.

His wife and son came to meet them at the hospital. 'What am I to say to them?' he asked himself, and then stayed silent, pretending to be overcome with emotion.

'Tomorrow I have to go away for about three days,' said his wife. 'A trip down south, to a conference organized by the association. I'm taking the boy with me. I'm sorry—it's not much of a way to celebrate your return.'

Friedmann felt hugely relieved. 'That's all right. I'll stay here in hospital to be near Mother,' he said. He was very fond of his wife and especially of his son. The boy felt an almost protective, even paternal, affection for his father. In response to the doctor's often eccentric monologues on medicine or on life he would reply: 'Yet another of your brilliant ideas!' And then, clapping his father on the back: 'Dad, Dad, you'll never change.' But you could hear the pleasure in his voice as he said it: it amused him that his father—or rather, his little boy—was the way he was.

Friedmann's wife on the other hand, beautiful, refined and at the same time sensitive, simply couldn't get used to her husband's way of looking at life. She couldn't get used to his curiosity—travelling round the world in search of some strain of bacillus whose identity he kept a secret—nor to his fervidly disorganized mind. 'One day it will all come to a halt,' was Friedmann's usual riposte. Now he wasn't so sure any more.

'There's a telegram here for you,' said his wife. 'I read it only because I didn't know when you'd be arriving. Is it something serious?'

The telegram was from Vera's mother, asking him to return immediately. The child was in danger, and only he knew enough about the case to save her.

He had that same feeling of emptiness that he had when he heard the news about his mother: a terrible, aching loss, unmitigated by any loss of consciousness. 'The child must not die,' he thought. 'The world would not be the same without her.'

His wife asked him what it was about.

'Oh, a unique case I came across quite by chance. Absolutely unique.'

'Dad, Dad,' his son interrupted, this time giving him a pat on the cheek. 'Not that again! We both know there's no such thing as by chance, at least not from one particular point of view. Why do you think I studied theology, Dad?'

His wife asked him not to pay any attention to the request. Doctors were exposed to far too much psychological pressure of that kind. He really couldn't afford to get involved. And anyway it was too late now, really much too late. The doctor promised not to give in. His wife and son left the next day and he went to his mother's house.

It had been years since they had slept under the same roof, and this, together with his resolve not to go back to Vera, made him feel young again. He spent the evening sitting beside his mother's bed looking at her kind face and listening to her soft voice. Together they spoke of happy memories, of the trials and certain successes of life and of his career.

But during the night the thought of Vera and her mother would not leave him. He couldn't sleep: the more he tried to picture all the earth's suffering multitudes and remind himself that death was a natural condition, the more those two feeble beings returned to his mind and to his senses.

Two days later another telegram arrived with a message even more desperate than the last. He talked it over with his mother.

'Yes, go, if that's what your conscience tells you to do,' she said. 'I won't hold you back. Don't worry about me. You have your work, your science, to think about.'

Friedmann's blood froze as he listened. His mother was so ill that he didn't feel able to discuss things completely candidly with her. Science had also taught him this: it's not always best to tell the truth. The whole business seemed much too complicated to explain.

'Why should I worry her with my emotional problems? She has already suffered enough. No, I'll spare her this final pain.'

On the fourth day he took her to dinner in a restaurant and they talked long and openly about the years of emigration, the suffering, the struggle for survival, the mishaps at school, the birth of his son. They recalled the funny events of his son's childhood with tears and laughter. They went to their beds in peace, as if the past had somehow served to plug the holes in the present.

At two in the morning the telephone rang. It was Vera's mother. 'I arrived three hours ago. I need to talk to you immediately.'

Before agreeing, Friedmann tried to weigh up everything that would happen and everything he needed to avoid and how to avoid anything which would compromise his relative equilibrium. Words, gestures, shouts, cries and every conceivable form of lie passed through his mind. He agreed.

Noiselessly he locked the door to his mother's bedroom. When Vera's mother arrived at the house, she found the gate, the outer door, the porch door and the door of the house all slightly ajar. Friedmann was relying on the intelligence of his persecutor. When he saw her in the doorway he took her arm and led her to the bedroom.

Before he had time to turn out the light she put her arms around his neck and whispered: 'Another minute without you and I'd have died.'

His mother having by now made as good a recovery as she was likely to, Doctor Friedmann was asked by the Ministry to return to Europe to continue his work there, since he was the only specialist they had in the field. In the meantime his wife and son had returned from the conference trip. On the morning of his departure, his son was particularly affectionate towards him and kissed him repeatedly on the cheeks as he was leaving. The doctor's mother was dressed up in her most elegant red dress with a pattern of black flowers; the hairdresser had come to the house at dawn to put her hair up.

'I'll be waiting for you, my sweet. I'll wait here and I won't go till you get back. You'll spend many more beautiful nights like these past few, while your mother sleeps on the other side of the door.'

His mother's declaration of complicity alarmed him deeply. 'My secret's out,' he thought. 'From now on anything could happen. But at least it shows that she really does know everything, and it means that there's someone I can be honest with.'

He decided to write to his mother every day and keep her up to date with everything that happened to him, the good and the bad. In that way his story would come out into the open; in a confused sort of way Doctor Friedmann was beginning to convince himself that his experiences were wholly exceptional, and that it was imperative they were documented.

They travelled separately, as they had arranged. Vera's mother departed one day before the famous scientist. On his arrival on 21 June, Friedmann reported to his superiors. The formalities completed, he was able, with the somewhat dubious consent of his general, to return to his previous lodgings in Acacia Avenue in the house of a widow who had lost her two sons in the war, and who treated him as if he were one of her sons brought back to life.

The first week passed without any news from Vera's mother. He resolved to put an end to their relationship and, if at all, to concern himself in the future with the child and only with her. He was aware, however, that circumstances cannot be changed quite that easily, neither for better nor for worse, and so he vowed that he would not descend voluntarily into that nest of vipers unless he received a specific request to visit the child.

He heard nothing from the woman. He continued collecting his statistics on diabetes. He wandered around the ruined neighbourhood, visited the sick for four hours every day, took notes, catalogued the cases worthy of most interest. And he wrote long letters to his mother in which he revealed the remotest thoughts of his waking hours as well as the labyrinths of his nocturnal visions. Every now and again his mother would reply with expressions—usually fairly conventional ones—of love and concern.

On his sixth day back in that strange and yet familiar country he was summoned to see the general.

'It has come to my attention that you are neglecting a case of the greatest interest for the treatment of neoplasia of the central nervous system. What sort of scientist are

you? We know, among other things, that this case has
been drawn to your attention on a number of occasions,
to no effect. This is not any old mission: it's a scientific
expedition, not a pleasure trip. I don't want to hear your
excuses. Just get to work!'

An hour later the woman was in the arms of her lover.

'I have to go and meet my poor husband's stepmother,'
she said, getting up and dressing hurriedly. 'She was so
good to me, the poor thing, and to him. Now she's all
alone in her bombed-out house. She has nobody in the
world. Will you stay here with the child? I'll never ask
you again, I swear it. I'll be back in an hour. Please, do
me this favour. I don't like leaving Vera with the
neighbours, like I did when I came to see you. I'm afraid
they'll mistreat her. I have this terrible suspicion. And
she, poor thing, can't speak, can't do anything. Will you
forgive me for asking you this one favour?'

Friedmann was happy. For some time he had wanted
to be alone with this creature who was such a mystery to
him. But at the same time the man became aware of a
vague sense of ill-boding which seemed to emanate from
some deep and unknown part of his being, like the failure
of some vital organ that was slowly spreading into all of
his limbs.

'If I agree to do what this woman is asking I'll be stuck
in this house for ever. I can feel it. But it was only to be
with Vera that I've put up with all of this. I have given

everything and everyone for this one opportunity. And now I am frightened and I'm trying to back off. It's grotesque.'

'It's no use,' she moaned through her tears. 'I can't let that dear old lady die of hunger. I'll take Vera to the neighbours. Or I'll take her with me, on my back.'

'Please don't. Leave her here. I'll wait till you get back. But hurry. Go to your mother-in-law.'

Vera's mother made herself up, dabbed herself with what was left of a bottle of perfume and left. As the door closed the doctor knew for certain that a part of his existence had finished for ever. He didn't know what would become of him from now on.

His heart beat loudly as he headed for Vera's room; he felt slightly ill, the way he used to at school when there was to be a test that day.

The child had been placed upright on a cushion just the other side of the door. As Friedmann entered he was harpooned by Vera's look. He struggled with himself for a moment, turned to go, then changed his mind. With one hand he wiped a drop of sweat from his brow, and with the other shielded his breast, as if to ward off a stabbing pain in his heart. Finally he calmed down enough to return the child's stare.

Her smooth, round face, her lips only slightly parted, her forehead, narrow, but high and even, her small perfect nose, all combined to the same effect, emphasizing her look of terrible mildness.

He sat down next to the child. The way he was acting, the clothes he was wearing, even the thoughts in his head seemed completely fake in the judgement of that purposeless stare. He felt a sense of shame, and wished that he too could be like that: exactly what he was, and nothing more.

'Little darling,' he said quietly. Something about the child filled him with a feeling of tenderness and respect such as he had never felt for anyone before.

A thread of saliva ran over the child's lower lip and dangled, extending little by little until it landed on her arm resting in her lap. Her legs were crossed and her hands held palms together in an attitude of absolute piety and gentleness.

'You have suffered so much, haven't you, little one?' the man asked, immediately aware of his own banality. But his impulses were now leading him from one ineptitude to another, almost as if he was trying to convince himself of his own worthlessness.

'My name is Abraham. Go on, try it. A-bra-ham.'

The child began to twist herself into unnatural poses which, if they didn't actually cause her pain, must certainly have been exhausting. Her head, almost completely hairless, followed the contortions of her body. Her eyes were almost closed, with just a tiny slit showing, enough to detect her constant stare, both present and absent at the same time.

'Come on, little one. Call your mummy, just like you did that morning on the landing. Call her, please. Ma-ma. Ma-ma.' The child stopped twisting and turned once again to face Doctor Friedmann. He was moved by the light of her expression.

'What can I do for you, little one? Do you want something? Is there something you'd like? Tell me what you want.' The child stared into a corner of the room.

'Who knows what thoughts are swarming in that little head of hers?' the doctor thought. 'Who can guess what she might have seen in that corner, or when? She's probably trying to evoke those memories now. Or maybe she really does see someone, someone we cannot see and will never be able to!'

'What was it you saw in that corner?'

Vera's features contorted into an expression that might be described as one of anger or of pain and remained fixed like that for what seemed like a long time.

'Is something wrong? What is it? Come on, tell me, please.'

The child didn't move. Another rivulet rolled off her lip, stretched in the air and dribbled on to her dress.

'I'm sure you know all the words to speak but don't want to use them. Why not? Go on, have a try. You're doing it to exasperate me, aren't you? You understand every word, but you're refusing to communicate with

VERA

anyone because of the way they hurt you. Your mummy
told me about your screaming fits, every night, for
months and months after the first operation. You shouted
at your father, your mother, your grandparents. And now
you're getting your own back, right? Go on, say
something. You're getting your revenge on the world for
betraying you, aren't you?'

Speaking these words—which he later scrupulously
noted down (or had they been altered by his memory?)—
Doctor Friedmann gave way to the temptation to
attribute ever widening significance to his interpretation
of the facts.

The child became rigid. Her face turned red, then a
darker colour, as if she were straining tremendously. Her
eyes filled with tears and her neck swelled and swelled.

'She's trying to say something,' Friedmann thought,
'but she can't get it out. Perhaps she's forgotten how to
speak. I must be patient.'

'My darling, my sweet, I love you, I love you more
than anyone else alive. I love you without conditions.
You're my heart, you're my angel, my soul, my
everything. My little baby, my little baby.'

The man shuddered to hear himself speaking like this,
so sincere and so false, to Vera. Tears filled his eyes, he
wanted to throw himself to the ground, prostrate himself
at the feet of that small, motionless figure. Suddenly he
felt her little hand touch his cheek and the gesture,

89

somewhat clumsy and uncontrolled, struck him as indescribably affectionate and sincere.

'My love, say something. Speak to me, my sweet, I beg you. Say Abraham, I implore you: Abraham.'

The child withdrew her hand and the expression of strain and tension disappeared, to be replaced by a look of disenchantment.

'Please, little one, I beg you with all my heart, in desperation, say something.'

Why did he want words? Why was he not content with the affection he had already been shown? Doctor Friedmann was unable to explain this to himself. It wasn't greed, nor was it poverty. It was something else.

His thoughts returned to the dream he'd had and he was filled with despair to see how obstinately reality refused to accord with it.

'I know you used to be able to read, write, play the piano. I know you used to dance beautifully. Where did it all go, tell me? And what are you now? What were you before you were born? What do you think of us, what do you see? How much life is left in you? Tell me about Rex, go on, tell me about your dog. Mummy told me everything. Rex, where are you? Bow, wow . . . Re-ex, Re-ex! Call Rex!'

Vera remained motionless and the expression on her lips reminded the doctor all of a sudden of the unfathomable misery of the hospital corridors: the excrement, the urine, the shame and the resignation of certain patients, and their tenacious hold on life, on illness and on death.

'Come on, little one, I won't torment you any more. Now I know you'll never speak again. But at least give me another little hug. Go on, give me another hug.'

The child did not move. She continued to look straight ahead, as if she were aware of her own smell, of her own filthiness, as if it disgusted her. But this pose made her appear even more graceful, arousing tenderness rather than pity.

'My love, my little darling, please give me another caress. I've been naughty to you. I won't do it again. Do you hear? Never again. Give me one more smile. Let me feel your gentle breath again, let me feel it deepen as you strain, or perhaps because you love me a little. Do like you did before.'

Vera shook her head, almost imperceptibly, as if to say: 'No, I don't want to.' Was it an illusion? Was it his state of excitement that made him think he saw the gesture? The man repeated his miserable request, he didn't hesitate to beg for Vera's affection. But the child didn't move.

'Why are you doing this? Are you trying to hurt me?'

With an effort that before would not have seemed possible, Vera began to pull herself upright; agonizingly slowly, pushing down on the arms of the chair, she managed to get to her feet. Her head and torso swayed wildly from side to side before she found her balance.

Then she began to walk towards her bed, one tiny step after another. The rays of the setting sun caught the outline of her figure and for a moment she appeared to be made of light. Vera's progress across the room was very slow. She pendulated from one leg to the other, looking as if she might fall at any minute to the right or to the left.

'Where are you going?' the doctor shouted. 'Stay here! You can't go hiding in your sleep! You're quite capable of sleeping all day and not saying a word to anyone. All you want is someone to dote on you, wait on you, feed and look after you, but you're not even prepared to give them a hug in return. I want to understand you! I want you! Do you hear? Do you hear?'

Vera reached her pitiful little bed with its satin-covered quilt the colour of gold. Gently she lowered herself down on to the edge of the bed. She was about to lay her head on the pillow when Friedmann took hold of her.

'No! You're not getting away that easily! I want to hear your voice! Can you cry?' The doctor took her by the shoulders and shook her hard. 'Let me hear your voice, now!'

The child's expression became even more vacant. A look of complete stupefaction flashed across her face, so breathtaking that for an instant the doctor's anger was stopped in its tracks. But the next moment his fury rose more violently.

'What is it? Are you surprised that I'm desperate? You don't think it might have been you who provoked me? You, you, you!' Friedmann began to rain slaps on her tender cheeks until they turned crimson. A muffled cry emerged from the child's throat.

'Louder! Louder! Let's hear what your voice sounds like!' The famous professor, the research scientist, was spotting the poor creature's face with blood. He wanted to hear her cry, louder and louder. He was aware of what he was doing, he knew how cowardly and how cruel he was being, and he knew that he was endangering Vera's life. The effort of holding himself back was making him sweat, but still he didn't stop until he saw blood mixed with saliva coming out of the child's mouth.

Vera was sobbing disconsolately, struggling to catch her breath.

'Darling, come here. Come here, and let's wash ourselves before mummy gets home. I won't do it again, I promise, I won't do it again. Come on little darling, come on my love.'

He tried to pull her towards the bathroom, but her body remained motionless. 'Come when I tell you!' the doctor shouted, tugging her roughly towards him.

And now the child's cries became louder and more desperate. 'Don't scream, they'll hear us!' he whispered, trying to cover her mouth with the palm of his hand. Finally he had to force his fist between her bloody lips.

He pulled a handkerchief from his pocket and wiped Vera's face, then sat her down on the sofa opposite him. When the child raised her eyes to meet his, Doctor Friedmann knew that judgement had been passed.

He took a sheet of paper and wrote a farewell note. Then he ran out of the apartment.

He arrived home bathed in sweat. Still out of breath, he stretched out on a couch and lay there pondering what he had discovered about himself that afternoon.

'I'll never feel at ease again. I'll never remove this stain of guilt, not even with my own blood. It's true: all I have to look forward to is a life of remorse, of atrocious suffering, infecting everyone around me with evil. Why did it all happen? How could I have acted the way I did? How could such cruelty have grown inside me? Or was it her, Vera? What is it within her that provokes such wickedness in an otherwise quiet soul? How could such an angelic looking creature evoke such injustice? It is her, it is her who's to blame!'

With this attempt to console himself, Friedmann dozed off, and as his conscience rushed headlong into sleep, it carried with it into the darkness the firm conviction that Vera was the cause of all his troubles.

At three in the morning he was woken by the telephone. 'I'm calling you now,' Vera's mother said, 'because in a few minutes' time I'll no longer be capable. So you want to leave me. You want to go. Well that's

fine. I've taken care of everything: the child and I are
fixed up for good. I'm so sleepy . . . I've taken some pills.
I've taken so many . . . Too bad, we loved you. We
loved you very much . . . '

Ten minutes later the doctor was once again in the dark
belly of the Eighth District. He groped for the gate, and
then found the door.

Vera's mother was stretched out on the quilt wearing a
white nightdress embroidered with threads of yellow silk
on the collar and bust. Her features looked relaxed in the
light of the lamp on the dresser. An empty bottle of
sleeping pills lay next to her hand, which was resting on
the quilt as if she were about to play a chord on the
piano. The whole posture of the body gave Friedmann
the impression of artificiality. He sat down on the edge of
the bed and listened to the mother's breathing. It was
regular and quite strong: there was no question of coma.
Then he thought he could see the woman peeping at him
through closed eyelids; lying the way she was, he found
the whole thing embarrassing. He went to examine the
child. Switching on the lamp above her bed, he couldn't
help sighing at the look of perfect calm on Vera's face:
He felt as if he were committing an act of sacrilege just
looking at her, and was surprised to find that he was still
alive. Life implied the onerous obligation to act. It
became even more onerous when every form of action
appeared to the doctor indecent and ridiculous in the face

of that dignified, absolute passivity.

He turned back to the child's mother. He had to slap her face repeatedly to bring her round. How often he had clasped that face, transfigured by passion, close to his chest! But what it was that moved her to such passion the doctor couldn't fathom. It certainly wasn't him; in his own opinion of himself, he was capable at most of evoking only pain or pity. Still she had chosen him to be the instrument of the emotions of her own body and soul. She had searched meticulously among the multitude of men for a compliant subject; and she had found him.

After two or three slaps on the cheek the woman came to. 'What are you doing here at this hour?' she asked the doctor who was appalled by the look of complete anguish on her face.

'What do you mean what am I doing?'

'Who let you into my house?'

'You did. I let myself in with the keys you gave me.'

'Keys? What keys?'

'You know well which keys I mean. Come on, get up, quickly, I'm taking you to hospital.'

'But I haven't done anything, I don't know what you're talking about . . .'

'You give me the keys then you don't know what I'm talking about. Don't be ridiculous.'

Minutes passed before she could be convinced that she had tried to kill herself by taking an overdose of sleeping pills. In her encounters with the doctor, Vera's mother was in the habit of trying to pass off as perfectly normal situations arising from her behaviour that were, to say the least, absurd. Perhaps it had been the protracted illness of her daughter, now accepted as a permanent condition and no longer thought of as something which might eventually come to an end, which had caused her to regard all the 'illnesses' of reality as quite normal occurrences. Vera's mother was completely at home in this eternity of sickness.

No sooner had she arrived at the hospital than she began to complain at how dirty and disorganized everything was. The nurses, veterans of the war and used to amputating arms and legs by the dozen, wouldn't look after her. She began to cry as she entrusted Vera to the doctor.

'Call the woman next door if you can't manage yourself, just don't let her die, I beg you. I didn't give her pills, I only took them myself.'

It occurred to the doctor that everything had been arranged so that he would be alone with Vera. As he returned once again to Grand Transport Street, he felt as if he were about to undergo the most decisive test of his existence and that the test was nothing more or less than the run to the finish. In fact he was afraid that his inadequacy with regard to Vera might have driven him to despair and to suicide. The child, on the other hand, symbolized for him an infinite duration: the spirit of life in her seemed indestructible. These thoughts both comforted and depressed him.

'She'll survive us all,' he thought, and then laughed bitterly to himself. 'We're all working to keep her alive, and dying in the process.'

When he arrived at Vera's house it was already dawn. He put out the light which he had left burning and turned again to stare at the child's pouting face. She looked as beautiful as ever in the bright rays of the moon. Friedmann resigned himself mentally to the situation. He had no idea how long this period of enforced togetherness would last, nor where to begin.

He fell asleep in a threadbare armchair which he had dragged into position alongside the child's bed. A short time later—or perhaps a long time later—he heard someone call out his name. He opened his eyes and saw Vera staring at him. She had called him! So she could speak! So it had all been a trick, an act, even her mother's attempted suicide.

Doctor Friedmann had slumped down a little into the armchair; now he adjusted his position, sitting up straight and looking solemnly ahead.

'Did you call me?' he asked the child, a little ironically. 'Here I am!' She didn't bat an eyelid. She just stared down at him, with the slightest hint of a smile in her eyes and in the corner of her mouth.

98

'If you can speak, why don't you tell me everything?'

The child remained silent, standing stiffly, her expression rigid on her face.

'Yesterday you reduced me to behaving like a wild animal,' he murmured. 'Today you won't succeed. You're trying to provoke me with your silence, but I won't fall for it.' But as he was saying these words, he was aware that he was in a state of near-delirium. That defenceless, motionless creature sitting opposite him wielded her power over him simply by existing, simply by being there. The paradox of her insistence on life made no sense to him, the scientist.

'Where did you learn to act like that? Standing there with one tiny hand on your cheek, your elbow raised, looking chaste and fearful, simpering and surprised. Where did you learn those gestures? Tell me! What are you trying to do? Seduce me?'

Vera's appearance moved the doctor almost to tears. 'Could anyone be wicked enough not to see in you a thing of beauty, not to want you for his own desires, to bruise your delicate flesh?' He was surprised by his own thought, but still he continued his peon. 'Men can be mad, perverse. But it's all part of life and the ways of nature. My little angel, my dear one, my beauty, my beauty . . . '

The doctor expected a little reward for his amorous words. But this time the child didn't move. Not a sound, nor an embrace. But now from Vera's snow-white bed a new odour assailed the doctor's sense of smell, and he realized that from that moment on he would have to devote himself to the most humiliating tasks just to keep that tiny body clean, that as well as feeding her, moving her around and caressing her it would be his job to wipe up even the lowliest excrement of her delicate organism.

'It doesn't frighten me,' he murmured as he set about cleaning her up. 'I'll do it all; not out of sacrifice, but with great joy. This is my love for you.'

Some days passed—exactly how many, his diary doesn't reveal, perhaps because the same Doctor Friedmann had lost all sense of time passing. He stopped looking after himself, lost all interest in his own needs, and took to caring for Vera with punctilious precision. But beyond providing for all her daily needs he continued his attempts to penetrate her unconquerable silence and indifference. Every now and again, when the sun's rays shone red, he would take her on his knees and sing her songs, recite poetry, make animal noises, speak to her tenderly in different languages. There were times when he felt his childish rage returning and was on the point of losing control. But when that happened Friedmann would tense his lips and clench his fists, repeating to himself: 'I musn't go backwards. I must erase my mistakes, with other mistakes perhaps, but I have to change. I'm sure Vera's strength will return to her, and

that her illness will not hold her back for ever. I have
faith. The more she makes me despair, the more faith I
have.'

Sometimes, having put Vera to bed when, either
through laziness or sheer physiological impossibility, she
was incapable of walking more than one or two steps,
Friedmann would sit down, eat a piece of bread or an
onion, and poke around in the drawers of the sumptuous
chests in the apartment.

He found a pile of photographs, each with a precise
caption on the reverse: 'Vera at one year old . . . at two . . .
at five years old.' 'Vera the day before the operation.' 'Vera
on the beach at . . . ' The names of some tiny places he
had never heard of, which perhaps didn't even exist.

'Vera three weeks after the operation.' No visible
difference. If anything she was more beautiful, much
more beautiful now. But beautiful wasn't quite the right
word.

He even found an old record with a label which read:
'Vera's voice.' He put it on the gramophone and listened.
The flat voice of a spoiled child: 'Mummy loves daddy
and daddy loves mummy. Vera loves mummy and daddy.
The dog says bow-wow, the cat says miaow-miaow.' A
woman's voice asks: 'How many fingers do you see?' and
she answers: 'Seventy!' She laughs. At the bottom of an
old suitcase he came across a number of exercise books.
Each bore a white label with a blue border. 'Six years old.

Seven years old. Eight years old.'

Simple, rather banal phrases, repeated ad infinitum across
the page between the thin grey lines. 'The sun shines. The
rain falls. Birds fly. Snakes crawl. Plants grow.' The world
she had created was obvious and monotonous and
indicated a period where time had no meaning. But
gradually, from one year to the next, the handwriting grew
less distinct, the letters became bigger and bigger, until
finally all that remained were gigantic scrawls.

'Vera says she wrote "today".' 'Vera says she has written
"you".' 'Vera says she has written something but she is
pointing at a blank space.'

One day Doctor Friedmann found an album containing
photographs of the family's dead. The photographs, some
of them rather mysterious looking, were stuck to sheets
of black card and showed well-groomed, well-dressed
men and women with radiant faces. Sacrificial victims,
silent, composed, not a coarse gesture or a dissonant
expression among them, conscious of the function of
their own deaths. So many photographs. The doctor
never would have believed she had such a large family.
He remembered his own, still alive, and he dashed off a
letter to his mother:

I'm getting used to this country, perhaps because I
know that Father's father and even Father himself
were born here. Once I would never have
considered staying here, living in this part of the

102

world. Today the thought no longer shocks me. If
you too wanted to return I think you'd be content
here; 'happy' would be too gross a word—you know
well how remote that possibility is for any of us.

Anyway, let me know what you think. My wife
and son will of course say no. I'll wait for your
answer before mentioning it to them. I cried a lot the
other night thinking about all the love I would be
leaving behind, but believe me, I absolutely have to
stay here. Don't ask me to explain. Let's just say that
I am compelled to by my desire to know, and for me
that is more important than anything else.

By now the lie came so naturally to him that to say or
write the truth—or a semblance of the truth—would
have struck him as an unprecedented transgression.

Then one morning a series of loud knocks on the door
brought the doctor back to the reality of the world
outside. He didn't know whether he ought to open it or
not. The house was by this stage in an intolerable state of
disorder. An acrid smell of urine pervaded the air, and the
triangular napkins he used to wipe the child lay in a soiled
heap in the corner. Saucepans and plates were strewn
about the table and across the wooden parquet floor.

'It doesn't matter; let them see my mess. I know I have
to let them in, I sense that something good will come of
it. My imprisonment is about to end.'

He opened the door. The general's adjutant was

waiting for him. 'I've been trying to reach you at your lodgings for days on end. I wanted to deliver this letter to you. The general wants to see you. I think he's a little angry. You disappeared completely. Do you know what they call that? Desertion.'

On the spur of the moment, the doctor couldn't think of anything better to say than to claim that he was only doing his duty as a scientist. But did this excuse stand up in the light of his duty as a soldier? The adjutant agreed with him but said that these things were decided 'very high up'.

It was only once the general's emissary had disappeared down the dark throat of the stairwell that Friedmann was able to recover a little of his calm and poise.

He opened the letter:

I have learned, from those who know you well, all about your infidelity and your ridiculous erotic intrigues. From this moment on you had better forget about me and about my son, whom you should no longer consider yours. We'll discuss the rest in court. You never loved anyone. Shame on you.

Your wife (but not for much longer)

Doctor Friedmann folded the letter, put it in the outside pocket of his uniform next to his heart, and turned to Vera. He ground some sleeping pills up in powdered milk, mixed it with a glass of water, and gave it to the child to drink.

After putting the child to bed, the doctor went out to face the general.

What a strange impression it made on him, coming out of the prison he had held on to so tenaciously! Compared to the rigours of Vera and the passions of her mother, so chaotic and yet so precise in her aims, the ruined city and the throngs of starving people in the streets seemed to him to be completely without purpose. The suffering on their faces, the piles of waste, the stench of filth, the crazed efforts at reconstruction were nothing compared to the child's mute dignity.

'This too is life, but real life is like Vera's,' he thought, and noted his thought down.

The Hotel Continental was full of women and soldiers in uniform. His fellow officers gave him a warm welcome —he was well-liked by everyone—and even the general greeted him in a friendly way, if a little stiffly.

'Sir, in contacting my wife you were interfering in our private affairs. I have not in any way acted against the interests of my country, or of the army, or of anyone else. By what right did you intervene? My conduct, as far as anyone knows, has always been rigorously within the boundaries of current standards of morality.'

'I know how much store you set by current standards of morality. Yes, and the boundaries are fairly flexible;

unfortunately there's a lot of hypocrisy around. But that doesn't change the fact that your conduct has been reprehensible, and I as your superior cannot tolerate that. Apart from anything else, that business with the child is highly suspect, I won't put it any more strongly than that, and if you can't give me an explanation right here and now, I will have no alternative but to . . . ' The general stopped.

'To?'

The general made a gesture of passive dejection. 'To punish you in an exemplary fashion,' he replied.

Punish him? Wasn't he already paying for his terrible, inexplicable violence towards Vera?

'Nevertheless you descended to the gutter in involving yourself in my private affairs. You wrote to my wife.'

'Your wife?' asked the general, raising his eyebrows. 'Your wife doesn't exist as far as I am concerned. I am not in the habit of writing to an abstraction.'

'Look what my wife wrote to me. Look.'

Doctor Friedmann pulled the letter out of the pocket of his uniform. The general glanced briefly at the crumpled sheet of paper, read a few lines, then, holding it between his index and his middle fingers, threw it down on the shining surface of his large table as if it were a playing card.

'Go away and take it up with someone on your level. You should be ashamed of yourself. From this day on as far as I'm concerned you don't exist. The machinery, not the person at the controls, will bring you to justice.'

The scientist left the building, not at all offended. The general's condemnation had been deserved, and he himself agreed with it. The only judgement that might have hurt him would come from the absence of Vera's look. 'And as for the anonymous letter, it must have been written by one of my fellow-officers. It's just what one would expect of an interfering colleague.'

He spent the morning making enquiries but was met with open laughter. By midday he was back at Vera's, none the wiser as to the identity of the secret informer.

He put the key in the lock with an increasing sense of discomfort: some old people were watching him from behind their windows as if he were a thief. Others were watching from the courtyard, their hands in the pockets of their worn-out dressing-gowns. What did those looks mean?

The key would not turn. The doctor tried and tried again, without success. 'What will become of the child if I can't get in? I'll have to break down the door. What awful luck! My life is going wrong at every turn. I'll never get it back on course.'

He put his shoulder to the door. The courtyard filled with spectators, silent and hostile. It was only to be expected of them.

Suddenly the door flew open of its own accord. In the

dark entrance he could just make out the slim figure of Vera's mother.

'I ran away from hospital. Come in, quickly, come in.'

The doctor had a sudden flash of inspiration: it made him desperately unhappy, yet at the same time he felt content, the way he felt after winning a game of chess.

'Was it you who wrote to my wife?' he asked nonchalantly.

Vera's mother closed the door with a smile. 'Don't bother asking me how I feel. Some welcome home!'

'I asked you a question and I'd like an answer,' the man shouted, perfectly conscious of the sad banality of the scene they were rehearsing.

'An answer? To what?'

'Look. Read this letter. Read what my wife has written to me. Who told her what I was doing, or what the two of you were doing to me?' He realized with horror that he was holding the child partly to blame. But perhaps she really was, and he was simply avoiding the . . .

'I see. You wanted to hide it all from your wife. You'd have preferred lying to this miserable truth. Shame on you. Well I didn't write anything to your wife.'

'Are you sure? You're not lying?'

'Quite sure. I'm not in the habit of telling lies. Still, if you insist on believing I did, then you can leave this instant. Vera and I don't need you.'

He hung his head. That evening, when he took Vera's

VERA

mother to bed, she showed him more passion than ever before.

The doctor fell into a sleep that was neither restful nor undisturbed: he felt a tiredness, a sort of deafness to the world which he had never felt before, and which he feared might turn out to be final and irreversible.

And yet in the depths of the night he got up, taking every care not to wake the woman, and tip-toed into Vera's room. He was naked, and the child appeared unflustered in the yellow glow of the nightlight. She looked at him: she looked at him and saw him, unmistakably, without the slightest reaction. He sat down and began to whisper quietly, telling her of himself, of his life, of all that he had had to leave behind him for ever, of past loves.

The tears fell on his bare knees and ran down his legs. Traces of expression flitted across Vera's face, disappearing as suddenly as they had appeared, until finally a faint sigh, a strangely prolonged and yet barely audible 'aah', issued from her lips: a sound without significance, or perhaps the sign of an intelligence that had understood everything and sympathized—for how could she not?—with all he had said.

These secret nighttime conversations continued for some time. During the day, Friedmann would get up only to eat, perhaps read a book, or make a few jottings in his notes. He moved all his belongings to the woman's

109

house after informing the general of his decision. He wasn't ashamed of anything.

Vera's state of torpor, during which she was sometimes unable even to move her limbs or turn her head, ended suddenly one night. The evening before the child's mother had forgotten to make her take her sleeping pills. The doctor found her sitting on the edge of the bed, her arms waving, trying to enunciate some syllable, or possibly a word, that sounded like 'darling, darling'. As soon as she saw him she tried to stand up. Her nightdress had rolled down around her perfect, slender, tapering legs. The doctor ran to her fearing she was about to fall. He crouched down beside her and held her up. Then, quite unexpectedly, she put her little arms around his neck and began to kiss his cheeks repeatedly with inimitable tenderness.

'My love, my love! I knew this would happen. I knew there was more to you than mere silence. Come on, let's go to mummy. No man on earth has ever been happier than I am. My darling, my little treasure.' He began to cry, and the more emotional he became, the more the child seemed to understand and to want to help set him free from the unhappiness inside him.

Many happy weeks went by. The scientist didn't stop to wonder what unforeseen coincidence had caused the neuron circuits in that enormous mass of cells crammed into Vera's little head to start working again. Now she

110

would speak his name every other minute, with such charm that she was able to transform the distressing appeal into a game. And her mother too found the child showing unusual confidence and affection towards her: Vera would stroke her face, press her little hands into hers, nuzzle her mother's forehead with her own. She had even recovered the strength in her legs, and on sunny afternoons all three would go for walks through the narrow streets of the neighbourhood, once again teeming with life after the rumble and the silence of the war. Vera walked in the middle and the doctor and her mother each held a hand. It seemed that she had grown a little and now looked nine or ten years old.

But the two people who knew her secret were a little anxious for her.

'Can it be that she has started growing again?' her mother asked, and the doctor replied with some elusive, meaningless and quite unintelligible scientific explanation.

But knowledge was of no use to him any more. 'I am overcome with happiness: I would never have believed that she could harbour so much affection, or that life could offer moments like this, that such joy was possible on earth.'

It had been worth sacrificing his other affections and duties. Now everything had a meaning for him. 'My wife and my son don't need me. And as for my mother . . . I'll see her again soon, I'll bring her here to live with me.'

The young body of Vera's mother no longer radiated agonizing distress in their lovemaking; now he found her presence reassuring. Doctor Friedmann had settled for once and for all the old doubt that nagged inside him about the goodness of man's existence on earth.

One Sunday afternoon they went into the pastry shop on Wednesday Street. They wanted to buy Vera some chestnut purée. As she saw the jar filled with threads of purée, her face lit up in happiness and gratitude, quickly replaced by the sly look of someone congratulating herself on having got exactly what she wanted by sheer cunning. The very next moment, without the slightest warning, Vera collapsed on the stone floor of the shop. The thud of her tiny head as it hit the floor was the most terrible sound Friedmann had ever heard. He was shaken to the bones, as if the sound heralded death itself. Not the child's death, or his own: the death of everything.

'My God,' cried Vera's mother in a thin voice that was almost a squeak. She began to cry over her daughter's motionless body. When Friedmann reopened his eyes the first thing he saw was Vera's bewildered look, her stare begging him to tell her what had happened.

'Why did this have to happen? Why does evil always have to visit this little creature? Why does it get mixed up with love and grace?'

Faced with the absurdity of this hysterical line of questioning, the doctor took refuge in logic and science.

He concluded that the scars of the operation, the prolonged use of drugs had probably caused permanent damage to Vera's cerebral tissue. Stopping the administration of the drugs, however, had probably led to a short-lived state of equilibrium which was neither controllable nor repeatable.

Throughout the next night the child's mother tried with great skill and some malice all her usual approaches, in a vain attempt to produce some reaction. In the end she fell asleep in a sulk, almost offended.

Friedmann got up and went to Vera. He stared at her by the light of the bedside lamp and stroked her head. He knew then that the feeling of complete happiness of the past weeks would never be his again. He told the child of his feelings, without pretending to hold a conversation, but in the sure conviction that she understood his every word, and much more than his words.

But Vera had once again shut herself away, absent and indifferent to him and to the world.

'Very well, I'll simply observe progress, and I won't make any more demands of you or of myself.' But moments later he wailed: 'Where have you gone to, and why?'

He loved her, without nourishing any hope, without any expectations; he was ready to confront the worst. He fell asleep in a chair beside the little white bed and when, the next morning, Vera's mother woke him, he realized he could no longer stand being near her.

They stopped going out together. The weather turned ugly. Another fit might cost Vera the loss of a tooth, or a fractured arm. Her perfect body was in danger, and with it Doctor Friedmann's life.

One night, rather than try again to communicate with Vera, he decided to continue another investigation. His suspicions on the subject of the anonymous letter to his wife had never been fully allayed and now he wanted to arrive at the truth. Why was the letter so important to him? It was obvious that he was looking for someone to blame for his fate.

Around five in the morning he began to caress Vera's mother's body tenderly. He started at her back, and when he felt her move, murmured sweetly: 'Was it you who wrote to my wife?'

The woman smiled in her sleep, stretched her limbs and mumbled a clear 'yes.'

His fury was immediate. He took her by the shoulders and began to shake her. 'Say that again, that you wrote to my wife. Say it again!' Her eyes flew wide open and she winced with the pain, but the doctor was not moved to stop.

'You wretch, it was you who took me away from everything good and sane in my life. Why? Why did you do it?' He repeated his ludicrous question five or six times, and when there was no response, he began to punch her in the face. 'You evil monster, you!'

Any attempt the woman might have made to cry for help was masked by her gasps for air. She panted and flailed about desperately in an effort to ward off the scientist's blows, which were becoming more ferocious by the second. 'Are you trying to destroy all that's good in me? Are you trying to drag me down into your cess, into your nothing, you bitch?'

The man no longer knew what he was doing: he was punching wildly at Vera's mother in an attempt, however blind, to lay all his own guilt and failure on to her.

'Are you mad? You'll kill me! Are you trying to kill me?' The woman's voice was flat, nasal, rather faint. Its sound infuriated him all the more. Yes, it would be better if she didn't exist. But now, even if he were to kill her, he could not wipe out her existence, merely shelve it.

'You're killing me!' wheezed the woman, ceasing for a moment to defend herself. In that instant he became aware of what he was doing. He ran to the bathroom, locked himself in, started to wash the blood from his hands, and then with a shout smashed his head against his image in the mirror on the bathroom wall.

Dear Mother,
I'm writing to you again from here. Will you listen to me, just this one more time? I need you like I did

when I was a child. I need your love, I need you to encourage me to get on with my studies, to get on with life! This time I'm not asking, I'm begging you to come and see me in this country where my fate is working itself out. I could leave quite soon, indeed I ought to, as you know; the international agreements stipulate that our unit should leave the country now and hand over to other foreign forces. But whatever happens I can't not stay here. Let's say that I have chanced upon the most interesting case of my career; but let's say also that I have become completely embroiled, body and soul, in a relationship which I am unable to bring to an end. We two have never been completely sincere with one another, but now I feel we must. Please agree to come and start a new life here with me. We're now the only members left alive of our original family. Our roots are here, even if they're hard to see these days. I will live for you as long as you come and rescue me, haul me out of the damnation from which I can't seem to save myself. You know it's useless to expect anything of Lilian and Michael: for them I'm already dead. Answer me, please, with haste.

Appealing to you for help,

Your son.

P.S. If you don't understand my situation, if I sound crazy, remember that I didn't ask to be born. If nothing else, then at least take your share of the responsibility for having cast me, from your belly, into the world.

His mother, seventy-five years old and afflicted with serious illnesses and disabilities, replied in a letter written in lines which became more and more tightly packed together as they neared the bottom of the page. It was full of justifications, digressions, evocations of events both happy and sorrowful, of characters and sayings from the past. In short, it was a listless refusal of his request. The letter held out no prospect for the future beyond a patient and resigned wait for death to arrive.

The carpet has unrolled before our feet and we are reaching its end. Only one more step to go. Let us take it at the appointed time and in peace. We can't turn back because there is nothing behind us: as we tread the carpet, it is consumed. So, dear son, you too should be content with your lot, and if you really wish me well, then come here to live with me until the end of my days, or until the end of yours. No one knows precisely when his hour will arrive: the young sometimes go before the old, the healthy before the sick. It is useless to protest. I'll wait for you, then. But if your interests, science, your career, your feelings force you to stay, don't have any regrets on my account, stay, and don't worry about me. I'll take the last step alone.

Kisses and all my love, which will never change,

Your mother.

As Doctor Friedmann read and re-read the letter, far-away images of a remote childhood paraded before his eyes and all around him in the void. This is how he arranged the figures of his imagination. He sensed the presence of someone else inside him, a smaller copy of himself, a little boy. The boy was running quickly through the streets, forcing a way through the crowds, singing a canticle. Then suddenly his double receded, contracted around his worn-out body and disappeared inside him

'There, I've settled my scores with the past,' he said to himself. 'Now I can devote myself to the agony of the present.' It didn't occur to him to exert his own will, to take steps to change his condition. He thought of himself as an inert object confronting the relentless advance of events that would overwhelm him, trample him underfoot, and annihilate him.

'How on earth did I get myself into this state? It must be due to nervous exhaustion, a psychosis perhaps. Or maybe there really is something poisonous at work to undermine all of us, and everything else is an illusion? This is a fine trap we're in.'

He looked at Vera's face, her precise features, her unchanging expression, the barely perceptible flicker in her eyes, a sly, slanted look. 'It is her I'll live with from this day on. But I'll never understand her. It's useless. Before her all I can do is remain inert. We can compete to see who is the most inert.'

He began to stay in bed, in his pyjamas, until late in the morning, by which time Vera's mother had long since returned from the market and begun to cook and clean.

'Good morning darling,' she would say to him when she saw him appear in the kitchen. 'Do you still love me a little?' This phrase sounded like some horrible joke to him. It made his blood pressure rise instantly. His head would begin to throb with discomfort. The woman's question sought to burden him with a responsibility he had never asked for, in the same way as he had never asked to be born.

'Not only do they want us to live, although after a bit there's little good in life: they want love as well, they want us to love.' The thought scandalized him.

'Yes, I love you,' was his usual reply, before going back to bed until lunchtime.

'There's always the possibility that life itself will finish me off. What's that pain in my chest? Maybe I'm having a heart-attack! My fingers are going numb. I've a shooting pain in my arm. This may be it. I don't have the will to resist. Why should I?'

Meanwhile Vera's mother looked after all his needs: he couldn't have found anyone more useful, more loving or more dedicated to him. And Vera sat on her little sofa—

she had now started to walk again, with difficulty—and stared ahead, stared into eyes of Doctor Friedmann and her mother. 'There's something wrong, isn't there?' said her look. Every now and again her eyes would moisten, her stare would become unbearably intense, she was transported by who knows what visions: these were her moments of crisis. It was as if she had been carried off to another world, to the origins of being. There was no lying or pretence about her; her condition unmasked everything and everybody.

Day and night, in his thoughts and in his feelings, Friedmann scrutinized his own entrails. He was waiting for a sign which would announce the end. In reality he would not admit the fallibility of his own body: he wanted to die of no cause, not weakened by illness.

One morning, after the woman had gone out on her usual trip to do the shopping, he heard a knock at the door. The doctor didn't reply.

'Friedmann, open up! We have to talk!' It was the general's voice. He had come all the way here for him!

The doctor rushed to open the door. A moment later the gaunt figure of the general stood before him.

'Yes, I have come in person,' he said. 'I must speak with you.'

'With me? You?'

'Yes, as a friend. We were both born in this country. We grew up here and in America. Your behaviour has

been most irregular and . . . but just look at the way
you're dressed.'

'Do you mean this dressing-gown? It belonged to the
child's father. He is dead. Now I'm wearing it. Until I die
too.'

'What child? What are you talking about?'

'I'm sure you've found out all about my situation, so
please speak frankly.'

'Are you asking me to dispense with the pretences, is
that what you mean? Social conventions, politeness, our
whole existence, all meaningless next to Vera, is that what
you're trying to say?'

'Yes, but there's one more thing I have to add,'
Friedmann interrupted. 'Everything is meaningless,
except blame. That solidifies as the rest evaporates,' he
said whispering each syllable distinctly. 'I am twice
guilty.'

'Fine, fine, but remember that a man must never
condemn himself. He must be judged by others, for he
cannot rise above his own person. Come away from here.
In America we'll think it all over.'

'America . . . America. No, I can't. And anyway I don't
need to think anything over.'

'You're right, why should you? When you're at the
centre of an event you don't believe in the existence of
other events, ones that were there before and ones that
will be there after. It all gets submerged in the moment,

blinded by the moment. Look at Vera: for her, the moment does not exist. In short: our mission is finished here. We're going home. Don't be a stubborn fool. Come with us!'

'No,' said Friedmann, with such firmness that the general took several steps backwards, as if the words had struck one of his legs.

'I'm staying here for ever. There's nothing else I want to do. I want to stay here.'

'You may not want to do anything else, but you do have obligations. And you can't simply duck them.'

'Obligations?' Friedmann demanded, motionless. 'What obligations? The obligation to live?'

'Yes, and to help others to live.'

'No, I can't think that far. Help who to live?'

The general hesitated for a moment. 'Your mother. Your son. Your wife.'

'I see. What came before, what came after, what came during. No. Prosecute me if you like, hand me over to the authorities, but I won't do it. That's not my job. I have still a lot to do today. Would you be kind enough to leave me to my tasks?'

'You have nothing to do, that I know. Don't you realize what it smells like in here? Open the windows.'

'Thanks all the same. It suits me fine.'

'So, you've decided you want to die?'

'What do you know of life and death? Go away.'

The general signalled to the two military policemen to take Friedmann away by force.

'Just one more day, I beg you,' the doctor pleaded, with unexpected humility. 'Just give me one more day. You don't know what scientific curiosity means. By tomorrow I may have discovered what I've been searching for all these months. This is a unique case, there isn't another one like it anywhere in the world. To have survived so long . . . I have to take one last set of samples, we can have the analysis done on the plane. Just one more day, please. For the sake of our childhood friendship . . . '

'Let him go!' the general said, and he left without a word, without even looking at him.

Going over what had happened in his mind, Friedmann knew that the general had not been the slightest bit taken in by his inventions and had only let him be to shame him all the more. 'But I won't let him, I swear I won't let him. He doesn't know how desperate my love can be. It's a pity I'll never see Vera's eyes and little face again. I'd like to know what she'd think if she were to see me in this state.'

What form should he choose for his own death? Yielding to his nightmares he pictured the nine hundred and seventy-six ways of dying he'd read about in some book. He began to sweat and felt faint. Now all he was waiting for was the moment of true decision. He went to Vera's room. He heard the gentle breathing of a creature who was full of grace and innocence, but terrible in condemnation. 'No, I will not be moved. I'll go my own way.'

And yet some moments passed before he had the courage to look into that face, to see her little hand resting on her cheek in her characteristic expression somewhere between chastity and pain, her arm bent, her elbow in the air. 'I'll go my own way,' he said loudly and turned to go out of the room. As he reached the door he heard her whisper his name.

'She called my name again! This time I won't react.' But the syllables of his name were hurled in his direction for a second time, this time louder than before. He turned around. 'Don't do that. Do you understand? Don't do that.'

The face of the child—but she was seventeen years old!—was relaxed and calm. Her eyes under her lids were indifferent, but alive. 'Why are you calling me? Tell me, why are you calling me? Would you call to anybody or do you just do it with me? Tell me!' He ran to the bed, took the child by the shoulders and shook her, shouting 'What do you want from me? Are you trying to hurt me again? I won't allow you to. No! And I won't let you see me dead. You'll come with me, wherever I go, you're coming too. I know nothing about you, but now it no longer matters.'

He ran into the kitchen and gathered all the bottles of

pills and a jug of water. 'We'll drink it together, it's nice, you'll see, it's nice.' He emptied the contents of five bottles, all that was left in the house, into a mortar and began to grind them up. The mortar rang like a bell under the blows of the pestle. He emptied the powder into a glass of water and turned to Vera.

'Yes, I've brought you some nice lemonade. Now we'll drink it together.' The contents of one bottle would have been enough to kill them both. Friedmann put the glass down and took Vera on to his lap. He began to sing an old lullaby, crying as he sang. He was deeply moved and felt that he was engaged in an act of great solemnity; it was a feeling he had felt as a child when, on certain holy days, he would put on his blue suit and his white shirt.

But before and after had vanished from his head. All that existed now was Vera's face and his own ego, a formless entity, and one that space and time would soon be rid of.

He raised the glass.

'Drink, my love. Whatever, whoever might be inside you no longer matters. It will remain our secret, your secret, for ever.'

Vera was staring at him, more intensely than usual. Her perfect lips, her nose, her clear brow, her cheeks, now a little pale, and unrelentingly soft, all these were beyond Friedmann's sense of awareness. Caressing the nape of her neck with one hand, he brought the glass to her lips with the other.

'My dear, sweet, innocent little creature . . . ' Slowly
and carefully he poured half the contents of the glass into
the red cavity of her mouth. Vera swallowed. 'It's over,'
he thought with relief. He brought the glass to his own
lips. And now all his feelings arose from the bottom of his
heart like a swarm of dreadful insects, a terrible chord that
came from within him, and yet also surrounded him. He
was drowning in an ocean, but he was the ocean: an
ocean of bitterness without end and without hope.
'Where to now?' he had time to wonder. 'Into nothing?
Into nothing at all, or is there someone else still watching
over me? An answer, before I cease to exist. An answer, I
beg you!' He drank the first draught.

That instant Vera gave out an awful sound, a deep,
tuneless, coughing, belching sound. The liquid she had
swallowed came rising out of her stomach and spewed
over Doctor Friedmann's face. She stared at him with
moist eyes, her expression that of someone who has just
done something unforgivable. She blinked, perplexed,
but freed.

'So I have to go through with it alone! You've killed
me. You've tricked me. The two of you will live and I
will die. No matter. I won't turn back. I've reached the
end of the carpet and there's nothing behind me, except
for the two of you, except for the two of us.'

He raised the glass again but it flew out of his hand,

smashing into fragments on the worm-eaten wooden floor of the old house.

Vera's mother stood behind him. She had arrived just in time. 'But why, my love? Why did you want to leave me?'

She took his head and pressed it to her breast. But Friedmann pushed her away, threw the dressing-gown around his shoulders, flung open the door of the house and walked out into the blinding sunlight.

He wandered through the Eighth District.

His admission to the neurological ward of St John's Hospital, his stay in the mental asylum on Lime Tree Mount, his return to America and his participation in the Korean War are not relevant to this story. Nor are the circumstances of his disappearance in that far away corner of Asia something we can go into here.

Doctor Friedmann's notes and his diary were delivered to his legitimate wife ten years later, and her agreement to having them examined has made this reconstruction possible.

It is said that Vera and her mother moved to the Stone Quarry district. There is no documentary evidence that they ever stayed there.

When a man is ill, they decide on his life and death in the Fourth Palace. No man should pass judgement on himself, lest someone hear it and try to carry out sentence. The world exists through secrets. In the dream that Friedmann had shortly after getting to know Vera, they talked together for a long while, but when he awoke, the words were gone. There is no evidence that they ever came back to the illustrious, if unlucky, man of science.

A. Friedmann, *US Army Magazine*, Connecticut, 1945, pp. 164–166

Bahdy's Disease

Speaking of Bahdy's Disease, these days increasingly widespread throughout the world, brings to mind a case I observed over the course of twenty years or so. I can still see the three patients in my mind's eye. Three patients—but only one disease. I always picture the three brothers together, but in fact I never saw them all at once. They came to me—why to me anyway?—at different times, with years between each visit. After the initial consultations, the diagnoses, the prescribed therapies, I was unable to follow the course of their illnesses any further: the men simply refused to undergo treatment. It was only from what the second brother told me that I found out what had happened to the first, just as the third was able to shed light on the fate of the second. What became of the last brother I never did find out.

It's all coming back to me now: I'm sitting in my old surgery in Karfenstein Street. I can almost taste the fresh raspberry drink made for me by old Esther, my nurse at the time.

The May sun was streaming through the window and the syncopated footfalls of a cripple echoed in the silent afternoon. Someone opened the door to my surgery and then closed it again with extreme delicacy so that I hardly noticed the noise of the handle and the click of the catch. I looked up from the prescription I was writing and saw in front of me a man who seemed suffused with a radiant glow. He would have been about thirty as I remember him: slim and broad shouldered, his thick brown hair combed back from his brow, he stood upright in front of me wearing a calm, somewhat ironic expression. On his left arm he carried a light raincoat. He smiled at me with shy embarrassment, but without a trace of fear or cowardice. His chief concern seemed to be to preserve a sense of decency, to appear neither pathetic nor sentimental. He introduced himself, then took another step before stopping again. I indicated to him to sit down, which seemed the pragmatic thing to do, and noticed as I did—I remember this so well—that I felt slightly ashamed, the way no doctor ever should, that I was about to intrude on the privacy of this patient's body.

On examining him, I could feel a lump about the size of a walnut on the distal part of his right thigh. It could have been a cyst or a tumour, or perhaps the consequence of a muscle trauma caused by a sudden movement, or by

a blow from, or a collision with, a blunt object. Or it
could have been a lipoma, a deposit of fat. I advised him
to make an appointment to see a surgeon, gave him the
address of a clinic where the friend with whom I played
tennis worked, and asked him to come back after the
operation with the results of the biopsy.

The summer passed. I spent a long, relaxing holiday on
the lakeside. My wife and my children, young at the
time, treated me to day after day of quiet charm.

One afternoon in September, before my clientele of
teenagers and little old ladies had gathered in the
darkened waiting-room to collect their pills against
pimples and hypertension, Esther announced the return
of my strange patient. Moments later the man with the
raincoat on his arm appeared in my doorway and the
surgery was filled with the solemn air of a holy day. I was
never able to explain to myself where this atmosphere
came from, nor indeed why he always carried the
raincoat. At first I thought it was a somewhat aristocratic
affectation, or perhaps a prop for the man's lack of self-
confidence, or maybe even a nod at the English style.
Only some months later, thinking of him quite by chance
by who knows what chain of associations, did it occur to
me that this article of clothing might actually allude to a
permanent state of departure, even of flight. What
response was he looking for in displaying this sign?
Understanding? Pity? Or the *coup de grâce*?

I opened the sealed envelope and rapidly scanned the results of the biopsy and the many tests and analyses. His was a very rare case of a tumour, not of itself unfavourable, which grows in the connective tissue. Today it even has a name, histiocytoma. Our knowledge of it in those days, however, was scanty, and very confused. Some sources talked of pulmonary metastasis in thirty per cent of cases, others disputed these statistics. All were agreed however in tracing the tumour's origins right back to the embryo. In other words, the man's destiny had been stamped in his tissues since birth. As is the case with many of us. Whether the already disordered cell would, in the body of the adult, migrate to an arm, or to the chest, or swell the right foot seemed to be down to the luck of the draw, if one could admit to the existence of such a thing in our universe. But the significance of the cancer, which tomorrow we may call by another name, and which in the not too distant future will most likely have disappeared forever, was not something that the young man could find words for. For him, in that context, it was unsayable.

I was very unsure about how to break the news to him. I think perhaps I underestimated his intelligence and his education. But in the end it was he who came to my aid— how often patients come to the aid of their doctors!— excusing himself for having put me in a difficult position.

'I've done a little reading on the significance of the

diagnosis,' he said with a smile, 'and I can see that there's nothing particularly unusual about my case. In fact, I wasn't sure whether I should even come back—after all, why should I bother you? But I thought it might seem rude if I ignored the usual formalities. You told me to come back with the results of the analysis, so here I am. I know you can't do anything to save me. But you have to carry out your check-ups, make your deductions, prescribe and give advice all the same, you poor man. Just don't ask me to go into hospital. It wouldn't help—I'd feel you'd written me off.'

I wanted to comfort him, to lie to him, to try and get him to believe in miracles, to talk of possible cures. But after only a few sentences he interrupted me most politely.

'Thank you, Doctor,' he said with good-humoured irony, 'you've given me a new lease of life.' His voice was deep and reassuring, his face gentle but disillusioned. 'Well, I suppose that's about it. I settle up with the nurse outside, do I?' The heavy tread of his footsteps soon disappeared down the length of the corridor. I didn't even hear the outside door close, as if he had faded through the wall, just as histiocytes pass through the capillary walls in diapedesis.

I felt a wave of gratitude towards my patient for having spared me the awkward lies and the agonizing scenes. And then I forgot him, as I had forgotten so many others

135

before him. Complete indifference is the only sort of humanity vouchsafed to those who care for their fellow men. Any sort of involvement—physical or emotional—would make helping impossible.

The years which followed saw my earnings increase and my career advance. I was invited to teach pathological anatomy at the University of M, a great honour in such a small city. But I didn't give up my surgery in the capital. I preferred to travel up and down three times a week than to content myself with making a reputation in a dull and unprofitable small-town practice.

It was May again—just a few days before it had snowed unexpectedly—when I made the acquaintance of the second brother. There would have been about three years difference in their ages, five at most. The second brother bore a striking resemblance to the first, both in appearance and in manner, even down to his dress. And yet seeing him didn't bring the other case to mind; as far as I was concerned it had been resolved—if not triumphantly—and wiped without a trace from my memory. Not even when he told me his name did I make the connection. In those days my memory was full of good things.

Only that, on looking up, I was struck by a look of radiance—that word again—on the man's face. He must have been about forty, well-dressed and elegant, a lawyer, I'd have guessed. He was standing in front of me, a smile

on his lips and a look of humility in his eyes. He described
in simple terms the pain he'd had for some months in his
right calf every time he walked up a slope or climbed
three or four stairs.

'The lift in our old apartment block breaks down fairly
often. The apartments themselves are nice and spacious,
but the old plumbing and antiquated electrics are a bit of
a nuisance.'

It was as if he was attributing the cause of his own illness
to entirely extraneous circumstances. But I wasn't having
any of it. Patients, when they're describing their symptoms,
often try and confuse doctors, hoping that fooling us into
making a less serious diagnosis will actually change the
nature of their illness, perhaps moving it from one organ to
another. I had him undress and examined his leg.

And while I was doing it—I'm only realizing it now—I
felt exactly the same sense of shame as I had done a few
years before. Still I didn't make the connection.

Stretched out on the rubber sheet, the second brother
stared at me throughout the examination. From my point
of view it was all a bit of a sham—the examination, the
diagnosis, everything. I had already made up my mind
what the trouble was.

And then all of a sudden he said: 'The reason I came to
you, Professor, was because you looked after my brother
so well.'

'Is that right?'

'Yes, he told me so much about you. "An extraordinary doctor", he called you.'

'I'm glad I was able to cure your brother,' I said, without the faintest idea who he was talking about.

'Cure him? No, unfortunately you weren't able to cure him. You didn't even try. But he still spoke very highly of you.'

'That's strange,' I said irritably, my pride a little wounded, 'I don't remember that. I remember your brother well, of course, but I had assumed . . . What was it he had? Remind me, if you would. I have so many patients in my care . . . '

He told me all about his brother's case, and how he had died only a few months before. 'And now it's my turn. I think I have the same illness. The symptoms are very similar, identical even. If you find it difficult, if you'd rather not see me turn white, then just write it all down on a prescription form and I'll read it at home.'

And at that precise moment the memory of my strange patient of a few years before came flooding back. I felt a pang of regret that he had died. I spoke comfortingly to his brother, reassuring him that his illness was quite different to the other, and advised him to have further clinical investigations. But as I said, my prognosis was already made, and according to it the outlook was not good. The right superficial femoral artery was partially obscured and in a few years it would lead to paralysis if a coronary or something else didn't finish him off first. The pipework was becoming blocked up, just like in his old apartment.

He too returned to the surgery a few months later. He brought with him folders full of X-rays and analyses, charts and electrocardiograms, and letters with their sentence written in Latin, clear and irrevocable.

Much of an individual's destiny has already been decided centuries before he comes into being—in this respect the machinery of the human body doesn't leave us much room for manoeuvre. The judgements handed down by science are more severe than the sentence of a court; in the end, there's not much that any one of us can do or say that's really relevant in the grand scheme of things. History itself is but a tiny scrap of that enormous fabric of death from which life on our planet has sprung.

The second brother handed me the pile of papers and limped off, his raincoat on his arm.

That year I closed my surgery on Karfenstein Street. Old Esther had died of viral hepatitis and with her a family tradition disappeared. What reason was there to stay in that street when I could move to an elegant part of the city, to Rose Hill or Liberty Mountain? The prospect of the change seemed enormous to me, like moving from one universe, or world or century to another. What would await me in those *fin de siècle* suburbs? I threw out the old leather armchairs that had belonged to my father—once the best diagnostician in the city—and fitted out my new surgery with fashionable furniture and the most up-to-date equipment. The grace of my new nurse Martha, a shapely blonde whose young body was as fragrant as the plains she came from, lent an idyllic atmosphere to the hours I spent at work. My wife for her part provided me with the cosy and undemanding love of the perfect conjugal relationship. Those were the happiest years of my life.

I obtained the chair in comparative anatomy in the science faculty of the capital's university. I was assiduous in keeping up with developments in my field; I neither chased breathlessly after every novelty, nor resigned myself to a life of leisure.

One afternoon last year, when the streets were already covered in muddy snow and I was making plans to take a nice winter holiday, Martha took a strange call for me. She entered my office quite out of breath.

'Excuse me, Professor, but there's a patient on the line who insists on speaking to you at all costs. He won't listen to reason.'

'Just put the phone down on him and leave it at that,' I said with a smile.

'I've done that twice already,' she said 'but this gentleman won't give up. He phoned back straight away, both times. He's very upset.'

'Very well, put him through to me, but don't let it

happen again. Can't you see I'm with a patient?'

In fact there was a girl stretched out quite naked on the examination couch, her shining body demanding my absolute attention.

I went to the telephone. 'Professor, help me, please. You're my only hope. I've been confined to bed for the last three years. Save me, I beg you. You're the only one who can help me.' Without asking what the matter was I advised him to call an ambulance and have himself taken to hospital.

'No, please don't turn me away. You looked after my two brothers, you were so good to them, now you're almost one of the family. Don't abandon me, I implore you.'

The man—who from his voice must have been fifty, possibly sixty—was pleading in utter desperation.

'But what is wrong with you, what are your symptoms?' I asked him as calmly as I could. 'I might not even be the specialist you need.'

'Please come, I beg you,' he insisted in heart-rending tones.

What could I do? My sense of humanity, my studies in geriatrics, and my image of myself as a doer of good deeds, even as a sort of miracle-worker, struggled against decades of ingrained professionalism which called for absolute resistance to emotional blackmail. On the other hand, the little old men and little old women who used

141

to visit me at my old surgery considered me a sort of demigod, only because I never refused them their weekly prescription of diuretics and laxatives.

I hesitated for a moment, and the man, bursting into tears of despair, knew it.

'Thank you, thank you, Professor. May God bless you. Come, come today or I'll die.'

He gave me his name and address and hung up.

I felt angry at having given in to the blackmail, especially since I had hoped to stay behind for a while with Martha after surgery hours. But in the event it was she who induced me, without knowing it, to keep my appointment with the sick man.

'I'm sorry, Doctor, but I won't be able to come in tomorrow,' she whispered as the last patient was leaving. 'I'm getting married at half past ten, and in the afternoon . . . '

As I heard this I was tempted to take her in my arms and exercise my dominance over her, to claim my rightful *droit de seigneur*. Fortunately I was able to control myself.

I was surprised to hear myself saying: 'Right, I have to hurry. I've an urgent case to visit. I just might be able to save his life. Congratulations, and see you the day after tomorrow. Don't forget to turn off all the lights.'

Half an hour later I was back in the old district where I grew up. The houses, once luxurious, now seemed lifeless ruins, but quite without any sense of tragedy. Crumbling plaster, patched up window panes, rotten wooden beams propping up courtyards and entrance halls. Tiny human beings wrapped up from head to foot scurried about on broken pavements. Every now and again they would stop for a little rest, moving on after five or six breaths.

Twenty years had gone by since I had last set foot in the Eighth District, still in the central part of town. I crossed Karfenstein Street, skirted past the market on Teleky Square and turned into People's Theatre Street. I entered the apartment block as directed by my troublesome patient-to-be.

Inside, I came face to face with the statue of a boy, of decidedly mediocre manufacture, and his eyes followed my progress across the hallway to a rickety elevator. On the fourth floor I had to walk all the way around the internal balcony, its wooden handrail supported on wrought iron railings painted an oily black.

Number five was an apartment whose windows faced in towards the courtyard. The glass door faced in the same direction.

I pushed the plastic bell button and the door was opened by a little old lady with thinning white hair, wearing a grease-stained dress with a faded pattern of red flowers. At that instant I recalled my new patient's mention of his two brothers. And as I entered the darkened apartment I came face to face with all three in an old family photograph hanging framed in the hallway.

I saw three boys sitting in a row with their arms folded, each wearing the radiant expression that I have never been able to define properly. The woman who had just shown me in I recognized immediately as their mother; she was sitting somewhat to the right of the three in the photograph, a little cut off from them and was the only one looking at the camera, wearing a sad and strangely allusive expression, almost as if she was sharing a secret with the viewer.

'Thank you, Doctor, thank you,' the old woman began, handing me a bundle of rags made up to look like a fancy parcel. 'Please don't be offended, it was my poor husband's. I thought you might like it.' I opened the bundle and took out a pocket watch, apparently made of solid gold. 'Please accept it, Doctor. You've been so good to my sons—may the earth not find them a burden—you looked after them so well, the poor things. Now it's the turn of the third. I don't have anyone else. Come, come and examine him.'

I showed an appropriate degree of reticence before accepting the present, but finally I concluded that it was merely a surrogate, no different from the fee which you pay today for practically everything, even a simple doctor's prescription. The poor woman obviously had no money and she must have thought long and hard before sacrificing the watch.

We entered the darkened bedroom the sole window of which opened on to the courtyard.

'Good day, Doctor. Excuse me if I don't get up, but you can see my condition. You did so much for my brothers, now I hope you'll help me. Do you remember them? One came to you ten years ago, the other fifteen or twenty, I don't remember any more. It was just after the war. Or maybe it was just after the revolution. I don't know.'

And then in the darkness of that little room, for the third time in so many years, I had the sensation of confronting someone surrounded by an aura of luminosity. Every aspect of him, every visible part of his body, was suffused with an air of solemn joyfulness, as if in expectation of some great event, the very proximity of which caused an irresistible euphoria.

The mother stood at the foot of the bed, watching over the invalid with a look of admiration and great tenderness. But the instant she turned away from him and looked towards me, her expression changed. A blank look of resigned objectivity spread across her face, in which, even at that age (she must have been about eighty), one could still detect the sweet and melancholy beauty of long ago. The photograph in the hall showed her with shining dark hair, white teeth and a penetrating look with just the hint of a sparkle in her pupils.

Now she was standing in front of me, leaning on a metal cane, pale, her narrow shoulders sagging. She smiled at me.

'You look after him, Doctor, the way you looked after the other two. You're such a good man.'

Good? What had I done to save those two men, or even to help them? And where was the second? Whatever had become of him? But the old woman spared me the awkward question by continuing: 'The second . . . you understand . . . Fifteen years ago. Ah, yes, how time flies by . . . '

'He died of a heart attack,' the remaining brother explained, 'but he had arterial stenosis in his legs. In the end he was unable to move from one side of the room to the other. I even had to carry him to the toilet. And now it's my turn. Look, look at this swelling here, in my right leg. It is so painful. Let me die quickly Doctor. You are so good.'

So the family had chosen me as their judge, but I could pass only one sentence: the penalty of death. The judgement had been handed down before either they or I had been born, and there was no appeal. The solemnity, the luminous aura was that of the sacrificial victim. And by agreeing to the visit I had accepted the role, however much it conflicted with my personal and professional ethics. It was too late now to turn back. There was only one thing I could do.

I had the patient undress and I began my examination. The swelling in the right leg near the ankle could have been a symptom of any number of organic disorders. However I was able to exclude diabetes, malignancy, and malfunctions of the kidneys and of the circulatory system from the list of possible causes.

'Sciatica, rheumatism or a simple injury,' I pronounced in tones of triumphal certainty. 'Don't worry, you certainly won't die of this illness.' Naturally I was happy to be able to give a hopeful diagnosis every now and then.

'Did you say I'll get better?' the invalid said, with an almost imperceptible hint of disappointment in his voice.

'Yes. The cure will not be easy, but you will get better, I can assure you of that.'

'But can it be cured, Doctor?'

'Yes. Some illnesses are transitory, and yours is one of those.'

'Are you being serious? There really are such things as transitory illnesses?'

'Yes.' I put an end to the discussion, suspecting I wasn't going to be able to convince them of the truth of what I was saying. 'And now I have to go.' In that instant I heard a feeble noise behind me, like the sound of someone sighing. I turned around. The mother was standing behind my back, sobbing tearlessly, but all the more desperately for that. Her shoulders, so narrow in relation to her hips, were shaking under a storm of inexpressible emotions.

'You astonish me,' she gasped, each syllable an effort to catch her breath in the turmoil of the moment. 'You astonish me. You're not content with having killed two of my children, now, heaven forbid, you want to take my last from me? Have you not even a spark of conscience? Can you not see what a state that leg is in? Even a newborn child would realize that my son's life is in danger. Either help him or let him die in peace, Doctor. I never thought I'd say this to you Doctor, but after all . . . How dare you claim that my son isn't seriously ill?'

Then it all became clear to me. The woman expected me to take responsibility for the death of the third son in addition to the other two. No remission was possible. If it came to it I would have to kill him. Yes, that was it: she wanted me to kill him. Not judge, but executioner, that was the part she wanted me to play.

The swelling was in all three cases the symptom of a completely different illness, but one that had struck each man in the same limb: the right leg. In view of the enormous progress medical science has made over the last few decades I know that it is madness to lose oneself in philosophical speculation of this sort, but Professor Bahdy's paper made me realize that forms of illness and even causes of death are no more than symbols. It is not the mechanism itself which is important (except insofar as we are able to intervene to change its course) but rather that which the mechanism is trying to express. Seen like this, our lives might only be the relatively insignificant preamble to the unique truth towards which we are all heading, the only indications of which are the illnesses of our bodies and, definitively, our own deaths.

Behind the radiant respectability of the three brothers I detected an inexplicable silence. Their own lives remained incomprehensible even to them. Their only possibility of communication was through the expression of their sickness and the form of their deaths.

The little old woman would not let go and continued to sob disconsolately.

Can I risk a hypothesis? These three brothers sacrificed themselves for a love which demanded such a sacrifice. What this love might have hidden, and what kind of love it was, are questions too difficult to comprehend, much less answer.

After this visit, which I ended in indignation, my career took a downward turn. Old enmities and petty jealousies deprived me of my chair at the university. But I bear no grudges now. A doctor, after all, seeks the truth. Philosophers gave that up some time ago. The current state of science gives me grounds for hope, but only hope. Without the certainty of truth, I am unable to practice science. That is why I am giving it up. I will keep the gold watch, and wait.

E.D.P

Professor Bahdy, 'A Lower Limb Disease', *Asiatic Medical Researches*, number 4, 1985
Professor E. D. Puster, 'Statistics about Bahdy's Disease and Chromosome Y Mutation', New York, 1988

CHOICES

St John's hospital covers a vast area, right in the heart of the First District, but its wards, which seem to be in a state of perpetual transformation, are connected by narrow, dusty corridors.

Eugene Shermann was brought here in a very serious condition. The original diagnosis, still in the archives, speaks of sarcomatosis.

He was moved into a room with six beds, in each of which lay a silent, well disciplined patient. Every day his wife Erna brought him his lunch from home. They would talk, exchange trivialities, gossip about the other residents in their apartment block on Wednesday Street. Then Erna would gather together the plates and the bowls, wave goodbye to Eugene and disappear swiftly down the passageway. She was sixty-five, he was seventy-two. They had been together for more than forty years.

They had got to know each other at a local dance, just after the end of what the history books now call the First

World War. He was already completely bald, with a substantial paunch. She was small and plump, with thick black hair gathered in around her neck. Her large eyes would open and close as if she was giving way to an overwhelming sleepiness whenever the person she was with began to bore her or otherwise failed to meet expectations. By the time she met Eugene she had already devastated one suitor, Ladislav Schwarz, a book-keeper at a firm of importers of tropical fruit. For a whole year Ladislav had gone to meet her every afternoon outside the women's fashions boutique in Vac Street where she worked as a seamstress, then walked her home to Karfenstein Street. They walked arm-in-arm, chatting about any old thing to avoid having nothing to say to each other. But after a time, Erna decided he was too beautiful for her. For as they walked home, Ladislav would keep turning around and staring at other girls, and the other girls stared back at him.

'Please don't come for me ever again,' Erna told him one day, without further explanation. 'I'm perfectly capable of going home by myself.' So Ladislav Schwarz disappeared from her life. And Erna wrote down the date in her diary: 20 March 1920.

The typographer Eugene Shermann was a rather awkward and overly formal sort of man. He lived with his mother whom he had been supporting since he was twelve years old. He was taken on as an apprentice at the typesetters and a few years later was promoted to machine compositor.

He was a swift worker; no one else could set as many ens per hour as he could. Typographical errors were unknown to him. He could decipher the most garbled manuscripts. And no spelling mistake ever escaped him, no matter how deeply buried in the work of some poet or novelist. He would sit at his machine for thirteen, fourteen hours a day. With his pliers he would pull the tiny pieces of lead, each one embossed with a letter, from the packed wooden cases, and from there slide them into position in lines of type. The thoughts enclosed in each symbol by his own two hands danced before his eyes; and messages born in dark rooms would find their way in the hands of other people into sumptuous buildings. Eugene sipped every now and again from a glass of milk placed on a chair. The milk was supposed to guard against lead poisoning. The monotonous clicking of the composing machine rang in his ears at night, providing a background to the sound of his sick mother's sighing and moaning. One day Shermann the typographer wrote a poem on this concerto of noises, full of melancholy and resignation.

As a boy he had supplemented his earnings performing every Thursday afternoon on the outer circle of People's Park as assistant to a fourth-rate magician. He would rehearse their tricks, changed every two or three months, on Saturday and Sunday mornings, getting up even earlier than usual. He learned to throw his voice and to imitate the sounds of a trumpet and a balalaika.

By the time he reached thirty the entire neighbourhood had taken to calling him simply 'Baldy' and he took pleasure in his nickname, rubbing his billiard ball-smooth head every time he heard his name mentioned.

His third source of income, and also occasionally of loss, was horse-racing. Every Friday and Saturday afternoon, armed with binoculars and specialist newspapers, he would go to the old race-track to place his bet. If he came home with money it was celebrations all round: sweets for his little nephews and his sisters and for the whole family a ride around town in a horse-drawn carriage or an afternoon at the Café Emke drinking hot chocolate and eating cake. When he lost he would come home and go to bed without a word.

But apart from the horses, Eugene Shermann's only vice was his habit of eating unthinkable quantities of whatever he could get into his stomach. It is hard to say whether his voracity was of a pathological nature. There was no mention of it in his medical records, nor in the yellowing prescriptions found lying in a wicker basket at his home. Nevertheless it was more than just a simple fact of his character; more probably some kind of irresistible imperative, something he was born with, stronger than his own will, stronger even than the laws of life itself. This overpowering impulse drove him to feed himself continuously, at any and every hour of the day, with the result that his stomach was permanently full of food and gas. To find temporary relief from the torment of indigestion he would often call in the children of his neighbours or of his sister and get them to do a little dance on his bare back, 'to straighten out the bones,' as he used to say, but more probably to help him release the wind from his belly. This happened often, much to the amusement of the children.

And it was like this, through an open door, that Erna, his wife-to-be, saw him for the first time. She had come to deliver a newly made suit to Eugene's neighbour.

At that time the Shermann family lived on Wednesday Street, in an apartment block full of Gypsies. Erna lived on Karfenstein Street. The prostitutes of Conti Street, for whom she, so chaste and demure, had learned to make working clothes which were, to say the least, on the provocative side expected her to come by every morning. And so she passed along Wednesday Street every day. Eugene Shermann would stare after her from the single window in his tiny, dark apartment at the end of the alley.

In those days they had all kinds of ceremonies which are unknown today: balls, engagement parties, official marriage requests. Both Eugene and Erna went along to a ball organized by the Jews of the Eighth District, each intending to come away engaged. Erna couldn't dance, and spent the entire evening in the darkest corner of the hall keeping her sisters company. Whoever wanted to find her knew where to look. Erna put her trust in destiny, that is, in the will of the Almighty.

Eugene Shermann found her. She said yes immediately. His lack of physical attractiveness was Erna's guarantee that their marriage would remain free of the cloying emotions of lovers and sweethearts. Her older brothers—Erna was an orphan—gave her permission to get married, and she gave up her job at the women's fashions boutique and started to work regularly making dresses for the prostitutes. She sewed on her old Singer under the window from which Eugene used to spy on her. She looked after his old mother who was ill with a bone tumour, helped her to die and the day after the funeral took her place in bed. Until then she had slept on the floor, between Eugene's bed and her mother-in-law's.

From her only union with Eugene, which took place at the end of the week of mourning, she gave birth to a son who was brought up in an atmosphere of love and severity.

Eugene was not a believer; he had even got involved in the socialist trade union at the typographers. Erna in her own way was religious and observant.

'My son,' Eugene said to the boy on the day of his bar mitzvah, 'I've had this ring specially made for you. The decoration, see, on both sides, I designed. The stone too, an emerald—I chose it.'

'And I saved the money to buy it,' said Erna, 'sewing

night and day. Just so you know that into this ring went all my effort, all my hours, all my thoughts. Take great care of it, and may God be a help to you.'

The boy, whose official name was Frederic, but who was called Aaron by the community, looked at the ring for a long time before trying it on at the door of the temple.

'It's too big!' he exclaimed anxiously.

'It will fit you perfectly once you've grown big enough,' said his father. 'Try it on once a month and you'll see.' And for the first time in his life he leaned down and kissed the boy.

Those three beings, their lives joined in the belly of that dark building, were visited one day by the poisonous currents of war and persecution. They were taken away, separated, then reunited again. The moment of their destruction, all at once or one at a time, never arrived. They survived the war.

Erna offered up prayer after prayer of thanksgiving; Eugene put it all down to the nemesis of history: many innocents, but also many evildoers, had been spared in that whirlpool of blood.

Aaron wore the ring on the day he first turned up for work, he too at the typographers. He began to go around with the girls of the district. He was now old enough to start thinking of having a family of his own. The day he packed his clothes and the few possessions he needed to go off and live an independent life, Eugene was terribly

159

agitated. He devoured everything he could lay his hands on in the kitchen, while Erna turned the wheel on her old machine, sewing more joyfully than usual.

'Even the birds, once their wings are fledged, fly away from the nest,' she said. 'The Lord ordained it that way. So don't be silly. Come to bed now.' They lay in each other's arms that night, and Eugene's heavy breath reminded Erna of the sweet milky smell of her son when he was little.

'Erna, come quickly,' Eugene said, pulling his wife along with him to the toilet, which was in a corner of the courtyard next to the back staircase. 'I don't know what's happening to me. Look.'

It was a few days after Frederic had said goodbye. The toilet bowl was covered in blood. A pile of faeces lay at the bottom like the decomposing corpse of a new-born baby.

With his wife's help, Eugene's haemorrhoids (that's what he thought they were) got better, and for a while he was well. He retired from his job at the typographers. Then a few weeks after his last day at work he was admitted to St John's Hospital for an operation on his rectum. He was fitted with a bag to wear at his side in which the waste products of his digestion would accumulate. Eugene had to try to keep this bag clean.

His son visited him often, but Eugene detected in him a sense of fear, or worse, revulsion, which made him cry at night in the dimly lit hospital ward. Erna left her dressmaking at three o'clock every day and walked from Wednesday Street to the hospital, praying for him all the way. She prayed calmly, without desperation.

Her husband was discharged, and not long after arriving home began to apply himself to the household chores. He would cook and clean, while Erna got on with her dressmaking, no longer for the inhabitants of the brothels—these had been abolished by the new government—but for other women whose requirements were less pointed, but all the more secure for that. Erna devoted much attention and imagination to bringing out every aspect of femininity in her clients, just as she denied it in herself. She went to them in the spirit of one who visits the sick, to do a good deed.

Then the country revolted, and this was followed by a counter-revolution. The people who organized the counter-revolution accused the original revolutionaries of being counter-revolutionaries and, having won, proclaimed themselves the real revolutionaries.

Eugene puzzled over these happenings with Erna for hours on end. He was a knowledgeable man, but finally, after endless discussion, he could only ascribe such violent changes to the unstoppable onward course of history. He would picture the onward course of history to himself as an immense river, down which floated so many boats full of human beings. Erna imagined the will of the Almighty as a giant fist thumping an enormous table.

In those tumultuous days Aaron came to visit them. He was in a rather solemn and mysterious mood.

'This place is not for me. You know what I mean, don't you, Dad? I want to be rich, and here you're not allowed to be rich. You know how quick-tempered I am, how I don't weigh my words very carefully. Here if you say certain things they stick you in gaol. So I've decided to leave, just as soon as I'm able. It'll have to be soon, before all this hullabaloo has quietened down. I know nothing of revolution and counter-revolution. All I know is that I want to be rich.'

Eugene and Erna remained silent for a long time. This was not how a good son should speak to his parents, and that counted for more than anything else in their family.

'I've brought the ring,' Aaron continued after a painful silence, 'not because I want to give it back, but for you to have as a reminder of me and as a token of my intention to come back one day and take you with me, so that we'll all be back together again as one family in another part of the world.'

'We'll never see each other again,' said Eugene, who had asked a lot of questions of the doctors and knew well what fate awaited him. And then he added: 'You're a grown man, you know what you're doing. May the Lord bless your footsteps.' He took back the ring he had given his son, kissed his forehead and didn't address another word to him for the rest of the evening.

Aaron left at dawn the next day and Eugene watched him go from the window of the tiny apartment on Wednesday Street. Outside on Matyas Square they had dug communal graves for dead of the revolution and the counter-revolution. Aaron had to pass by the graves to get to the lorry which was waiting at the corner of the square to take him far away from his native land.

From that day on Eugene was never the same again. Although he loved and respected his wife and treated her with a rather clumsy formality, he would now lose his temper from time to time, and answer rudely back at her. When this happened little Erna would stop, wipe her hands in her apron, fix him with her eyes, and say: 'Are you crazy, Eugene?' Then she would lower her eyelids, shutting him out of her world.

Eugene Shermann began, more assiduously than before, to frequent the races, but now he no longer stopped at betting small sums. It was as if he wanted to bring about his own downfall before the Almighty ordered him to leave the chessboard. Eugene would sometimes lay half of his pension on one bet, until one day he bet the whole of it and lost.

Leaving the race-track he didn't know where to go. He didn't have the courage to tell Erna how he had brought disgrace down upon his head. He wandered about the city, his great paunch thrusting out before him, his bald head bobbing up and down in the grey crowds. He began humming to himself in desperation. Suddenly he had an idea. He smacked his forehead and set off quickly back home. After greeting Erna with his usual affectionate respect he went straight off to bed. Erna, who was waiting with his supper, looked long and hard at him, then decided not to ask any questions that day.

The next morning Eugene was up and out by seven. Erna woke and looked all around for him. 'Where has that *meschügge* got to now?' she muttered, dressing hastily. 'He wouldn't be playing some trick on me, would he? You can't get any peace and quiet in this life.'

She searched for him in the market, in the cafés, in the shops, she even telephoned his old workplace, the typographers. She took the thirty-six tram to the corner of People's Theatre Street. Then, just as she was about to get on the number six to the East Station, she stopped. She knotted her headscarf under her chin and said to herself: 'I'm not going to let him drive me crazy, that's for sure. Why all the fuss? If he wants to act like a madman, why should I follow suit?'

She turned around and began to walk home. As she passed by the grey building on the corner of Adam Vaj Street, the sound of a guitar reached her ears. Drawn by her own curiosity rather than by the unusual sound, Erna went into the courtyard. There in the middle, standing on yellow tiles, his hat by his feet, his bald head held up high against the black railings, Eugene Shermann was imitating the sounds of a guitar and a mandolin. An audience of toothless pensioners and astonished children watched the busker's impromptu performance from various floors in the building. Two or three coins fell, bouncing and rolling nearby.

'Have you gone mad?' Erna shouted, seizing her husband by the jacket. 'Come away this minute! For shame! The things I have to put up with in my life!'

'Erna, dearest,' Eugene replied, following his wife like a puppy, 'I obviously owe you an explanation, and you'll get it in time.'

'There's nothing to explain,' said Erna with a note of finality, as she continued to drag her husband, whose eyes were by now popping and brimful of tears with the pain, along the street towards home. 'The only thing to do is to go away and hide, and *schluss!*'

'You're right, I'm thoroughly ashamed of myself,' whispered Eugene as he crossed the threshold of the house in Wednesday Street. 'I've lost all my dignity—and all my money. I bet it away on the horses.'

Erna stopped, gave a deep sigh and said: 'May it all turn out for the best.' She stood still for a moment, then started off again, but not as quickly now.

Later that day Eugene felt a tremendous pain in his back as he lay down so that he had to spend the night lying on his front, with his stomach in continual agitation under the weight. After a week the pain had become unbearable and they had to call a doctor.

'You should prepare yourself for the worst,' the doctor told Erna after the examination. 'It has metastasized to the bone, I'm sure. There's a small chance I could be wrong.'

'Metastasized? What does that mean?' Erna asked.

'Madam, the disease your husband had before in his rectum has now moved to his bones. I wouldn't wish it on my worst enemy.'

'Why did He invent all these tortures?'

'Who?'

'I know who,' she replied, raising her eyes to the heavens. Then she lowered her eyelids, as if with this rather emphatic gesture she could abolish heaven itself.

Eugene was taken off to hospital, and at the same time the first letters began to arrive from Aaron in far-off Canada.

'Everything's beautiful here, everything's new,' he wrote. 'The only thing missing is you.' Erna read the letter to her husband, now frighteningly thin and weak, writhing in his hospital bed.

'I have to go home,' Eugene murmured when he heard those words.

'Go home? Have you gone mad? What would you do at home, with you in so much pain?'

'I want to say goodbye to him, for the last time.'

'Who do you want to say goodbye to?'

'Aaron.'

'Now come on! Aren't you too old for such nonsense? You know very well that Aaron is in Ottawa, on the other side of the ocean. Do you want to fly over to see him?'

'No, I don't have the money for the journey.'

'Exactly. So what do you want to go home for?'

'To say goodbye. To the ring.'

Erna was struck dumb. She fixed him with her big grey eyes. 'I'll bring it to you,' she said solemnly.

'No, please, not here, not into the midst of all this sickness. It might get infected.'

Eugene fell back on the bed, exhausted by the effort of talking so much, of wanting so much. Erna stayed by him until he dozed off, then she tucked in his sheets and left the ward, taking her leave politely of the other patients. They responded with weak, tearful goodbyes.

When she returned the following afternoon, Erna found Eugene sitting up on the side of the bed wearing all his clothes.

'They've allowed me to leave. Let's go.'

'Will you manage on foot?'

'Of course I'll manage, angel,' Eugene whispered, and he set off with shaky steps. Erna took him by the arm without a word.

Once home she made him sit down on a stool in the kitchen. The tiny apartment hummed with the faint noises of the afternoon.

'Would you like a coffee?'

'No, thank you, angel,' Eugene answered, and turned his head towards the room. Erna understood the significance of this slight movement. She went to the cupboard and opened one of the doors. She reached in with her arm, ignoring the shelves bursting with sheets, pillowcases and towels, all folded neatly and drowned in a strong odour of naphthalene. She groped to one side and then the other, then from under a pile of never-worn nightshirts, she pulled a red leather-covered box.

'There you are, since you care so much about it. I only hope the Lord doesn't let any evil come of it.'

Erna opened the lid of the box. The ring, with its great green stone, flashed in the darkness of the kitchen. Eugene put it in the palm of his hand, and Erna put the coffee on. Eugene's bulging eyes filled with tears. 'Be good to your mother, since you weren't good to me,' murmured the typographer. He put the ring back in the box and closed the lid.

The X-ray plates developed over the following two weeks showed a diminution of the opaque area which corresponded to the spread of the tumour. During that fortnight Eugene had peaceful and triumphant dreams, and he and Erna talked together about the future and about the possibility of going to visit their son. It was the happiest time of their lives. The doctors were astounded, speechless. Then one day Eugene had an attack of excruciating pains in his spine.

A week after this he entered the terminal phase of his illness. Shooting pains ran through all his bones, as if the framework of his clumsy construction of flesh was threatening to collapse and leave a formless mass, deprived of support and of dignity.

Eugene implored the doctors to give him an injection which would put an end to it all instantly. 'I'm sorry, but our professional ethics do not permit it,' was Dr Klein's firm response, taking the dying man's hand in his.

Then one day Erna arrived with a letter from their son. She had written to him about his father's condition, and warned him of his imminent death. Aaron didn't know how to address his father: in the face of such a solemn event, one of greater significance than any other instant in one's own or anyone else's life, all he could find to write was: 'Here the weather is fine; the sun is shining and it's not at all windy.'

'Yes, yes, the sun is shining over there, but for me it is evening,' Eugene said, his eyes full of tears. 'Look, Erna dear, from here down'—and he pointed to his side with a tired wave of his hand—'I'm already dead. Only here am I still alive,' and he indicated his chest, 'and here in my head. But not for much longer.' After an hour of silence he added, 'I'm grateful to you for everything,' then fell asleep.

'What are you doing here?' demanded the duty doctor of Erna who was staring fixedly at her husband's face.

'Visiting hours finished some time ago. Why don't you go home. Tomorrow morning you'll get a telegram. Your husband won't survive the night.'

Erna took the letter, tucked it into Eugene's pyjamas, gave a hundred florin note to the doctor and then turned to the invalid who was by now in a coma. 'Well, goodbye then.'

Eugene seemed shrunken, as if an irresistible force had pulled all the molecules of his body in towards a single point where all his pain was concentrated. Erna lowered her eyelids and left.

At Eugene's funeral she said a prayer on behalf of their son, then she approached the coffin and murmured in a quiet voice: 'Take me away from here. Do you hear me? Goodbye for now.' She didn't shed a single tear. 'I can't cry,' she said, as if to excuse herself to the rabbi who, so everyone said, was in the habit of eating a couple of onions or one or two cloves of garlic before making a funeral oration.

Not many months after this Aaron wrote her a letter full of bitterness, confessing all his failures, his inability to get on in life without the help of those who taught him everything he knew. 'Come over here to this wonderful country, we'll live together and you'll have everything you want, even if I never become rich.'

Erna loved her son and she cried long and hard when she read the letter. She went to the cemetery and sat down next to her husband's still fresh grave and began to reason with him.

'A little while ago I asked you to take me with you. Life without you and without Aaron seemed meaningless to me then. You'll have to forgive me, but I've come to ask you for an extension. I've changed my mind—I want to stay here. Maybe not for long, just to come here and chat to you, perhaps make a dress for some girl or other—I'm still good with my hands. The fact of the matter is I want to see things, feel things from down here, not from up there. I don't need a lot: a coffee with milk, a little bread and butter, a biscuit or two, does me for a whole day. Somebody might need me, one of my sisters perhaps; you know how I like helping the sick, how it doesn't upset me at all. And who knows, even you might need me, from up there. I'll never forget you. There, and now I'll have to get home. There's a bit of tidying to do and I have to write a nice letter to Aaron. By the way, he wants me to go and live with him. What do you say to that?'

And in this way Erna finally worked up the courage to broach the subject with him. Then she stood for a long time in silence, listening, and going over her own thoughts. At dusk she walked back along the dusty road from that remote spot in the Stone Quarry district and took the tram back into town. She spent the entire journey working out word for word in her head the text of the letter she would send to Canada. Once home she took paper and pencil, put on her spectacles, sat down and began to write.

Dear Aaron,
You asked me to make a choice. I've been to talk with your father and I've asked him for an extension. I have always admired your father: he was an honest man, hard-working, he never showed me anything but respect, and he always gave me all his pay. Honesty and respect mean everything to me, they are the real proof of love. You too are an honest boy, if a bit headstrong. May the Almighty help you. My place is here: that is my choice. Your father needs me. I'll think of you always, but I'll never leave here, I'll always stay close to your father, to the piece of earth where he rests. But let us change the subject. The weather is fine here and the sun is shining. What's it like with you? Write to me soon. Goodbye, and may the Almighty bless your footsteps.

Erna is ninety-eight years old. Her love for her husband and her son are 'a memorial' according to Dr Klein, who has been treating her for thirty years for mildly oscillating blood pressure.

'Sarcoma Generale Regressum', in *Review of Oncology*, Siracuse (Canada) and Jerusalem, 1958
Interviews on Regressed Cancer Cases, New York, 1987

VINTAGE INTERNATIONAL

TIME'S ARROW
by Martin Amis

Dr. Tod T. Friendly dies and then feels markedly better, breaks up with his lovers as a prelude to seducing them, and mangles his patients before he sends them home, in this ingenious novel that not only rethinks history but dreastically revises our notion of time itself.

"Splendid...bold...*Time's Arrow* is Martin Amis's most thrilling book...gripping from start to finish."
—*Los Angeles Times Book Review*

Fiction/Literature/0-679-73572-0

FLAUBERT'S PARROT
by Julian Barnes

An elegant work of literary imagination involving a cranky amateur scholar's obsessive search for the truth about Gustave Flaubert, *Flaubert's Parrot* also investigates the obsession of the detective, whose passion for the page is fed by personal bitterness—and whose life seems oddly to mirror those of Flaubert's characters.

"A high literary entertainment carried off with great brio...rich in parody and parrotry, full of insight and wit...a great success."
—*The New York Times Book Review*

Fiction/Literature/0-679-73136-9

POSSESSION
by A. S. Byatt

An intellectual mystery and a triumphant love story of a pair of young scholars researching the lives of two Victorian poets.

"Gorgeously written...dazzling...a tour de force."
—*The New York Times Book Review*

Fiction/Literature/0-679-73590-9

THE STRANGER
by Albert Camus

Through the story of an ordinary man who unwittingly gets drawn into a senseless murder, Camus explores what he termed "the nakedness of man faced with the absurd."

Fiction/Literature/0-679-72020-0

IN COLD BLOOD
by Truman Capote

As Capote reconstructs the 1959 murder of a Kansas farm family and the investigation that led to the capture, trial, and execution of the killers, he generates both mesmerizing suspense and astonishing empathy. The resulting work transcends its moment, yielding poignant insights into the nature of American violence.

"A masterpiece...a spellbinding work."   —*Life*

Nonfiction/Literature/0-679-74558-0

INVISIBLE MAN
by Ralph Ellison

This searing record of a black man's journey through contemporary America reveals, in Ralph Ellison's words, "the sheer rhetorical challenge involved in communicating across our barriers of race and religion, class, color and region."

"The greatest American novel in the second half of the twentieth century...the classic representation of American black experience."   —R.W. B. Lewis

Fiction/Literature/0-679-72313-7

THE SOUND AND THE FURY
by William Faulkner

The tragedy of the Compson family, featuring some of the most memorable characters in American literature: beautiful, rebellious Caddy; the manchild Benjy; haunted, neurotic Quentin; Jason, the brutal cynic; and Dilsey, their black servant.

"For range of effect, philosophical weight, originality of style, variety of characterization, humor, and tragic intensity, [Faulkner's works] are without equal in our time and country."   —Robert Penn Warren

Fiction/Literature/0-679-73224-1

THE REMAINS OF THE DAY
by Kazuo Ishiguro

A profoundly compelling portrait of the perfect English butler and of his fading, insular world in postwar England.

"One of the best books of the year."   —*The New York Times Book Review*

Fiction/Literature/0-679-73172-5

THE WOMAN WARRIOR
by Maxine Hong Kingston

"A remarkable book...As an account of growing up female and Chinese-American in California, in a laundry of course, it is anti-nostalgic; it burns the fat right out of the mind. As a dream—of the 'female avenger'—it is dizzying, elemental, a poem turned into a sword."   —*The New York Times*

Nonfiction/Literature/0-679-72188-6